Using the Creative Arts in Therapy and Healthcare

Using the Creative Arts in Therapy and Healthcare provides a practical introduction to the uses of arts and other creative processes to promote health and encourage healing.

This latest edition includes newly edited chapters from the original and second edition covering the therapeutic use of dance, drama, folklore and ritual, storytelling and the visual arts. Information on guidelines, preparations and practical hints for leaders and facilitators has also been updated. New chapters provide an international perspective in the field of the arts and healthcare, and show how the artist can alleviate distress for patients through art, music and drama.

Illustrated throughout with ideas and examples of how the arts can be used in a range of healthcare settings, this book will be essential reading for creative arts therapists and healthcare professionals throughout the world.

Bernie Warren PhD is Professor of Drama and Education in the Community in the School of Dramatic Arts, University of Windsor, Ontario Canada. He is also the Artistic Director of the Fools for Health clown-doctor program.

Using the Creative Arts in Therapy and Healthcare

A practical introduction

Edited by Bernie Warren

 Routledge
Taylor & Francis Group

LONDON AND NEW YORK

First published 2008
by Routledge
27 Church Road, Hove, East Sussex BN3 2FA

Simultaneously published in the USA and Canada
by Routledge
270 Madison Ave, New York, NY 10016

*Routledge is an imprint of the Taylor & Francis Group,
an informa business*

Typeset in Times by
RefineCatch Limited, Bungay, Suffolk
Printed and bound in Great Britain by
TJ International Ltd, Padstow, Cornwall
Paperback cover design by Lisa Dynan

This publication has been produced with paper manufactured to
strict environmental standards and with pulp derived from
sustainable forests.

British Library Cataloguing in Publication Data
A catalogue record for this book is available from the British Library

Library of Congress Cataloging in Publication Data
Using the creative arts in therapy and healthcare / edited by Bernie
Warren. – [3rd ed.].
      p. ; cm.
   Rev. ed. of: Using the creative arts in therapy / edited by Bernie
Warren. 2nd ed. 1993.
   Includes bibliographical references and index.
   ISBN-13: 978-0-415-40403-7 (hardback)
   ISBN-13: 978-0-415-40404-4 (pbk.)
1. Arts–Therapeutic use. 2. Movement therapy. 3. Creation (Literary,
artistic, etc.)–Therapeutic use. I. Warren, Bernie, 1953– II. Using
the creative arts in therapy.
[DNLM: 1. Sensory Art Therapies. 2. Creativeness. 3. Laughter
Therapy. WM 450 U851 2008]
   RM931.A77U75 2008
   616.89′1656 – dc22

                                        2007032798

ISBN: 978-0-415-40403-7 (hbk)
ISBN: 978-0-415-40404-4 (pbk)

Contents

Illustrations

Figures

Tables

Contributors

Richard Coaten trained initially in dance and theatre at Dartington College of Arts. Since then he has specialised in a range of different arts based practices involving management development, street theatre, community dance, and arts/health work having been an Arts Co-ordinator in hospitals in Sheffield and Stoke-on-Trent in the UK. In 2000 he became registered as a Movement Psychotherapist and now works part-time for the South West Yorkshire Mental Health NHS Trust in Older People's Services in Calderdale. Richard is also in the last year of a doctorate in "Dance & Dementia" at Roehampton University, London and is Training Programme Director for Woldgate College's Dance Development Team in the East Riding of Yorkshire, pioneering the use of free-movement play & dance in early year's settings in the county.

Veronica James was born in England and has lived in Wales and Scotland. She is Professor of Nursing Studies at the University of Nottingham having previously worked in hospices, law courts and prisons, and with homeless street drinkers. Veronica works as a practice nurse in the community, and is undertaking a five-year course on transactional analysis.

Roberta Nadeau was born in the western United States and emigrated to Canada in 1973. She studied psychology and sociology as an undergraduate, graduating cum laude. She pursued graduate studies at Purdue University in the sociology of art, and is a painter who has exhibited her works across Canada, a writer and an arts therapist. She taught part-time at the University of Calgary and at the University of British Columbia and lectured in the United States, Canada, Europe and the Middle East. Until recently she worked as an art therapist in private practice in Vancouver, British Columbia where she also taught painting. Her own art work has been exhibited internationally. Sadly Roberta died in 2007.

Cheryl Neill is a musician, storyteller and teacher living in Montreal, Canada. She has over 20 years experience teaching people of all ages and abilities. She has extensive experience in conducting professional development workshops in storytelling and drama and is the author of many original musicals. A published poet and author, she has taught developmental drama and storytelling at Concordia University. Currently she works full time as a storyteller and singer/songwriter.

Susan Pointe directed the McMullen Gallery, Art Collection and Artists On the Wards for eight years. Pointe left her position as Art Advisor to work with Cohos Evamy Integratedesign™ on the Lois Hole Hospital for Women in Edmonton. She has since opened S. Pointe & Co. Inc., an arts consulting business to assist other healthcare organizations and private corporations in integrating original artwork into their facilities and professional artists into staff and client wellness programs.

Judy Rollins is a researcher and consultant with Rollins and Associates, Inc., in Washington, DC. Initially trained as a nurse, she has a BFA in Art, an MS in Child Development/Family Studies, and a PhD in Health and Community Studies. She is on the faculty in the Department of Health Sciences at Montgomery College, adjunct faculty in the Department of Family Medicine at Georgetown University School of Medicine, and associate editor of *Pediatric Nursing*. She developed 'ART is the heART', a program for children and families in hospice care, and 'Arts for Children in Hospitals', a course for medical students, both of which are being replicated worldwide. She developed and directs arts-in-healthcare programming for children and families at Georgetown University Hospital and Hospital for Sick Children in Washington, DC. Dr Rollins consults, writes, and researches on children's issues internationally, with a special interest in the use of the arts for children with cancer. She currently serves as Treasurer on the board of the Society for the Arts in Healthcare.

Magdalena Schamberger is the Executive Director of Hearts&Minds, a registered charity established in 1997 to promote the quality of life for people in hospital and hospice care. It promotes clown doctoring for children's services and an Elderflowers program for elderly people with dementia in hospital. Last year Hearts&Minds benefited over 10,000 children, older people and their families in Scotland. Schamberger's experience in visual/physical theatre companies covers three continents. She has worked as a director in her native Austria, as a performer in New York as well as performing and directing with many leading UK companies, such as Théatre sans Frontières and Benchtours and Hullaballoo Children's Theatre, in Scotland, where she now lives.

Peter Spitzer is a western trained physician who also actively uses acupuncture, hypnosis, counseling, psychotherapy, provocative therapy, nutrition, vitamin therapy and herbal medicine in his general practice. He is the founder, chairman and medical director of The Humour Foundation Australia, for whom he works as a professional clown-doctor (Dr Fruit-Loop). In addition, he is involved in the training of clown-doctors in hospital issues and establishing clown-doctor teams. A sought-after speaker worldwide, he has presented papers and workshops to the corporate sector, community groups and medical students. In 2001, Dr Spitzer was awarded a Churchill Fellowship to study the international impact of hospital clown units on the healthcare system.

Bernie Warren was born in England. He has worked as an actor, choreographer and musician. As a community worker, drama teacher and drama therapist he has worked with people of all ages and abilities. In addition he has studied Chinese and Japanese healing and martial arts for more than 35 years. His research and practice brings together his Eastern and Western training in his work with children with disabilities, seniors and people living with life threatening conditions (e.g. cancer). In 2001 Bernie was the recipient of the University of Windsor's Alumni Award for Distinguished Contributions to University Teaching, and has been included in Canadian *Who's Who* since 1994. Currently he is Professor of Drama in Education and Community at the University of Windsor and Director of Fools For Health clown-doctor programs, Windsor. He regularly works in hospitals and healthcare facilities as Dr Haven't-a-Clue.

Rob Watling was born in England. He began his career as a drama therapist, before working in community arts, local government, higher education, and the BBC. He studied English and folklore at the University of Stirling, media studies at the Polytechnic of Wales, and leadership at Ashridge Business School. He wrote his PhD at the University of Nottingham on the links between education and community development. He has written extensively on these subjects and is particularly interested in the role of the arts in tackling social exclusion. He has worked with European, national and local government departments; a range of community groups and trade unions; Southern Arts and the Welsh Arts Council; the Universities of Leicester and Nottingham; as a Learning Executive at the BBC; and most recently as an educational consultant for the BBC World Service Trust. He now runs his own consultancy, providing coaching and facilitation services for individuals, teams and whole organizations.

Wende Welch trained as a dancer, actress, puppeteer and mask-maker and has an MFA in theatre performance from York University, Canada. She has worked as a performer, designer and director with a number of professional companies in Canada and the United States most notably 50/50 Theatre Co. – a company dedicated to integration through the theatre arts. In addition to her professional work, she has taught theatre performance at Concordia University, Montreal and at the University of Windsor.

Keith Yon was born on the island of St Helena and received his professional training in England at the Royal College of Music, the Guildhall School of Music and Drama, and the Central School of Speech and Drama. His work bridged the boundaries between dance, drama and music and he employed his innovative and eclectic style of working with a broad spectrum of people, covering a wide range of ages and abilities. Yon worked for over 20 years at Dartington College of Arts, Totnes, Devon where he taught acting-directing and voice music. Sadly Yon died in 2002.

Acknowledgements

Many people were involved in the genesis and evolution of the current book. First, I wish to mention Bert Amies, George Hu, George Mager, Peter Senior, Caroline Simonds and Keith Yon, whose work and friendship have influenced and inspired me in my work over the years.

In addition, I wish to thank all those who contributed to the development of previous editions of this book, especially Donna Harling, Roberta Nadeau, Julie Ortynsky and Kerrin Patterson. I must also mention Tim Hardwick (Croom Helm) who first suggested I write this book and Edwina Welham (Routledge) who suggested the second edition.

For several reasons this third edition took a lot longer to put together than either of the previous ones and as a result many people helped me. First, I wish to thank Joanne Forshaw and Routledge for first suggesting and later agreeing to publish this current edition. I also wish to thank Claire Lipscomb and Jane Harris and everyone at Routledge who has helped transform an idea into a manuscript and finally into this book.

I wish to thank all those assistants who over the past two years helped to do various tasks in the development of this volume. In particular I wish to thank Candace Hind who was given the task of reading everything and commenting on it critically from a reader's perspective: her observations and comments were invaluable. I also wish to thank Mandy Boreskie who did an excellent job correcting the proofs and creating an index for this book.

My greatest praise and thanks go to my research associate, Nicole Gervais, who has worked on all my research and literary projects for the past four years. Sadly this project will be her last with me before she takes up her new job. Without her sage advice, her eye for detail and her persistence I doubt if anything would have been completed!

Lastly I would like to take this space to express my sincerest gratitude to all those people with whom I have worked as facilitator, teacher, therapist and friend. The amount I have learned from you, about the strength of the human spirit struggling against adversity, is truly immeasurable.

To all these people (friends, students, colleagues and clients alike) I dedicate this book.

Chapter 1

Looking backwards, looking forwards

A preface and introduction to using the creative arts in therapy and healthcare

Bernie Warren

What follows is a personal retrospective in which I briefly look back at the first two editions of this book, try to place them in context and introduce the changes in this new edition.

The more the world changes

This book was first conceived over 25 years ago. In 1982 when I was first approached by Tim Hardwick to write this book the world was a very different place. The United Nations International Year of the Disabled Person had just finished. I had just completed my work with the LUDUS Dance-in-Education company's Special School Project 'Learning Through Dance' and had recently moved to Canada to begin what has turned out to be my career as an academic.

So much has happened since then. There have been incredible discoveries in technology and medicine that have positively affected people's lives. At the same time, the events of 11 September 2001 and its aftermath have changed the world immeasurably. Moreover, if all leading experts are to be believed we seem to be facing potential ecological disasters of incomprehensible proportions.

Yet while the world may have become a scarier place, the arts not only continue to exist but also, with the advent of new technologies and media, continue to evolve. Throughout all the many changes to the world and our place within it, the arts in all their forms (visual, performing, electronic, written, mixed media) remain expressions of personal vision and belief, ways of conveying emotion and thought.

Expanding human horizons

The focus of the first editions

When this book was first considered, it was against a backdrop where, for the first time, persons with a disability were seen as human beings who should be empowered, enabled and encouraged to express themselves creatively. The subtitle for the original book, 'The Power of the Arts Experience to Expand Human Horizons', in part reflected this.

The goal of the first edition was to provide a practical introduction to the use of the arts not as therapy or treatment but rather as a way of expressing each individual's humanity. Most particularly it was focused on working with persons with a disability to help them find a creative voice and to use it to express themselves. In 1984 I wrote the following:

> We have created the concept that artistic creation is the responsibility of a few gifted individuals. In so doing, we have denied the majority of individuals within our urban and technologically advanced society their birthrights: that, as a human being, everyone has the right to make his or her own 'unique creative thumbprint'[1] – one that no one else could make. We all have a need to make this 'mark', not because we necessarily wish to be the reminders to a future generation of a long-lost culture but because each creative mark reaffirms the self. It says 'I am here', 'I have something to express.'
>
> (p. 4)

In the 1993 edition I elaborated on this point:

> In using the creative arts in health care, rehabilitation and special education settings, and seeing the resulting growth in self-image, self-esteem and healthy social interactions, society as a whole is being handed a mirror concerning what is possible for all its members if only they are given the opportunity. . . . Slowly people are becoming aware of their creative potential, their need to make their mark. As a result more and more individuals, who because of birth, crisis or accident had previously been denied their rights as 'full members' of their society, are finally gaining access to the arts. The results, in some cases, are quite staggering. Individuals, previously seen as useless, incapacitated or catatonic, have begun to speak, move more freely and in some cases, over a time, take a full and active part in society.
>
> (p. 4)

In 1983 when I began writing the first edition, there was no internet. When I was writing the revised edition, the world wide web was only just beginning. Now in 2007, it is possible for anyone to place their personal blogs, videos and music on the web enabling them to share their thoughts and creativity instantly with anyone who wishes to hear. Some may still question the 'quality' of these transmissions. Nevertheless the ability to make this mark certainly provides the opportunity for individuals to reaffirm themselves.

'You say potato, I say . . .'

A few words about 'arts for health' and 'arts therapy'

From the beginning I actively fought against using the word 'therapy' in the title of the book – a battle which I lost. In 1993 I put my disagreement with the notion of the arts being used as therapy with persons with a disability into the Introduction:

> As the workplace has become increasingly dehumanising and sterile (with fewer and fewer outlets for creative expression) it is not surprising that the arts have come to be seen as therapy. However, *Therapy* (which implies a prescribed course of treatment with predetermined expected results for a specific diagnosed condition) and *the Art(s)* (which at least in part suggests an exploration, one that usually finds the notion of predetermined expectation anathema) are strange bedfellows. Art is not a medicine that must be taken three times a day after meals. However, it can feed the soul, motivate an individual to want to recover and, in certain circumstances, cause physiological changes in the body.
>
> (pp. 3–4)

These comments did not endear me to some arts therapists. However, it must be noted that I have always believed in the therapeutic power of the arts. What I took and continue to take issue with was the practice of calling *any* artistic experience or exploration therapy simply because the participants had disabilities. I did try to clarify this point by penning a working definition of 'creative therapy':

> the use of the arts . . . and other creative processes to promote health and encourage healing. Implied in this working definition is the use of artistic and creative activities to help individuals accommodate to a specific disability; or recover from a specific medical or surgical procedure; or simply improve the quality of an individual's life.
>
> (p. 8)

However, in the revised edition I did also observe that there had been more opportunities for people to participate in arts activities, not because they necessarily wanted to be a professional dancer, painter or singer but because participating in the process made them feel good about themselves:

> More and more people are becoming aware that being involved in the process of artistic creation is every bit as important as and in many cases more important than the end product. . . . The recent move towards

'Arts for Health' (which suggests the benefits of participation in creative activity) as distinct from arts therapy (which implies the treatment of a condition that produces 'ill-health') is a healthy and honest extension of these developments.

(p. xi)

Since the publication of the original book there have been huge developments in the fields of arts therapy and arts for health.[2] Over the past 25 years there has been a rise in the use of the arts therapies in healthcare and with it a concomitance to professionalism and organizations to promote it.[3] Parallel to this there has been an upsurge in the role of the arts and artists in healthcare settings and organizations dedicated to their work.[4]

While some jurisdictions have clearly articulated their different scopes of practice (most notably in the UK),[5] professional organizations representing these distant 'cousins' often still eye each other warily. Nevertheless, many professional artists and arts therapists not only work amicably shoulder to shoulder in the same healthcare structure, but are also members of organizations representing both approaches to the work.

Putting the arts into professionals' practice

In 1984, I was hoping that the book would encourage professionals to incorporate arts activities into their practice. It was designed as a practical introduction to be accessible not just to trained artists and arts therapists but also for occupational therapists, nurses, psychologists, social workers and others working with persons with a disability or individuals who were in some way disadvantaged. Over the years I know that some professional arts therapists took issue with this. In part the problem can be attributed to the book's title which still contained the word 'therapy'. However, I wholeheartedly agree with their argument that therapists need to be trained in therapeutic procedures and should not be in the hands of untrained 'amateurs'. It should nevertheless be noted that the book's intended readership were already trained professionals. Nevertheless, in 1993 I did try to address what I felt were the therapists' concerns:

It is important to realize that this book does not provide a panacea for all problems, nor will it make the reader an instant creative specialist. However, it will give an insight into *some* of the techniques, originating in the creative arts, that have proved beneficial in health care, rehabilitation and special education settings in aiding individuals to gain better understanding and control of their bodies and emotions. One outcome of this is that they are better able to explore their own 'unique creative thumbprints' within the fabric of their daily lives.

(p. xii)

However, it is important to remember that the arts do not stand in isolation and are most definitely not in themselves a cure for all ills. Nevertheless, in each individual's act of creation, the arts engage the emotions and free the spirit. This can encourage individuals to do something because they want to and not just because someone else decides it is good for them. The arts can motivate in a way possibly no other force can. It is only through making a mark that no one else could make, that we express the individual spark of our own humanity.

(p. 4)

Changes to the second edition

While the world has changed markedly in the last 25 years, much of the material contained in the original and second editions remains relatively timeless. Included in this volume are edited chapters from the original and second editions of the book. Some such as Cheryl Neill's chapter on storytelling (Chapter 9), my own on drama (Chapter 8), and Wende Welch's chapter on masks and puppets in ensemble performance (Chapter 10) have only had superficial editing. The chapter on dance (Chapter 6) once again has been updated and revised.

Sadly, Yon's sudden and unexpected death in July 2002 not only robbed the world of one of the most dynamic, innovative and interdisciplinary teachers of the arts, but also meant that he could not revise his own chapter on music (Chapter 7). I have tried my best to be true to the essence of my late friend's work while streamlining his chapter.

Roberta Nadeau's chapter on visual art (Chapter 5) has also been streamlined a little,[6] while Rob Watling's chapter on the significance of folklore and other traditional material has been added to and brought up to date by Veronica James to include reference to rituals within modern society (Chapter 4).

New chapters in the third edition

The chapters in the third section provide stories with an international perspective in the field of arts in healthcare that focus not so much on activities (the focus of the original book[s]) but rather on the area of developing programs in hospital and other healthcare settings.

Judy Rollins' 'Arts for children in hospitals: Helping to put the "art" back in medicine', and Susan Pointe's and Shirley Serviss' 'Friends' art in healthcare program at the University of Alberta Hospital: Fostering a healing environment' look at the ways in which artists can alleviate distress for patients in the hospital, regardless of their age.

My piece on 'Healing laughter: The role and benefits of clown-doctors working in hospitals and healthcare' takes a look at Fools for Health's clown-doctor and familial clown programs and suggests ways that readers may develop similar programs even if they do not live in a large urban centre.

These themes are picked up in Magdalena Shamberger's 'Songlines: Developing innovative arts programmes with children who are visually impaired or brain injured' and Peter Spitzer's 'LaughterBoss: Introducing a new position in aged care'. They show some of the other ways in which clown-doctor programs have branched beyond solely clowning in the hospitals.

The contributors to this book are from many different professional backgrounds (psychology, nursing, medicine and the arts), but all have seen the therapeutic benefits of the arts at first hand. Whether they work in Scotland, Australia, England, the USA, Canada or elsewhere, the authors cite examples of how their work has touched the lives of the people with whom they work and where possible link their experiences to the appropriate research.

Final thoughts

Using the creative arts in therapy and healthcare, like its predecessors, is conceived as a practical book written in easily readable language that weaves theory into practice; distills research and theoretical models into simple conceptual frameworks; and then provides easily accessible ideas and examples that may be used by readers in a wide range of professional settings (e.g. seniors centers, hospitals, etc.) around the world.

As the observant reader will notice, the language used throughout this book is not uniform. However, it is important to note that finding socially acceptable language concerning 'disability' is always problematic and has changed many times during the last 25 years. Some early readers suggested I unify the language. However, as this volume is intended for a broad readership of people, from many geographical locations, each with its own particular political, cultural and linguistic concerns, I chose not to go into each of the chapters and tinker with the words used by individual authors – who are themselves from different professional backgrounds, geographical locations and times. I appreciate that some of the authors may use words differently to your usual experience. I hope that any minor inconsistencies will not get in the way of the essential fact that each writer believes passionately in the power of the arts experience.

The authors believe, and research tends to support, that providing arts and arts therapy experiences within healthcare settings improves the delivery of healthcare, helps healing and improves an individual's sense of well-being and quality of life. Moreover, if we succeed in providing everybody irrespective of age, ability or state of health with access to meaningful avenues for creative expression, there will be a noticeable reduction in stress levels, increased feelings of 'wellness', a perceived improvement in quality of life and ultimately fewer healthcare visits for clinical interventions, surgery and medication.

Bernie Warren
Harrow, Ontario
Canada
September 2007

Notes

1 All human beings, irrespective of their abilities or limitations, are capable of making their own 'thumbprint', that is a 'mark' made in sound, line, color, form, shape or movement that no one else could ever make in exactly the same way. It is this mark which states, 'I exist. I have meaning' and it is a reflection on an individual as a unique human being. Most importantly, this unique creative thumbprint can be thought of as the essential building block of all creative expression.
2 To illustrate this point, here is a selection of 'classic' and recent writings on the arts for health and the arts therapies:

  E. Feder and B. Feder, *The Expressive Arts Therapies*, Englewood Cliffs, NJ: Prentice-Hall, 1981.
  P. Jones, *The Arts Therapies: A Revolution in Healthcare*, London: Brunner-Routledge, 2005.
  L. Moss, *Art for Health's Sake*, Dunfermline: Carnegie Trust, 1987.
  F. Turner and P. Senior (eds), *A Powerful Force For Good: Culture, Health and The Arts – An Anthology*, Manchester: Manchester Metropolitan University Press, 2000.

3 For example: National Coalition of Creative Arts Therapy Associations USA (http://www.nccata.org/); Irish Association of Creative Arts Therapists (http://www.iacat.ie/links.html), as well as a multitude of organizations representing individual arts forms, e.g. British Association of Art Therapists (www.baat.org), Dance-Movement Therapy Association of Australia (http://www.dtaa.org/), Canadian Association for Music Therapy (http://www.musictherapy.ca/), National Association of Drama Therapy USA (http://www.nadt.org/).
4 For example: in the UK, Arts For Health (http://www.mmu.ac.uk/artsforhealth/); National Network for Arts in Health (http://www.nnah.co.uk). In the USA, Society for the Arts in Healthcare (http://www.thesah.org).
5 In 1997, the UK Health Professions Council was revised to include art therapy as a government regulated profession (*Health Professions Council: Art Therapist*. March 26, 2006, www.hpc-uk.org). In 2002 the state of New York recognized creative arts therapy as a legitimate mental health profession, the first US state to do so (*New York State Office of the Professionals: Creative Art Therapy Licence Agreement*. March 22, 2006, http://www.op.nysed.gov/catlic.htm). However it should be noted that at this time (2007) in most parts of the world the arts therapies have yet to be acknowledged as a legally recognized profession(s).
6 Since writing this Introduction it was with great sadness that I learned by chance that Roberta Nadeau had died. Roberta was a great champion for the arts, especially for persons with a disability, and will be missed by many, especially her family. As I write this my thoughts and best wishes are with her children.

Chapter 2

Guidelines, preparations and practical hints

A brief checklist for workshop leaders

Bernie Warren

Some basic guidelines

Before we begin

While it may it may be obvious to some, it bears stating that:

- What follows is not intended to be a substitute for proper training and will not make any one an instantly successful 'creative therapist'.
- Given the professional and geographical diversity of this book's readership, some of the points presented below may be different to what is considered 'best practice' in your area.
- Before you begin any practical session make sure that you are familiar with your own professional association's guidelines concerning code(s) of conduct, ethics and best practice.[1]

A few thoughts on the ethics and politics of healthy touch

- In an age where we work with a wide range of people it is essential that time be taken to consider individuals' personal cultural and religious beliefs concerning touch.
- In many countries, because of the odious, inappropriate and wholly unacceptable behaviour of a few, touching another individual has become a minefield fraught with legal difficulties.
- However, it is important to note that touch is a natural human activity, essential to healthy development. As Dr Roy Brown used to remark 'in some ways touch is like a scalpel'. For while a scalpel is a very sharp instrument and in the wrong hands can do a lot of damage, you wouldn't want to take it away from a skilled surgeon.
- As physical contact is often an essential element of working in the creative arts, here are a few things to consider when navigating the 'minefield' which will go a long way towards preventing awkward misunderstandings:

- *'There but for fortune'*: treat others as you would wish to be treated yourself, namely with dignity and respect
- *Be aware*: whenever possible get notes from the relevant contact person regarding each individual's cultural and religious beliefs on touch.
- *Be sensitive*: ask permission wherever possible of the individual, prior to *any* physical contact.

- In this era of 'superbugs' (e.g. MRSA, VRE, C. Diff, etc.) when working in hospitals and other healthcare facilities you cannot wash your hands too often.[2]

  - Wash with soap under warm water for as long as it takes you to sing the 'ABC Song'.
  - If water and soap isn't available, use a hand sanitizer.

A few words about contracts and clarity

- Most creative specialists are employed by public or private institutions or organizations, to deliver programs within very specific limits with a particular group. Before agreeing to any 'program' it is very important that you clarify the conditions of your contract. Always ask yourself:

  - *Who* will I be working with?
  - *Why* am I being employed?
  - *What* am I expected to achieve?
  - *When* are we expected to meet?
  - *Where* do these meetings take place?

- Make sure, in establishing the *why* and *what* of your contract, that you are willing and able to do what is asked of you. In this era of account-ability and malpractice suits, and simply to avoid misunderstandings, it is *essential* that you clearly identify your expertise and orientation. There is no point pursuing a contract where you are doing something beyond your experience and training or where it is just not your way of working. In both cases you, your group and your employer are unlikely to benefit from or be satisfied with the situation. The result is that your contract is likely to be a short and unhappy one.
- Always remember that each group, and each individual within a group, has specific needs; sensitively choosing material suited to those needs will go a long way to making your sessions both enjoyable and successful.
- Try not to become so entrenched in the goals you are seeking to achieve that you stop being sensitive to a particular individual's immediate needs, or lose sight of the importance for all your group to become actively and enthusiastically involved in the session.
- If you are working in a clinical setting, always remember that the games,

activities and ideas presented here are merely starting points for therapeutic work and they do not transform you magically into a 'therapist'.
This requires many years of training, something that can neither be
substituted by nor conveyed in a book.

- Activities in any session should above all else be enjoyable.
- Often when working with the creative process, individuals will do something that is not only unexpected but also beyond their previously
exhibited capabilities.
- Enabling individuals to enjoy each session, to have fun with you, goes a
long way towards the transformation of these sessions from simply being
labeled as therapy to being truly beneficial, enabling participants to
overcome their limitations:

  – There are times when this guideline may be broken as some of the
  material that may surface might be anything but pleasant.
  – However, there is little benefit to be gained from participating in a
  creative therapy session if it is viewed in the same light as having to
  take medication.

- Volunteer help is essential when working with individuals with profound
disabilities:

  – I have enlisted help from janitors and kitchen staff as well as the
  more obvious professional colleagues, interns and students.
  – While extra helpers, whether volunteers or paid aides, can be a great
  help, often so much time is spent helping the helpers understand a
  particular way of working, or an individual's specific needs, that a
  moment is lost.
  – Nevertheless, sensitive or well-trained helpers who support those in
  greatest need without becoming too obtrusive can make the leader's
  job so much simpler.

- To be a successful leader you need to be a '*creative detective*'.
- Read the information given to you about the group briefly before the first
session; try to 'forget' it, or at least not refer to it consciously, during the
running of the first session.
- Always try to pay attention to everything you see and hear in each session.
Where appropriate, keep notes!
- Try to place the information you gain first hand in context.
- Try to make your first sessions simple and fairly undemanding but try to
employ one exercise that can act as a *diagnostic tool*. 'Diagnostic tool'
describes any activity that provides some insight into the capabilities and/
or feelings of the group, allowing you to build a picture of the individual
that supplements and quite often contradicts the existing clinical reports.
- After the session is over, compare your perceptions of the group members,
based on observations during the session, with those given to you before

you started. It is surprising how happy, co-operative and creative some individuals, whom others see as aggressive, withdrawn or disturbed, can be when given a warm and friendly environment in which they have a chance to express themselves. Also, it is important to be aware that an individual's talents or abilities may lie dormant for a long period, surfacing only when a particular activity engages them.

- Developing your own personal style and making the material used your 'own' is often as important as the material itself.
- It is important to model each activity wherever and whenever possible.
- *Remember that discussions after activities are often as or more important than the activity itself.*

Preparation and planning

Below I have outlined some observations and questions that I feel are important to the running of a successful session of creative therapy. The following checklist reflects my personal concerns:

- being clear on my responsibilities as leader
- treating the people I work with, irrespective of age or ability, as unique human beings
- providing a structure in which people can enjoy themselves, be creative and work towards overcoming the mental, physical or emotional conditions that they face in their daily lives.

The checklist, which is annotated, covers the three basic phases of running a practical session of creative therapy, that is before, during and after each session:

- Some of the items reiterate points made above.
- Many of the points may be obvious to you, some you may think about only occasionally, and others you may not have thought about before.
- After a while, most of the suggestions and questions that follow become so much an integral part of a leader's way of working that you can strike them from your checklist, as you will be doing them automatically.

Questions to be answered before starting the session

I Who am I working with?

(a) How many people will be in the group? Will this number be constant?

- Often this number will fluctuate. Someone may be ill, need to go to surgery, X-ray, dentist, hairdresser, or a million and one other places.

- Be patient and be prepared for these changing numbers.

(b) What are the ages of the group members? Are they approximately the same age?

- Knowing the ages of participants is particularly important as this will be a factor to be considered when choosing your material.

(c) What are the *abilities* of the group members? Wherever possible, try to get specific information about each individual who will be in your sessions:

- All too often you will be provided with a very sketchy outline of the people with whom you are expected to work. In many cases this will provide you with little or no useful information.
- If someone uses vague terms to describe an individual's behavior, such as 'she exhibits schizophrenic tendencies', try to get them to explain what they mean.
- Also, try to find out under what circumstances any described behaviors occur.

The kinds of basic questions you need to ask are:

- How many people will be in the session?
- Does anyone use a wheelchair or other ambulatory aids?
- Is everyone able to communicate?
- Do any individuals have difficulties with speaking, hearing, seeing?
- Does anyone have epilepsy? A heart condition?
- Will I have any professional or voluntary assistance in my sessions?
- Is there a common link between members of the group? For example, are all the individuals in the group recovering from a stroke?

(d) Do I know everything I need to know about the members of this group? For example, are any members of the group on medication that will limit their creative potential (e.g. heavy sedation)?

- No two groups are ever exactly the same, but obviously experience gained with similar groups is very valuable.
- It is always important to plan *specifically* for your group.
- The key is in choosing activities that allow group members to succeed.
- It is highly unlikely that you will know everything you would like to know before the start of the first session.
- You will almost certainly gain valuable information from your own work.

2 What are my responsibilities as leader?

(a) In what capacity am I being employed: teacher, facilitator, leader, therapist?

(b) What am I expected to do with the group? Is my job to engage the group directly in creative activities, or am I employed to seek actively to change specific behaviors?

(c) If my job is to change specific behaviors, what is the time frame in which I am expected to do this? Is this realistic?

(d) Am I capable of carrying out what has been asked of me?

(e) Do I need to renegotiate my 'contract'? That is, what I am expected to achieve with the group through my creative medium (see also 'Questions to be answered after the session is over', p. 17).

- If your job description and your duties clash, there is a need to clarify exactly what is expected of you.
- There is also a need for you to make clear to your employer/supervisor what skills you possess.
- There is a vast difference between accepting a challenge and misrepresenting your abilities.
- Often you may need to re-educate your employer or supervisor about why you work creatively and what skills you possess in relation to the perceived needs of your group.

3 Pre-session planning

(a) When is the session scheduled? How often do I see the group and for how long each session?

(b) Do the group members know where and when we meet? Do the other professional staff who work with them also know this information?

- Often you will have no say in the frequency or timing of your sessions.
- If your sessions are too long, allow time for simply talking and being with the members of the group. If the session is too short, allow yourself time before and/or after the session to be with the group.
- This unstructured 'talk time' is often essential to allow an individual to develop a trust in you. It also provides a time to share what has been happening in the group's lives.

(c) What space do I need to work in? Does the space I have been allocated meet these needs? For example, does it have running water and enough chairs? Is it comfortable? If not, how can I make do with the space allocated?

- It is essential that you make clear to the person dealing with scheduling and administration exactly what your needs are.

- Demand the impossible – go for what you would want ideally and barter from there!

(d) Will I have any assistants? Will they be volunteers or professionals? Do they know the group members? Do they know my way of working? Do they know what my goals are?

- It is not unusual for your assistants to know the group better than you. This can be an extremely valuable asset. Make use of these people.
- Wherever possible, run workshops for them before working with your group. Take them into your confidence; share ideas and information with them.
- One word of caution – always remember that, no matter what happens, you are responsible for the running of the creative sessions, consequently when push comes to shove you must have the final word.

4 Planning the session

(a) Given all the information I now have, how can I best achieve my goals? These may be different from those suggested by your employer or supervisor.

(b) What activities will best match my strengths with the perceived needs of the group and their abilities?

- Plan for ability: always seek to plan for what people *can* do.
- Accept that everyone has some limitation or other; however, as John Swann said, 'I am not my disability, I am me.'[3]

(c) How much structure do I need to provide for the group so they can actively engage in these activities?

- Much of this may have to be left open until after your first session.
- Try to provide, in the first few sessions, activities, structures and language systems that allow you room to change direction without breaking the trust and security you are developing.

(d) What equipment will I need? Is this to be provided for me? Am I expected to take my own art supplies? Tape recorder? Musical instruments?

- Many creative specialists always carry their own materials around with them. It is perhaps the one way of ensuring you have exactly the materials you need.
- Try to be reimbursed, or given an equipment budget to cover these costs.

(e) Is the room with which I have been provided still going to function well for me? Do I need to negotiate another space?

- This may be difficult, but always try to get the room that suits you.
- If you need a sink for art work, or a piano, or a clean floor to roll on, keep on pressing for your needs.
- It may be difficult explaining to someone unfamiliar with your creative medium why you need these facilities, but keep on trying.

Points to look for and questions to ask yourself during the session

1 Immediately prior to the session

(a) Is all the equipment I need for this session here?
(b) Are all the group members here? What is the general mood of the group? Is it in keeping with my plans for this session?

- In some cases you may want to keep that mood. In others, you may wish to dispel it. Either way, you may feel the need to change your plans.
- Flexibility of approach is one of the keys to successful and creative leadership.

2 Running the session

(a) Did I introduce myself? Does the group know why I am here and what we will be doing together? How do they react to this?
(b) Do I know the individuals in this group?

- Every group is different.
- Every individual in every group is unique. Each makes their mark differently. The medium in which they are most creative differs.
- Name games, sharing information and allowing group members to feel they are part of the group's decision-making process is essential.
- All too often, leaders do not even consider asking a group what they would like to do.

(c) Am I warming up the group for the activities to come?

- The warm-up sets the tone for the rest of the session.
- If the session is to be 'physically strenuous', it is important to warm up the joints and muscles.
- If imagination is to be the focus of the session, exercises to warm up the imagination will be needed.
- If there is lethargy at the beginning of an active session, it's very unlikely that your group will be prepared to expend any energy without being coaxed.

(d) How are group members responding? Who is outgoing? Who is shy?

(e) Am I introducing the activities in a way that people can understand? Am I working at their pace?

(f) Am I providing the right amount of structure to allow the group to be creative?

(g) Am I meeting the individual needs of the group? Am I aware of changes occurring in these needs throughout the session?

- Throughout the session, no matter how actively involved you are, you must be sensitive to the needs of the entire group.
- This requires tremendous amounts of concentration and, in particular, paying close attention to all the observed behaviors of your group.
- Make sure you are using language that the group understands. You may need to vary your language level (that is, the complexity of words) and your language system – the way you put sentences together, and try to reinforce your requests with gestural clues to communicate with all the group's members.
- Always remember to work at your group's pace, but also always start each activity at the beginning and not just where you finished last time with this or some other group.
- As to the structure, you will have to sense if you need to let go of the reins or pull them in even more. This is something one learns with experience and unfortunately experience can not be gained from any book.

(h) Am I simply filling up the session with 'busy time'?

(i) Am I enjoying myself?

- If you are not enjoying yourself, it is almost certain that no one else will be.
- However, be careful that you are not the only person enjoying yourself. Remember who the session is for; it is often important to remind your assistants about this too.
- If you do get caught in a 'playing to the crowd' mentality, the session may degenerate into 'busy time' with a lot happening but nothing being done.

(j) How can I end this session on a positive but relaxing note?

- Lying on the floor, listening to tranquil music, gentle rocking in pairs, telling the group a story, while they lie on the floor with their eyes closed, working with a parachute, are all examples of ends to a session that are both relaxing and positive.

3 Immediately after the session

(a) Does everyone know when the next session will be? Do I need to send notes back with certain individuals?
(b) Does everyone have all the possessions they arrived with?
(c) Do I have everything I came with?
(d) Have I checked all the lights are out? Water turned off? Is the room in reasonably the same state I found it?

- This is particularly necessary as janitors and cleaners are possibly the most important professionals we encounter.

Questions to be answered after the session is over

I Evaluating the session

(a) How did the group respond? To me? To my material? To other members of the group? Was this as I expected?
(b) How did I feel about the session – good, uneasy, bad? Can I pinpoint a reason for this? The room? My presentation? My contract? My material?
(c) Did I meet any of my goals this session? Did I identify new goals during the session?
(d) Have I made a written note of my observations and feelings about the session yet?

- Even in this age where 'personal privacy' is protected by 'legislative acts' I feel it is extremely important to keep written records.
- However, I also suggest you seek counsel from your employers concerning who may have access to your session notes.
- Session notes should not just be a clinical account of what happened. They should include observations of what went on, how the group members participated and how you felt the session went.
- I have kept a journal of every session I have ever run and these have proved invaluable, not only during but also after the sessions have finished.

2 Planning for the next session

(a) Am I on the right track? Do I need to change my approach? My material? My medium? Do I need to renegotiate my contract?
(b) Who are the individuals in the group who need special attention? How can I best meet these needs without disturbing other members of the group?
(c) What shall I do next time? How can I link it to what we have already done so that it builds on these experiences?

- The answers to these questions will be extremely specific.
- The only observation I will make is that it is essential that you link your material to your own personality and to the personalities in your group.

(d) Have I scheduled time for a break between sessions?

- In the long run it is essential that you timetable 'space' for yourself to replenish the energy you have expended. You cannot pour from an empty cup.

(e) The most important thing to remember is that everyone in the room is a human being.

- You, your assistants and the members of your group all have good and bad days. All of you will experience frustration and elation, failure and success.
- If you can bear that in mind, you will be a long way down the road to allowing the people you work with the opportunity to expand their own horizons through creative activity.

Notes

1 For information related to training, accreditation and other related matters see the Appendix.
2 Any toys, props or instruments you are using should also be washed and/or disinfected after each use.
3 Quoted in H. Exley, *What It's Like To Be Me*, Watford: Exley Publications, 1981.

Chapter 3

Don't forget to breathe and smile

Breathing exercises as warm-ups for art activities in healthcare settings

Bernie Warren

> A thousand mile journey begins with one step.
>
> (Lao-tzu)

I began my study of the Eastern martial arts in 1970. Since that time I have continuously immersed myself in the forms, philosophies and healing applications of various martial arts, particularly Taoism and the Chinese internal martial arts.[1] In 1975 I began to pursue a career in the performing arts with a particular focus on the applications of these arts in education, healthcare and therapy. For many years I kept these two aspects of my life separate.

In 1991 on a research trip to Britain, a dear friend and I engaged in a discussion about our root discipline. We both had studied various aspects of the performing arts and taught courses that crossed disciplinary and artistic boundaries. After some discussion he proclaimed that while he taught drama and dance, his discipline was music. He then asked me what my discipline was. For a few moments I was completely speechless. However, as we conversed it became clear to us both that all my creative work was (and still is) based on notions of breath and energy rooted through my training in the internal martial arts.

Wei wu wei – 'do without doing'

> One must transcend techniques so that the art becomes an artless art, growing out of the unconscious.
>
> (Daisetsu Suzuki)

There are many similarities between studying the internal martial arts and the creative arts. An artist seeks a meditative state in which mind, body and spirit are balanced; for effortless action is one of the goals of both the martial arts and creative activity. To accomplish this, one must let go of conscious thought (for all too often thinking gets in the way of doing) and step beyond technical knowledge (e.g. the physical repetition of steps) and seek the balance between inner knowledge and external form.

When an individual is immersed in creative activity they can become lost in a creative moment, a liminal state that may potentially bring together physical, intellectual, emotional and spiritual aspects of our being in a way that offers unique opportunities for transformation and healing to take place. Moreover, this immersion provides opportunities for the participant to achieve a meditative state remarkably similar to that of the martial artist.

From a Taoist perspective creative moments provide a way of creating a *double balance*: a time when the energies of the body are in balance with themselves and the body is in harmony with its surroundings. At this time, when we are 'lost to the world', it is also possible that we may become open to change. Within the balanced stillness of the *creative moment*, individuals focus all their being into a *unique creative act* and it is in that creative moment, when Qi^2 flows freely, that they may be provided with the catalyst through which they may transcend their limitations. The potential exists for changes to take place, 'in spite of ourselves'.

Taoist concepts of health and healing

> Pure energy is the root of the human body.
>
> (Lu 1978)

For the Taoist the universe is alive with a kind of primal power, a force they refer to as Qi. In traditional Chinese medicine, Qi is said to flow through meridians in the body and blockage of the flow of Qi through these meridians is believed to be one of the major causes of illness.

Qigong is a Chinese system of fitness and health promotion. It is one of the 'three pillars' of traditional Chinese medicine[3] and the use of exercises for health and physical development that are now called Qigong has a documented history of over 2000 years.

There are many different Qigong exercises. Each exercise uses a specific posture and breathing pattern to stimulate hormone secretion and immune function, oxygenation of body cells and to generate bio-electrical energy for healing purposes.

Research pertaining to Qigong indicates remarkable results for persons with medical conditions such as high blood pressure, cancer and even spinal cord injuries. Regular Qigong practice helps to prevent illness, sustain an active lifestyle and increase longevity.

Breathing and the creative arts

> When done correctly all will appear effortless.
>
> (Taoist proverb)

My practical explorations with creative artists into the relationships among breath, thought and action lead me to believe that:

• sound must come from and return to silence
• movement must come from and returns to stillness.

More than this, *movement and sound must be a purposeful expression of the feelings and thoughts which the artist is experiencing.* To achieve this, ideally artists need to work in a relaxed state of creative tension so that their breath preparation and the physical process of breathing shape their thoughts and feelings.

From this perspective, breathing (something we do most usually without a conscious thought) is perhaps the most important skill that any artist must learn irrespective of the social, professional or therapeutic context in which they work.

Simple Qigong exercises

> Concentrate entirely on your breathing, as if you had nothing else to do.
> (Kenzo Awa)

For more than 20 years I have been using Qigong exercises with people with life-changing conditions and in the training of actors, dancers, musicians and visual artists. Below I present some simple breathing exercises that not only help individuals prepare for creative endeavors but also if done regularly can help reduce stress and prevent many illnesses.

All creative arts demand a great deal of physical, intellectual and emotional energy. The primary purpose of the exercises presented here is to help individuals to develop, control and shape the personal energy that in large measure is needed in any creative undertaking. These exercises emphasize self-discipline and concentration and will help you slowly become more attuned to your own body and can help you improve posture, breathing patterns and energy flow.

When may I use these exercises?

The exercises presented below are simple forms that you may perform for health benefits at any time during the day. In addition, here are some guidelines for their use during a creative activity session:

• Opening and Closing Breaths is a good exercise to start or finish any creative session.
• Crane Stepping into Water may be used as a break from periods of sedentary work or long periods of sitting.

- Tranquil Sitting or Standing like a Tree are good exercises either as a pause point in the middle of a physically demanding or energetic session or in the cool-down.
- Lighting the Candle may be used as part of a guided imagery session or as a means of calming an individual or group.

All the exercises can be done indoors in a room with good ventilation or outside. They can be performed in silence or you may want to play quiet meditative music. Throughout your experience, try to quiet your ever-questioning mind. Keep the following very important aspects in mind while performing the exercises:

- Breathe in and out through your nose, quietly and softly so that you can barely hear your breathing.
- Never force or hold your breath.
- If at any time you start to feel light headed or faint, *think about* but *do not* look at your feet.

Standing like a Tree[4]

Don't just act; stand there.

(Elia Kazan)

This self-healing exercise, one of the so-called 'Medical Treasures' of classical Qigong, is a simple but potent weapon in the fight against stress and stress-related diseases. Moreover, research suggests standing for five minutes in this position has the same cardiovascular effect as walking for 20 minutes on a treadmill at a moderate pace:

- Stand with your legs hip width apart and your feet flat on the floor parallel to one another.
- Bend your knees but do not let them extend beyond your toes.
- Keep your shoulders relaxed and your spine straight but not rigid.
- Imagine that your head is suspended from the sky by a silken thread, that there is a small cushion of air between each vertebrae and that your chin rests on a silken pillow – so that your eyes remain parallel to the floor.
- Move your hips slightly backwards, as if sitting down on a high bar stool, so that your shoulders are slightly forward of your hips.
- Point your elbows away from your body with your palms facing towards your thighs. (Pose 1 in Figure 3.1)
- Do *not* tighten your stomach muscles; rather keep the front of your body soft.
- Throughout this exercise think of your head 'floating up' and your tailbone 'drifting down'.

- When properly aligned you should feel a gentle stretching sensation in your inner thighs and buttocks.
- Close your mouth, so that your teeth touch and your tongue lightly touches the roof of your mouth.
- You should imagine that you are like a tree rooted to the ground through your legs and feet, and reaching upward to the sky through the top of your head.
- In the beginning, hold this position for about 30–45 seconds. As you become more comfortable with the position, you can slowly increase your time in this position until you can stand like a tree for five minutes.

This posture can be done while waiting for a bus or in a line up, before or after doing the dishes or anywhere where you are standing.

Opening and Closing Breaths

I begin my daily Qigong practice with a physical clearing and cleansing using a set of three linked exercises which together are known as the Opening and Closing Breaths. These exercises help to 'guide' Qi through the main meridians, energize the body and expel 'stale' air.

This set of exercises is also referred to as the Three Healing Breaths because they help to strengthen the immune system, cleanse the body of impurities and in traditional Chinese medical practice are used to help prevent and treat cancers and stress-related diseases.

- These exercises are best performed at the beginning and/or at the end of every session.
- Ideally *breathe in (IN)* or *breathe out (OUT)* through your nose where indicated below *or* breathe naturally without holding or forcing your breath.
- Repeat each exercise three or more times; then proceed to the next.

Assume the Standing like a Tree posture described above (Pose 1 in Figure 3.1).

Lotus flower opening

- (IN) Lift your arms up from floor, elbows pointing away from your body so that your palms move towards the sky.
- At your navel turn palms down, pointing your fingers towards the ground (Figure 3.1.2).
- Slowly lift your hands above your head until your fingers point towards the top of your head (Figure 3.1.3).
- Open your hands outwards, your palms towards the sky (Figure 3.1.4).

Figure 3.1 Opening and Closing Breaths: lotus flower opening.

Photographs taken by Nicole Gervais

- When your hands reach shoulder height (OUT), turn your palms down towards the ground (Figure 3.1.5).
- Continue until your arms are at your side (Figure 3.1.6).

Lotus flower closing

- (IN) Open your arms away from your body with palms pointing to the ground as if a large balloon is inflating underneath them. (Pose 2 in Figure 3.2).
- At heart height turn your palms towards the sky (Figure 3.2.3).
- Lift your arms in an upward circular motion until your palms face the top of your head (Figure 3.2.4).
- Bring your elbows together so that they face forward.

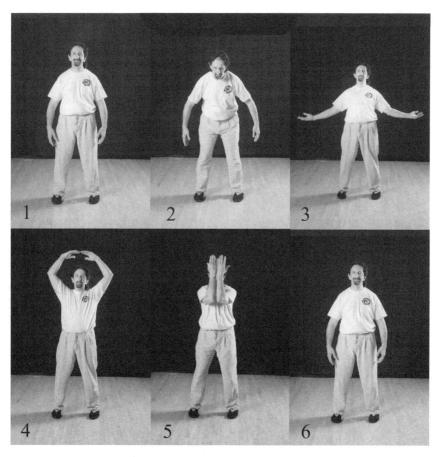

Figure 3.2 Opening and Closing Breaths: lotus flower closing.

Photographs taken by Nicole Gervais

- (OUT) Slowly move your elbows towards floor with your palms facing your body and your fingers pointing towards the sky. (Figure 3.2.5).
- At navel height open your elbows sideways and move your hands towards the ground.
- Continue until your arms are at your side (Figure 3.2.6).

Petals floating on the water

- Raise your hands to navel height turning them until your palms face towards your navel (Figure 3.3.1).
- (IN) Float your elbows away from your body; your palms follow the motion of your elbows (Figures 3.3.2, 3.3.3).

Figure 3.3 Opening and Closing Breaths: petals floating on the water.

Photographs taken by Nicole Gervais

- (OUT) Begin to bring your elbows towards body with your palms following the motion of your elbows (Figures 3.3.4, 3.3.5).
- At end of exercise cover your navel, one palm on top of the other. Breathe naturally (Figure 3.3.6).

Crane Stepping into Water

There are hundreds of walking exercises. Here is an exercise adapted from a version of Hua To's Five Animal Frolics.[5]

- Stand with your legs straight, your heels together with your toes pointing away from one another at a 90-degree angle (do *not* lock your knees).

Figure 3.4 Crane Stepping into Water.

Photographs taken by Nicole Gervais

    – Let your arms rest against your body, palms towards your thighs. *Imagine your arms are wings* (Figure 3.4.1).

Moving to the right

- As you breathe IN:

    – Bend your *left* knee.
    – Turn your hips to the *right*.
    – Pick up your *right* heel (Figure 3.4.3).
    – *At the same time*, float your arms away from your body up to shoulder height keeping your palms towards the ground.
    – Take a *small* step out at a diagonal to your *right* (Figure 3.4.5).

- As you breathe OUT:

    – Place your *right* foot on the floor heel first (Figure 3.4.6).
    – *At the same time* float your arms back towards your thighs (Figure 3.4.6).

- Bring your *left* leg in to meet your *right* leg so that your heels return to rest (Figure 3.4.7).
- Turn your hips back to the centre (Figure 3.4.8).

Moving to the left

- As you breathe IN:

  - Bend your *right* knee.
  - Turn your hips to the *left*.
  - Pick up your *left* heel.
  - *At the same time* float your arms away from your body up to shoulder height keeping your palms towards the ground.
  - Take a small step out at a diagonal to your left.

- As you breathe OUT:

  - Place your *left* foot on the floor heel first.
  - *At the same time* float your arms back towards your thighs.
  - Bring your *right* leg in to meet your *left* leg so that your heels return to rest.
  - Turn your hips back to the centre.

Continue walking forward alternating right and left legs. At the end, return to the Standing like a Tree posture or try the following exercise, Tranquil Sitting.

Tranquil Sitting

Seated Qigong exercises can be done anywhere: at home, at the office or when traveling. Any chair will do; however, for best results choose a straight-backed armless chair.

- Sit comfortably on the chair with your legs hip width apart and your feet flat on the floor in parallel.
- As for Standing like a Tree, keep your spine straight but not rigid with your shoulders slightly forward of your hips. Do *not* tighten your stomach muscles; rather keep the front of your body soft.
- Place one hand on top of the other resting just below the navel, palms toward the body.
- Close your mouth, with your teeth touching and your tongue lightly in contact with the roof of your mouth.
- Breathe in and out through your nose, quietly and softly so that you can barely hear your breath.
- *Never hold or force your breath.*

Lighting the candle

Qigong helps lower stress levels and helps us to relax. This exercise can be done lying back in a recliner chair or lying flat in bed (if lying flat in bed, place a small pillow under your head) and can help you rest and sleep:

- Do *not* cross your legs, as this blocks circulation.
- If you wish, play soft calming music during this exercise.
- Place your left hand palm down, at the top of your breast bone just below your collar bone.
- Place your right hand palm down, just below your navel.
- Allow your elbows to rest close to your body.
- Close your eyes.
- Breathe slowly and regularly through your nose.
- Never force or hold your breath.
- Imagine there is a lighted candle in the space under your right hand.
- As you breathe in, imagine the flame of this candle extending upwards towards your left hand.
- As you breathe out, imagine this flame returning to its original position.

Don't be surprised if during this exercise your palms get very warm. You can continue in this position for as long as you like or until you fall asleep.

Endnote

Unfortunately words are no substitute for experience and trying to capture the essence of Qigong on paper is like trying to catch the wind, one may feel it but never contain it. So if all else fails:

DON'T FORGET

BREATHE and SMILE

FOR THIS IS THE ESSENCE OF QIGONG

Acknowledgements

I shall always be indebted to my teacher Master George Ling Hu who, since our first meeting in 1993, has opened my eyes to the real essence of the Chinese martial arts.

I must also acknowledge my late friend Yon who opened my eyes to the connections between the performing and the martial arts and whose work has always been an inspiration to me as I struggle to find my way along the path.

Finally, I wish to thank John Taylor who ten years ago came to me as a student and from whom I have learned at least as much as I have taught.

Notes

1 Since 1994 I have studied and taught primarily Chinese forms such as Qigong, Tai Chi.
2 Qi (also written as Chi, or Ch'i) has no direct translation in English. It is often translated simply as 'energy'. However, 'vital force', 'life force' or even 'creative force' more accurately describe it.
3 The other two are acupuncture and healing with food and herbs. Some occasionally refer to a fourth pillar, namely bone setting and manipulation.
4 This is the basic standing exercise for all stationary Qigong.
5 The Five Animal Frolics, introduced by Hua To, is an ancient exercise based on the natural movements and postures of five animals: the Crane, Bear, Monkey, Deer, and Tiger. It is reputed to be the oldest written exercise program for preventive medicine.

Further reading

Cohen, K. (1996) *Qigong: Traditional Chinese Exercises for Healing Body, Mind and Spirit*, Boulder, Co: Sounds True (DVD).

Lam Kam Chuen, (1991) *The Way of Energy: Mastering the Chinese Art of Internal Strength with Chi Kung Exercise*, New York: Gaia.

Ling Hu, G. (1996) *Swimming Dragon Chi Kung and 6 Simple Chi Kung Methods for Health*, Houston, TX: Hu Ling Instructional Video Series (DVD).

Requena, Y. (1996) *Chi Kung: The Chinese Art of Mastering Energy*, Rochester, VT: Healing Arts Press.

Sheng Keng Yun, (1997) *Walking Kung: Breathing for Health*, York Beach, ME: Samuel Weiser.

Chapter 4

Folklore and ritual as a basis for creative therapy

Rob Watling and Veronica James

Folklore is formal, performative and thematic and becomes delightfully, dynamically alive as it is integrated into life and custom through 'the sieve of communal approval'.[1] Folklore is that active part of any culture which is transmitted by word of mouth or by habit and practice. Predominantly passed on in daily life through oral, physical and written traditions, and increasingly through the media, it is a moral repository which is renewed though repeated folksay (proverbs, riddles, rhymes, dialect), games, folk literature (folktales, poems, songs, dramas), customs and beliefs, music, dance and ethnography (the study of arts, crafts and the manufacture and use of artifacts). Folklore is as much part of the modern urban cultures of industrialized societies as it is of American Indians, Australian aborigines and ancient and modern Greek and Egyptian cultures. It is something we all do, not just 'the things our grandparents used to do' for it is a vital part of the way all societies operate. There is folklore for children and adults. It can be found at home, school, hospitals and work; in politics, religion and banking; in self-help and therapeutic groups; in cities, towns and rural areas and in both complex and simple organizations. By convention folklore draws on themes that are anonymous, but universally shared, although it is given life and continuity through individual communities and groups.

Wherever it is found, folklore belongs to the people who use it. They have devised it when they have wanted it and needed it, transmitted it down and across generations, adapted it when necessary, and discarded it when they have no further need for it. Interestingly, the internet is replete with folklore. Archived material gives new and international access to old materials whilst also offering new applications and projects for teaching and therapy. In addition it generates its own folklore – such as the contemplative story of the young man addicted to an internet game which ruined his life and led to his death, which is reminiscent of ancient tales of isolation and the struggle for survival. Here we can see that folklore is constantly adapting, and almost infinitely variable. While folklore is often considered to be 'traditional', in the sense of being handed down from the past, it is also generated anew. The custom of passengers clapping when a plane touched down was a measure of the wonder of flight, but one which passed as flying became taken for granted. Above all, folklore is functional and strong folklore stands the test of time because familiarity, predictability and repetition can bring the comfort and ease of generating structures which are critical to the facilitation of communal engagement.

Making use of the functionality of folklore, we believe that clients can be assisted to tackle their problems by applying folklore to enable safe, trusting connectivity and shared experience, as well as for creative therapeutic challenge. Without making a romantic appeal for some sort of return to a simpler, more ethnocentric way of life, we believe that there are important lessons to learn from tradition and ritual. We have found that a working knowledge of folklore is invaluable in engaging with a range of groups and individuals. It has served both as a source of material and as part of a theoretical model of what happens in creative therapy sessions. However, before we look at some of the applications of folklore we need to know a little more about the subject.

Many of the early folklorists, working in the nineteenth century, concentrated purely on collecting large quantities of material. They wanted to list the things people did – the songs they sang, the rituals they performed, the tales they told or the tools they used. Collections of this information were compiled but it was some years before people began to realize that the material was not enough by itself. It was not sufficient to know that 'Waly Waly' was a Scottish ballad. They wanted to observe it freshly, and connect it with how it was expressed, who sang it, to whom, where and when. Where was it learned, how was it remembered and why does it exist at all? Is it just a sad song? Is it a cautionary tale? Is it a record of an important event in a society unable to perpetuate its history with pen and ink? This new generation of students wanted to know about how folklore exists in social reality, looking at the context and the function of the living material. It is the social reality of context and function that interest us, too.

Folklore can serve an enormous range of functions. A simple folktale can, in certain contexts: relate the history and wisdom of a society; reinforce custom alongside taboo and prejudice; teach multiple skills by example; offer personality types against which to understand our personal hopes and fears and responses; explain the mysteries of the universe and our place within it; amuse and entertain; warn of danger and keep us safe; offer solutions to personal and family problems, as well as suggesting activities to solve practical issues. The list of the contributions of folktales can be made very long yet other types of material increase the range of these varied functions. To illustrate some of these are five examples. Four are old and established. The fifth is, apparently, a new one, but incorporates the forms seen in the previous four.

The Anang in Nigeria, like many other African peoples, use proverbs as a central part of their judicial system. Plaintiff and defendant quote proverbs (widely used as the embodiment of tribal wisdom) to support their cases.[2]

In China, while the tyrannical Chin Shih Whang was having the Great Wall built, folksongs emerged as one of the few possible expressions of the people's feelings: their grief at the death of so many laborers, their fury at the enforced break-up of so many families as men were sent away to build the wall, their opposition to the capital punishment of those who refused to go. Popular protest songs, passed on by word of mouth, are still around today.

In Norse mythology, combatants indulge in an insult-flinging competition as a precursor to a battle. Here the idea seems to be to goad your partner into action and to prepare yourself for victory.

The Inuit of North America will sometimes have a singing duel to settle a dispute in a non-violent way (violence is not welcome in the close confines of a winter settlement). The combatants sing songs at each other with the intention of ridiculing their opponent into submission. They channel their antagonism into a functional, conclusive ritual.[3]

Spectators of competitive team sports combine the use of ritualized sporting sayings to explain how the team will or will not perform well and as a defense against the anxiety of losing; ritual actions and dance (the New Zealand All Black Rugby team using a Maori chant and dance before the start of a game); and channeled antagonism through ritualized insult-flinging at the opposition, with singing duels and chanting duels aimed at undermining the opposition and enhancing team spirit.[4]

The notion that folklore can and should be studied in terms of its context and function is central to us if we wish to apply traditional material to creative therapy. We could sit in a circle and sing war chants. We could perform traditional Swiss dances, tell each other Russian fairy tales or play Welsh street games. However, as leaders we need to understand what it is we are doing and with whom. We too need a firm notion of the context and function of our material and the way in which these elements relate to each other. This relationship can be described by a simple diagram (Figure 4.1), in which the shading denotes areas of change and mutual influence. When any one of the variables in the figure alters, it may affect one or both or neither of the others.

Take, for example, the game of London described later in this chapter. Traditionally when played by a group of children, it is 'just a game'. Its context might be described as a backstreet game, played by friends in their leisure time. The function of the game appears to be fun; something to pass the time; perhaps a chance to consolidate friendship or to practice competitiveness. If we change the context by playing this game in a creative therapy session, what else do we change? Perhaps we change nothing, as we can play this game for its own sake. However, we could decide to use this game with a group who need to develop gross motor control. Now we could add the function of teaching people to stop quickly and to control their balance to our list. It is still the same material but now with new context and function. We can go further (as in the 'collective' version of the game

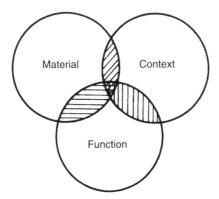

Figure 4.1 Schematic relationships between context, function and traditional material.

described below and change the rules of the game. It is no longer everyone for themselves but an exercise in co-operation. Context, function and material are variables for us and the group to alter as we wish.

Folklore is a powerful, accessible, adaptable source of material, which offers us insights into the way people act and interact with each other and the environment. Once we understand some basic principles of the way in which it operates, we are able to apply some of this material in a therapeutic way. The rest of this chapter outlines some practical ways in which this can be done, with particular reference to traditional games, folk narratives and simple rituals.

Traditional games[5]

We have tried to suggest games of different types in this section, varying from the energetic to the slow and contemplative. All of them, we hope, contain the essential element of fun referred to in other parts of this book. By way of explanation, we have used the term 'It' to describe the player who is working against the rest of the group, usually in an effort to catch them. 'It' is often called 'He', 'Her', 'On' or 'On it' in Britain.[6]

Stick in the mud

This is an excellent game with which to start a session with young active people and one that is always a great favorite. It is also called Sticky Glue, Release, Ticky Underlegs, Underground Tag, Ice Witch, and in Latvia is known as Salt Posts, where it used in everyday language to describe someone who is too scared to move.

One player is 'It' and chases the others. Anyone 'It' touches must stand with their arms outstretched and their legs apart – they are 'stuck in the mud'.

They must stand still until another player frees them by crawling between their legs. They may then run off again. Sometimes players are required to call 'SOS' or 'Release' while they are stuck in the mud. 'Its' job is to get everyone stuck in the mud, which is not easy. Having two 'Its' helps make the game less frustrating. The first and/or last people to be caught are 'It' next time round.

This is a fast, energetic game involving a variety of movement and body shapes, basic teamwork and usually quite a lot of noise. It can be useful as an exercise for those needing to develop simple spatial awareness and can easily be adapted for different ability groups. Slowing the game down to a walking pace can be useful, so can changing the 'freeing' act for a simpler maneuver. Some people find it easier to stand near a wall when they have been tagged and to hold up an arm or a stick to form an archway. They are released when someone goes through the arch (this is sometimes called Tunnel Touch). Alternatively, the game can be made more demanding: players must move around the room in a particular way; you must crawl backwards through a captive's legs to free them; play the game linked to a partner so that pairs of people have to crawl through two sets of legs. As ever, the possibilities are endless and can be matched to the abilities of your group or used to lead them into new areas of movement and activity.

Sun and frost

This is a version of Stick in the Mud played in Stornoway on the Isle of Lewis, Scotland and was collected by the Opies from an 11-year-old girl who said:

> You all stand in a row and one person picks the nicest face for the sun, and the rest that's left they all put on ugly faces and pick the ugliest [for the frost]. The people that's left all go out and the frost goes after them and if they're caught they have to stand still till the sun tips them and they will get free. That's how you play the Sun and Frost.[7]

The obvious symbolism in this game can be of use to many groups over and above the physical benefits of movement. Rob has sometimes extended the idea and asked the Frost to 'really freeze' the players and the Sun to thaw them out with a warm hug and a nice sigh. There are many other traditional games where quite intimate body contact is perfectly acceptable, and they can be used, among other things, for the recognition of body parts.

London

A game with exceptionally wide circulation, this is known in various parts of the world as Red Light, Green Light, Ochs am Berg, Eros zwei drei – sauer Hering! Uno, Due, Tre, Stella, Grandmother's Footsteps or simply Freeze.

Originally played across a street or a yard, 'It' stands facing a wall with all the other players on the opposite side of the road. The object is for them to creep up and tap 'It' on the shoulder, but at any moment 'It' may suddenly turn round. Anyone 'It' sees moving (even a hand) is sent back to the start. 'It' may look round any number of times but is often required to count silently to ten between each go or to say a short phrase in his or her head to give the others a chance. The first player to get right across is the next 'It'.

This game is immensely popular and nearly always played with complete equanimity. This has much to do with the quality of the 'It' role, for 'It' has considerably more control over the proceedings than in chasing and tagging games. This is one of those rare games where 'It' is the coveted role, but has the additional advantage that everyone else can feel that they are succeeding – even the ones who are sent to the back, for they are now hidden by the people in front of them and can move forward more quickly. A headstrong dash for the finish is rarely successful and the quiet individual can often win by stealth. We have seen many players delight in the attention they receive in being sent back over and over again. It is rare for players to accuse one another of cheating or to refuse to accept 'Its' verdict.

In creative therapy sessions the game is useful in a number of ways. It is fun, of course, and can relax a group very quickly, helping to create a good working atmosphere. It improves concentration and alertness and can be used to develop body awareness, balance and gross motor control. Faced with a group of adolescent boys who were having difficulty making group decisions and acting co-operatively, Rob developed a variation called Group London. There was still one 'It' but the rest of the group had secretly to select one of their number as the one they wanted to 'make it' to the other side. Their job was to help him get across by shielding him from view, or by 'sacrificing' themselves and drawing 'Its' attention away from him. The dynamic of the game changed dramatically and it was used on a number of occasions as a link between more self-centered games and exercises to develop group cohesion. A more gentle variation is from Italy, called Beautiful Queen in which the Queen faces the children and calls the name of an animal and the number of steps and children approach in small or big steps as befits the animal. The first one to arrive is next Queen.

As a widely known game, London also serves as a good example of another benefit of traditional material. Many people playing these games will remember their own variant and can make a positive contribution to the session (something they might otherwise find difficult). Whole sessions can be run with all the activities suggested by group members from their own repertoire of traditional material.

Muk

This game is part of the traditional winter activity of the Inuit. The players sit talking and joking in a circle with 'It' in the centre. Suddenly 'It' will say 'Muk' (the Inuit word for silence) whereupon no one must make a sound. However, 'It' is allowed to tell jokes, fool around, pull faces or whatever until someone breaks the Muk. Then the group gives that person a comic name (traditionally the name of an animal). This person then either replaces the 'It' or joins them as part of a growing team of animals who will eventually descend on the last silent member of the group.

Ostensibly a game about the breaking down of barriers between individuals (one of the social functions for the Inuit), in our society this game can easily become an exercise in reinforcing these barriers. This is particularly likely in a group where people have problems with communication and self-presentation and 'It' can quite quickly feel threatened and ostracized. The leader is at liberty to make capital out of this (perhaps moving on to more intensive work) or to defuse the situation by having more than one person in the middle. You may wish to stop the game when there are still three or four people in the outer circle to avoid the group applying all its coercion on one individual, but this last breakdown can have a unifying effect on the group and restore the element of fun.

Irish wake games[8]

The traditional Irish funeral was a fascinating mixture of solemnity and joviality. In common with the funeral rites of many cultures, it served as an opportunity not only to pay respect to the dead but also to celebrate life and the living. Most if not all of the amusements have now been separated from the modern Irish wake, largely in response to the disapproval of the Church, but we still know enough about them and the way they were played to understand at least some of their functions in this context.

The wake itself, where relatives and neighbors would watch over the coffin until the funeral, was partly a chance for people to express their respect and to show their mourning. It also served to guard the coffin overnight from evil influences – which could mean spirits, the devil, bodysnatchers, or all three. There would be much drinking and eating at a wake and there was as much singing and dancing as at any other Irish gathering. However, there were also these games to help people stay awake and relatively sober at their task. There were riddles, trials of strength and dexterity, tricks of all sorts and forfeits galore, all acting as a confirmation, a celebration of the living at a time of deep respect for the dead.

Pig in the sty

One person (traditionally a woman) stands in the middle of a ring of players who link arms as securely as possible. Outside the ring is another player (usually a man). His job is to kiss or tag the girl in the middle either by reaching over the ring of linked players or by forcing his way through. (At this stage the ring may decide to let the girl escape and to keep the man prisoner.) All the other players try to frustrate the man's attempts until he is successful or resigns.

This game can be used in a number of ways: to act as a warm-up, to channel physical aggression, to develop co-operative energy, to break down barriers to physical contact (which can here be intimate but safe), to illustrate rejection and corporate disapproval or to promote a discussion of traditional sex roles. The game can easily be adapted by encouraging different techniques: use no hands; everyone has eyes closed; tickling is allowed; use persuasion to gain entry into the circle; cheat; etc.

Do the opposite

This was a common amusement at the wakes and one that has been popular with all sorts of groups, the object being to trick people into making simple mistakes. Two players, for example, hold a scarf between them and are told to do the opposite of any instruction you give them. You tell them to hold it tight and they should let go, you tell them to pick it up and they should leave it alone, you tell them to keep it away from other people and they should give it to a new couple. Any mistake (and there are many) is punished with a forfeit – a hit on the head with a balloon is a cheerful option. The game is, once again, infinitely variable and can easily be adapted to the abilities and concentrative powers of most groups. It is great fun to watch, for humor is a great leveler. Once everyone has been fooled (including you, for the leader should join in whenever possible in these games) the whole group has greater access to each other as individuals.

Cumulative games

Another adaptable concentration exercise is the cumulative memory game. The first player in a circle, for example, says 'I went to market yesterday and bought a cow.' The second player says, 'I went to market yesterday and bought a cow and a sheep.' The third says, 'I went to market yesterday and bought a cow, a sheep and a sack of corn.' This continues with each player adding something new to the list. Again it must be used at an appropriate level for the group. Some groups will be able to go round the circle several times without making a mistake. For others it will be a considerable achievement if they can repeat what their neighbor has just said. Be prepared to use memory aids (pictures, mime, sound clues) and look for ways to develop additional skills in the same game (recognizing the idea of 'sets of things', counting, non-verbal communication, etc.).

Narratives

Storytelling, recounting and ritualised metaphor[9]

Storytelling can be a fulfilling experience in its own right. Traditional tales, fairy stories, family stories, poems, ballads and dramas, as well as some modern literary ones, embody all sorts of wisdom: teachings, history, parables and advice; for folk narratives are often the living encyclopedia and life manual of an oral society. Even the simple act of being a member of an audience can be calming and nearly everyone loves to be told a story. We need not limit ourselves to straightforward tale-telling sessions, however useful they may be, but can reinforce their meanings and messages in a number of ways. It can often be valuable to ask groups to externalize their reactions to a narrative in discussions, in paintings and sculptures, in a dance perhaps, or by acting out some of the scenes. Ask your group to project their ideas of what happened before the start of the story and what happens afterwards. Use the narrative and its accessibility as a platform for all sorts of expression and discovery.

Since it is often the hero or protagonist with whom we are meant to identify, who encounters our own predicament and symbolizes ourselves, it can often be valuable to use a traditional narrative as the basis of a guided fantasy. In this exercise each member of the group listens to the story and acts out the part of the central character as the adventure unfolds: doing what the protagonist does; 'seeing' what he sees; 'feeling' what he feels; and learning (often intuitively) what the hero learns. A whole wealth of human experiences can be fed into each group member, who need not be self-conscious about the quality of their performance as it is directed inwards rather than out at an audience.

A version useful in a mixed-sex group, or mature group, is getting an individual to identify themselves as a folk hero or heroine and tell a very short story (45–90 seconds) about an incident that is an example of them in that character. Children's storybook characters are often favorites, for example, being Snow White and getting lost. Following this, the same story is repeated one by one by each member of the group. During the retellings, the initial storyteller hears minor differences which can help them see their experience or their hero/heroine in a different light, while the rest of the group enjoy the creativity of their own storytelling, or 'picture making', and hear how the same event can be heard or seen differently. An adaptation is for other group members to tell the same story but as different characters: the witch, the animals in the forest, the dwarves, the prince, the night-time, the sun. At the end the group may want to discuss what it felt like from their own character. An 'Oh, I didn't realize' is often the mark of new insights.

As a development of these applications, the use of 'modernized' sporting rituals and metaphors, albeit with ancient origins, can help access hard to reach groups such as young men with depression.[10] The group leader can be, but need not be an expert in the particular sport, as asking naïve questions can encourage the rest of the group to work together to explain. In the group, a post mortem of a recent match is initiated, and working with the language of the group – 'he was useless' – discussion of what the player might have thought and felt about being 'useless' can be explored, often using banter and humor. Without danger of the issue becoming personalized to an individual or their family, this can encourage group contributions, ideas, solutions and activities. The same group technique, with optional extras such as getting the group to use flipcharts to draw team diagrams or giving a commentary as the player, uses sporting stereotypes as a metaphor to explore what it is like to live alongside such people, or be such people. The brilliant goalkeeper, central to team success, but also at the back of the team, taciturn and a loner can be used to discuss the strategies and feelings that the goalie might employ, and how others might feel about the strategies being used off the field.

Ritual and creative therapy

Rituals have always formed an important part of the collective and individual actions of people throughout the world. From the Indian dance to the swinging of Catholic incense, from the blood sacrifice on a new boat to the distribution of sweets on the birth of a baby amongst some South Asian communities, from the rain dance to the children trying not to step on the cracks of the sidewalk, rituals are anchors of certainty in a precarious sea. Rituals are endemic because at the moment of ritual we know exactly where we stand.

There are many times every day when an individual or group needs to know where they stand. With groups this can be: at the start of a session; when a new member joins the group; when a group member faces a crisis or shares a moving experience; at the close of the session; or when someone leaves the group. At moments like these it can sometimes be helpful for a group to use some sort of ritual as a collective expression of a shared experience. The predictability of ritual can help to take the slightly frightening edge off uncertainty. There was one regular weekly group that Rob attended whose members were comforted not just by the occasional use of simple ritual but by the predictable, almost ritualistic use of traditional games as a mainstay of their work. They knew what to expect from the sessions and learned to understand their place within them.

But a word of warning. We have been members of several workshops and sessions where a ritual has been artificially imposed on a group, actively discouraging the authenticity it sought to generate. 'We are now going to show our unity for each other's feelings and experiences by joining with everyone in the room and silently communing with each other,' said the therapist. Unfortunately, it was obvious that the group wanted, on this occasion, to reflect individually on their own experiences. They were a square peg being tapped remorselessly into a round hole. Any worthwhile ritual expression must have its roots in the nature of the therapeutic experience. It is material that must be appropriate to the context and personalities of the participants, and suited to its intended function. It is not hard to develop rituals with and for a group, but we must insist that our modern-day material takes a lesson from its traditional counterpart. All creative activity must work as an expression, not as an imposition, and folklore (the carrier of wisdom, faith, joy and learning for thousands of years) has never successfully been imposed on anyone.

Notes

1 D. Ben-Amos, 'The idea of folklore: an essay', in I. Ben-Ami and J. Dan (eds) *Studies in Aggadah and Jewish Folklore*, Folklore Research Center Studies VII, Jerusalem: Magnes Press, 1983, pp. 11–17.
2 J. C. Messenger, Jr, 'The role of proverbs in a Nigerian judicial system', in A. Dundes *The Study of Folklore*, London: Prentice-Hall, 1965, pp. 299–307.
3 K. Burket-Smith, *Eskimos*, New York: Crown 1971.
4 A. Pringle, 'Can watching football be a component in developing good mental health in men?', *Journal of the Royal Society for the Promotion of Health* 124(3), 2004, 124–128.
5 Over 35 years old and still the international definitive work on the traditional children's games from England and Wales is the Opies' (1969) *Children's Games in Street and Playground*. There is an enormous wealth of material in the Opies' work, including versions of the first three games in this section.
6 P. V. Gump and B. Sutton-Smith, 'The it role in children's games', in A. Dundes *The Study of Folklore*, London: Prentice-Hall, 1965, pp. 329–336. This chapter contains a fascinating preliminary discussion of some of the possible functional applications of selected it games.
7 I. Opie and P. Opie, *Children's Games in Street and Playground*, Oxford: Oxford University Press, 1969, p. 111.
8 For a fuller study of this material in context, see S. O'Suillebahn, *Irish Wake Amusements*, Cork: Merrier, 1969.
9 For a more elaborate discussion see Cheryl Neill, Chapter 9 this volume.
10 A. Pringle, 'Can watching football be a component in developing good mental health in men?', *Journal of the Royal Society for the Promotion of Health* 124(3), 2004, 124–128.

Further reading

Bettelheim, B. (1978) *The Uses of Enchantment*, Harmondsworth: Penguin.
Briggs, K. (2002) *British Folk Tales and Legends*, London: Routledge.
Brunvand, J.H. (1998) *The Study of American Folklore*, 4th edn, New York: Norton.
Brunvand, J.H. and Hickman, R. (2001) *Encyclopedia of Urban Legends*, New York: Norton.
Burket-Smith, K. (1971) *Eskimos*, New York: Crown.
Child, F.J. (1965) *The English and Scottish Popular Ballads*, 5 vols, New York: Dover, (original 1882–1898, papers held at Harvard. CD version available in USA).

Clark, E.E. (1960) *Indian Legends of Canada*, Toronto: McLelland and Stewart.

Ferretti, F. (1975) *The Great American Book of Sidewalk, Stoop, Dirt, Curb and Alley Games*, New York: Workman Press.

Frazer, J.G. *The Golden Bough*, London: Macmillan.

Grimes, R. (1965) *Readings in Ritual Studies*, New York: Prentice Hall.

Opie, I. and Opie, P. (1969) *Children's Games in Street and Playground*, Oxford: Oxford University Press.

Orlick, T. (2006) *The Cooperative Sports and Games Book*, 2nd edn, London: Readers and Writers.

O'Suillebahn, S. (1969) *Irish Wake Amusements*, Cork: Merrier.

Pringle, A. (2004) 'Can watching football be a component in developing good mental health in men?', *Journal of the Royal Society for the Promotion of Health* 124, 3: 124–128.

Van Gennep, A. (1960) *The Rites of Passage*, London: Routledge.

Websites:

Useful search terms include: folklore, legends, myths, traditional, children's games; children's folk games; therapeutic games, as well as country or group, e.g. Canada, Eskimos/Inuit. Examples include: children's folk games (www.estcomp.ro/~cfg/), wonderful examples from round the world; Native American and Canadian legends and myths (www.kstrom.net/isk/stories/myths.html).

Chapter 5

Using the visual arts to expand personal creativity

Roberta Nadeau

Because of the quiet contemplative, personal approach needed to produce in the visual arts, there are large expansive areas of inner exploration that go hand in hand. These inner experiences are of particular value to those who are using the arts with persons with a disability. Most other art forms require another person to have a full encounter with what that particular art form can give. In the visual arts we can provide tools, knowledge of materials and experience with drawing and painting, which can allow individuals to take with them, wherever they go, the potential for further work. We have the wonderful opportunity to enrich their lives and creative potential.

Even in a crowd, the visual arts encourage a capacity to work in solitude. The artist's eye is always seeing, sensing and feeling the atmosphere around at that moment. If the inner peace for such exploration is not present in the person or persons we are working with in our initial contacts, we can at least see such peace of mind as part of our goal in introducing visual arts sessions. In this hectic, fast-paced world, all people can gain from knowing greater inner peace. Such peace comes from self-knowledge and an appreciation of each person's unique, individual, creative mark which may in turn provide opportunities for increasing self-confidence and self-esteem.

The wonderful beauty of the arts, in all forms, is that human emotion is involved in a raw and uncensored manner. Feelings flowing are essential for artistic experience. The professional artist and the inexperienced participant have in common the fact of being at their best as creators of visual imagery by their capacity to tap the unconscious and, as a result, to present in line, color and form a mark that is individually their own, unable to be produced by any other individual in exactly the same way, ever.

All artists will testify to the fact that in producing one drawing or painting ideas are therein born for another ten or more works. The finished product may at times be a great success or a great failure. It does not matter. What does matter is the continuation of discovery. This process is what we have to share with the people with whom we work. As Fred Gettings has said: 'Art is of value for the way it improves the mind and sensibilities more than for its end products.'[1] Because of this exciting process and all-inclusive *seeing and feeling*, which are essential, it becomes easier to understand the enormous value of encouraging experience in the visual arts for those persons with a disability. Through teaching individuals to see what is around them, to express their feelings and constantly affirm the fact that they, and only they, can make those particular marks on paper or canvas, you increase opportunities for those people to know more about themselves and their unique rights for respect and self-love.

The uses of line, form and color are emotional encounters. There is even greater emotion involved once color is introduced. It is important to know and to feel sure about the fact that art deals with human emotion, as quite often the act of putting line or color on paper can produce cathartic emotional responses for the individual producing the work. Their excitement, tears and frustrations are to be dealt with sensitively – not in any way dismissed. For they are an integral part of the art process, and the arts play a vital role allowing for increased quality of life experience for those with whom we are working.

Preface to practical activities

I believe in the arts. My intense personal conviction regarding the healthiness of the arts experience for all people relates to their essential nature, to provide for every person irrespective of their age or ability an avenue of personal expression. The visual arts have a hand-in-hand friendship with craft or, as I prefer to call it, the applied arts. The trap is that too many people administrating, giving economic support for arts programming, have in mind something very different. For so very many 'arts programs' kits are seen as the root of creative action and the final products can be sold as commodities in gift shops. These kits, green ware, paint-by-number sets, etc. do not allow an individual to express his or her feelings, to expand his or her capacity as a human being to feel, see or respond. Wherever possible, such kits should be avoided as they tend to lead to the stereotypical reproduction of emotion. Our aim is to allow participants every opportunity to discover how wonderfully unique and special is the fact that they have known life and can share their feelings with us. To that aim, all our work should be directed.

Art materials

The art materials of concern to me in this writing are those that allow for two-dimensional expression: graphite, charcoal, conte, ink, pastels, paint, paper, pens, brushes, canvas and board. For a person who already has a limitation in physical or mental skills, it is essential not to create more barriers by improper selection of materials. The materials should be of the best amateur artist's quality available to you. Papers, canvas or boards must be of good size and quality. How destructive to say that you care to share the visual arts experience with a person with a disability and then to see only frustration because of easily torn paper, limp or lifeless colors, or 'self-destruct' creations, which are a pain to produce and a sorrow to the individual as their work is deposited in a waste can.

Pencils (graphite)

Art pencils range from very hard leads to soft and very soft leads. For the purposes we are talking of here, purchase and use only HB, 2B, 4B or 6B pencils. Art pencils can be purchased from the HB end of the range to 10B; however, too soft a lead will defeat your purposes as the work created too easily smears. The importance of the soft leads is that it takes less physical pressure to produce a mark and even the most inhibited person will not find it difficult to deal with having once begun. We all are guilty of concluding that we cannot do something and of being terrified to try. A simple well-chosen pencil and a large piece of drawing paper can provide hours of exploration and accomplishment.

Charcoal

Like graphite pencils, charcoal comes in varying weights or degrees of hard to soft. Again, buy large sticks, which are easy to grasp, soft and, as a result, quick to make distinctive marks and absolutely excellent for the intense black areas that can be created. Charcoal does get messy and for some people that alone can be a healthy and constructive experience because 'institutional' preference is for 'clean at all times'. For a person to be told, 'You have done nothing wrong, all will wash off when we are finished' is to be allowed to feel good, and is an affirmation of your belief in the individual's right to experience the joys at all levels of the tactile beauty and pleasure which the creating of visual art allows.

Charcoal can also add new dimensions when an art gum eraser is employed to lift areas of black away. The 'positive space' imagery or design can be created through the efforts of working into a large black space. Positive space is the actual design area. Negative space is the artistic term used for the space around the initial or essential design. For some people this can be particularly gratifying, for they are creating an element of magic. I try to employ as much fantasy and magic-related conversation as is fitting to inspire and excite exploration.

Conte

Conte is a stick resembling a unique blending of oil pastel and charcoal. It is available in a variety of soft to hard selections and in raw sienna and burnt umber (beautiful earth tones), black and white. Here, as before, buy the softer, easier to use materials. The beauty of conte is the feel of silk in your fingers and the tremendous variation of marks, designs, lines and forms that can be made. The sticks, as with charcoal, have great versatility. A stick worked on its side gives wide sweeping flows of color. The conte is easily smoothed or varied in intensity with the fingers or a tissue rubbing the paper. Persons with limited muscle control can achieve delightful results because of the fluid capacities of the medium itself, and you will be happy to know that there is not as much washing up needed as happens with charcoal.

Pastels

These come in the form of chalk pastels or oil pastels. I use both in my work and recommend that both be a part of your art supplies. Poor quality in choice will lead to two unfortunate problems: (a) the colors will be pale and bland; (b) there will be great difficulty for some people to experience the goals you wish to achieve, in that the pigment simply will not move easily over the paper. One of the great beauties of pastel is that you are working with pure pigment, which has been rolled with a limited amount of oil to create a medium of pure color. There are many varieties of good pastels for student or amateur work. Before buying, however, make certain that the colors are bright and the pigment is easily transferred to whatever surface would be worked upon. Even the most frightened or restrained individual can be moved to do preliminary explorations, purely by the excitement of the brilliant colors. The chalk pastels are soft and chalk-like in their feel in your hand. The oil pastels are more similar to crayon in feel, and yet are pastels, with all their wonderful qualities of color intensity and capacity to be manipulated or mixed using fingers or tissues.

Paint

Painting is a joyous experience that, as you will read later, must be introduced at the correct time to people to avoid frustrations and thus limitations to the gains that can come from the process. Again, your purchases must be made with concern for intensity of true color and the manufacturer's quality of pigment transfer. I choose to buy tube watercolors, as so often the cake watercolors are difficult for many of those with whom I work to be able to know the fun of flowing color as it explodes before them.

I repeat: in working with people who already have imposed physical, mental or emotional difficulties, it is essential that we as facilitators for the arts do not put more barriers in their way by poor choices of materials. I never work with oil paints with groups. If a certain person wants to paint in oils, that becomes an individual decision between myself and the person involved. The turpentine needed as medium for moving the pigment in oil paints is very poisonous, and if an individual has allergic reactions to the turpentine, you have great problems on your hands. Acrylic paints are water based, and water is used as the painting medium to vary thickness of paint and to clean brushes or hands. For many people interested in moving to thicker paints, I advise the purchase of acrylics.

Watercolors, particularly from the tube, are most adaptable. You can teach a person or group how to obtain gradations in washes or to paint in wild, bright colors. To produce a gradient of washes, you take a brush fully loaded with pigment. Strokes are made on the paper, and then, adding only water to the brush, a progressively lighter wash can be obtained. This provides, in work with persons with a developmental disability or persons with dementia, opportunities to spark imagination with suggestions of a certain element of magic, which has become theirs with the use of the paints, the brush and water.

Brushes

As mentioned before, buy good quality brushes. If cared for well, they will provide years of service to the artist's hand. I am not suggesting the purchase of sable brushes, but I hope to make it clear that a cheap 'bargain' will soon leave parts of the brush on a person's work. Efforts to remove a bristle can lead the way to the famous 'self-destruction' activity, which frustrates and can be heartbreaking. Also, brushes must be large – at least size ten or larger – with adequate handles. There are some brushes produced by art supply companies that have a plain, unpainted and unvarnished handle. If you are able to buy a variety of these brushes, you will see how their less slippery finish is a true blessing for certain individuals. The brush is an extension of the hand or foot of the person painting, and should be introduced as a tool. I will speak later of the importance of this understanding. As a tool, the brush can add variety to the experience with paint. It can provide unlimited variety in stroke, and in dabbing, pulling and swirling of color. If you are unfamiliar with all a brush can do in your hands, I advise many lovely hours of exploration and fun before you introduce paintbrushes to a person with a disability. As with any element of knowledge or experience, we can only teach what we know.

Inks

These come in many colors and can be applied with pen or brush. The uses of inks as a medium of expression should be judged according to the people you are working with and their particular interests, capabilities and desires to express themselves in various media. Inks, rather like oil paints, take closer supervision or, at times, a one-to-one working relationship. Inks can produce great delight when used in mixed media works, and again, for certain individuals, much excitement when waterproof inks are used and then watercolor or pastel is painted 'magically' over the original line. For individuals with limited imagination, you as the facilitator may at times need to suggest media and approaches that can unlock some of the imagination that is simply lying dormant, since no one before has given it much of a chance. This is true for everyone, not simply those with a disability. The opportunities provided to people all through life to explore their creative potential are so very limited that they seem proof enough to me that we are tapping a powerful source.

General beginnings

Medium

Introduce one art medium at a time and allow for full exploration and understanding of all the things one can do with a pencil, charcoal, pastel, etc.

Paper size

Encourage an end to timidity by only providing large pieces of paper – paper at least 18 by 24 in (45 by 60 cm). Even the person with extreme limitations in movement will be able to feel the desire to extend their reach. In my experience (as facilitator of such extension of motor skills) I have quite often seen attempts to reach the top and sides of the paper that have surprised the care professionals in charge of the particular individuals on a daily basis. Such extension was seen as unlikely if not impossible.

Some people can be assisted if you keep Velcro as part of your supplies, to wrap around the hand of someone who has little muscle extension to assist in holding a drawing medium or a paintbrush. Also, putting mixed watercolors or tempera paint in empty liquid soap bottles (any plastic bottle that can easily be squeezed) may enable those with little fine motor control to enjoy all the glorious feelings of the painting experience.

Remain aware

Remain continually observant of persons in need of help or encouragement, but please constantly remind yourself that the beauty of the visual arts is the essential nature of *quiet inner discovery*. Constant interruptions or comment can break the inner peace of another person. We have been given a birthright to produce. We have not been given the right to disturb another's creative space. In my experience I have found that, presented with a quiet, mutually respectful atmosphere, the individual or group with whom you are working will wish to create an atmosphere respectful of all in the room. For some people, just to feel such mutual regard for their own thoughts, work and capacity to think can be as beneficial to them as the entire creative process or their finished products.

Music

Classical music, well chosen and played softly, can be a tremendous aid in producing an atmosphere conducive to creative activity. Here, however, I warn: know the music you choose and why it will work. If you are unsure or uncomfortable with the music, you can do harm rather than good. Bach's music for classical guitar and lute have been standbys for me, in that they produce steady, quiet, soothing conditions of great musical beauty.

Storage and transport

Provide a means of storage or transport to protect the creations of the people with whom you are working. Very few individuals have financial opportunities to buy proper portfolios. However, these can be made by you and the persons in the group by saving all cardboard, sheets from packing cases, backs from drawing pads, etc. These simple materials and a little masking tape and time provide the person creating with a means of safe transport, and in some cases the only storage they personally can know, as this packaging protects their work while it is stored under their beds or in a closet in one particular type of institution or another.

If you have an arts or crafts room to work in, it is essential to provide storage for works finished or in progress. Some 'special populations' require that you find a way to lock up their work safely. Destruction or misuse of their completed works by another person, no matter how innocent or accidental the initial cause of such damage, may mean months of effort to re-establish the same quality of freedom in their artistic expression.

Plentiful supplies

Have plenty of supplies and a large amount of paper. There is at times nothing so inhibiting to artistic creativity than to see limited supplies and thus, for example, to fear using the last remnant of a stick of red pastel. Having adequate supplies available has also, in my experience, produced a mutual regard and patience within a group. They know that even if they must wait a few minutes for the use of a certain material, it will not be gone.

Erasers

Erasers should be viewed as tools and not as means of instant correction. Far more exciting results can be obtained by looking at other options of correction, such as darkening negative space or creating variations in shape and form that may not have been thought of if there were not a desire to change a form.

Volunteer help

There is a great need for volunteer help if you are working with a group larger than three or four in number. Also I have had occasions where sisters, mothers, fathers, etc. have come along to a session to observe, as they also provide transport. After numerous occasions on which comments were made such as 'No, that isn't the way a tree looks', or 'No one has hair that color' I decided that all volunteers or visitors would be given paper and encouraged to work. Suddenly, they too were having the same explorations and discoveries; soon negative and sometimes destructive comments stopped. Do remember that your volunteers are there to help you. Give them clear directions and encourage them to learn by doing what the artistic process involves. Otherwise they are more of a hindrance than a help.

Written records

Keep written records for yourself of your interactions with the various people with whom you work. These records are essential to your personal effectiveness as a leader and to your preparation in creating the proper time-and-space elements for each individual. The goal of one aiding others through the visual arts is to see positive change in self-esteem and self-expression, and an increase in motor skills and the quality of physical and emotional health of the persons with whom we work.

Patience

Be patient, very patient, if you have an individual who sits back only watching for a number of sessions. There have often been so many terrifying experiences piled one upon another to cause true and justified alarm when introduced to a new situation. Having created an atmosphere respectful of creative work, we then must learn to accept the flow of individual personalities. The rewards for such patience are great. An elected mute surprised all when she began to speak to me during an art session. She had sat watching for four sessions before participating. A severely handicapped young man made the first efforts ever to do things by himself and was so convinced that he had found his special way of successful expression that he asked if I could arrange a proper exhibition for his works. His family took him on holidays and he took all his completed creations in the makeshift portfolio I provided to show everyone. He had sat watching for five weeks before becoming involved. These are but two examples of the success that comes with patience and understanding. As certain people sit around the room watching, for sometimes even three to five sessions, when they, of their own will, approach you there is a rush of excitement and creative expression. For as they have watched, they have come to terms with the situation and have answered for themselves all the ever so important questions regarding how far to trust you as a person. Once the gift of trust has been exchanged, there is no end to the opportunities for creative self-expression.

Name recognition

The recognition of a person's name and the time spent in helping others to know names can be very important. All that some individuals may have that they can truly call their own is their name. By recognizing the importance of their name, you recognize the value you place on their existence. Start each group art session with introductions. These exchanges of names can vary as the weeks of sessions move on. For example, members can give their name and then state their favorite color or name of their favorite medium or image to draw or paint, etc.

Art history

As many people in the populations we work with have been isolated from society, the sharing and showing of art history books can be time well spent. There is a whole other world within the realm of the visual reproductions of other artists. Too many people are exposed to nothing other than calendar art, television and a few, poorly done, entertainment-geared publications. Select the best and share the names of artists and the time in history in which they lived. Talk about what kind of painting you are looking at or what the sculpture was carved from, etc. One or two pieces of work to share each session can be an amazing catalyst. If you are still working in pencil, charcoal and conte, show black and white drawings. Once working in color, move into sharing reproductions of paintings.

I had one young woman in a group of people with developmental disabilities ask me very honestly one session, 'Roberta, could you help me make a Mona Lisa?' I responded with the gentle remark that it would help us both if one of us were a Leonardo da Vinci. That exchange led to many small discussions: never present too much to absorb at any time about Leonardo da Vinci. The purity of her keen interest was a true joy. Many an art history professor should be as lucky as I have been with students so enthusiastic and thirsty for knowledge.

Respect

It is essential, in helping others create art, that you have respect for the independent and unique mark they, and only they, can make. Even in a clinical setting, it is essential not to intrude, ask unneeded questions or interrupt unethically the process of which we are privileged to be a part. If a person wishes to tell you about their work, you have received a double gift.

You were initiator of the process and are included in the individual's enthusiasm and emotions about what they are producing or have produced.

One such exchange I shall cherish always. There was a severely multihandicapped young man of 24 years who was in a group art session. He always arrived ready and eager to start. At this time the Falklands war was in full turmoil and he seemed to produce nothing but images of what he felt was going on. These images began to flow once we had worked together for a couple of months and he had all the media, except the paints, to choose from. One painting in pastel had a dark stormy sea, a dark troubled land, and a number of buildings. One of those buildings was a brilliant mix of pink, orange and yellow. The structure absolutely glowed from the paper. He asked, 'Do you know why that building is there?' I had no idea. 'That building is where the peace talks are going on.' This exchange opened a door for us to discuss all his many weeks of battleships, tanks, etc. He had hoped that by drawing all these images he could get the war to stop. His words were, 'War is such a horrible waste of life.' Interference in his process of emotional release regarding the war, which was getting so much press and television coverage, would have been unethical. Possibly such interruption might even have stopped his process of slowly creating adequate visual armies displayed on sheet after sheet of paper until he was ready to create the peace talks within his gloriously colored building. Then there was, in the news media, only discussion of future peace talks. This young man was ahead of the politicians and more capable of producing honest images than some professional artists I know about.

Encouragement of honest expression

Lastly, an important element regarding the value of the creative process upon which I could easily write an entire chapter: do encourage honest expression. Even if a person has ugly, angry feelings, which are finding their way to the work, you are succeeding, for these expressions are real. Work towards integrity and quality in the work of all people, and encourage truth of experience and sight. There is great damage done through allowing overly sentimental and stereotypical art to be produced by any individual. The value of involving anyone, particularly those defined within 'special populations', is lost if you passively allow the 'pretty' images. Because of lack of or limited exposure – and then at times only to the 'kit' art experiences, some people can easily arrive in your session knowing no other imagery than the sickly sweetness of stereotyped art forms. By encouraging the reawakening of inner self and presenting activities that remove one immediately from such production, you can begin to encourage expressions of truth and personal satisfaction.

Practical activities

My focus in this section will be on the use of the visual arts with a variety of people, with suggested activities which readers can adapt to their own particular theoretical frameworks or job descriptions. Personally, my professional approach is to offer actual experience within the visual arts and to know that the individuals involved will need to be attended to differently and responded to differently, and that the use of the arts in their lives must be individually defined.

Initial experience

People are often concerned and reluctant to participate fully when presented with a new experience. We must judge carefully what we introduce to an individual as a first visual arts experience. There are very few people who have not known, experienced, the use of the pencil. Even people I have known lacking arms have used a pencil from very early in their lives. A good graphite pencil, as I have described, should be used on large sheets of paper. Have everyone begin with drawing circles all over the paper and, depending upon their individual abilities, encourage them to try to make the circles as similar in size as possible. The same should be done with ovals, lines and scribbles, the effort being to make the person comfortable with producing a line another person is seeing, and to break down all barriers to the famous saying 'I cannot do art'.

These elemental forms are basic to most motor efforts used in writing. The fact is that such simple efforts can bring true feelings of accomplishment and are worth every minute spent. Every experience from there forward will reduce further and further an individual's inner fear. My own years of work with others has shown that there are people who will repeat, over and over again, the same imagery because they received such true pleasure from the first encounter. The circles or ovals will recur in works in pastel and paint enhanced or matured through other experiences, yet a reminder of how important the first good feelings were.

Pencil

Pencil circles, rectangles and scribbling all over the page. Tell the group: 'You can do nothing wrong. Art gives you freedom to express yourself as you wish.' If I see a person being particularly withdrawn and afraid to begin, I ask them to hold the pencil or other drawing or painting medium. Then I slowly begin to move that person's hand (or foot). There will come a point where you can feel the person begin to take over the action. At that point I slowly release guidance and simply let my hand go for a ride. It will be obvious when you can lift your hand away and not have to give such assistance. For an individual with a limited range of muscle movement or motor control, this can be most important in assisting their efforts.

Charcoal and conte

After a session or two with a pencil, I then introduce charcoal, a messy breaking-free experience which renders on paper intense blacks and assorted variations thereof. Charcoal should be demonstrated as used in a direct drawing form; then with the stick on its side with the wonderful swirling effects that can be produced; smudging of the charcoal once laid upon paper; erasing – 'lifting' of charcoal with an art gum or charcoal eraser; encouraging people to feel the exciting fun of rubbing the charcoal on their fingers and then using their fingers as tools to create design elements. Hours of much pleasure to all can be spent. Simply make certain you have taken soap and towels.

Conte, although a different medium, can be used in much the same manner. The stick on its side can produce wonderful areas of variation. Into that area of pigment a person can again utilize the art gum eraser, or a tissue, to produce a variety of special effects. Actually, conte is more easily manipulated than charcoal.

Pastels

The chalk pastel is my personal choice as the medium through which I introduce people to color. I have very specific reasons for this. When we as artists are working with a person with a disability, there is great advantage in keeping, for as long as necessary, the pigment in contact with the fingers or toes. Not only are we, as people, more aware of the feeling of the medium against our skin, but we are also closer to the transfer of color to paper, canvas or board. The intimacy of this process can be cathartic for some people experiencing the arts for the first time.

Colors can be layered, mixed, smudged or wiped away, leaving hints of pigment. All varieties of creative activity with color teach fundamental understanding about color and about mixing. The rich pigment of the chalk pastel allows for easy demonstrations and explorations of the *primary* colors: red, yellow and blue, and the *secondary* colors: violet, green and orange, which are derived from the mixing of the primary ones.

Each person responds differently on an emotional level to color. The emotions and feelings evoked by certain colors are good to discuss. Small dramatic activities can be introduced where a person shows how a color makes them feel – by the use of facial expression or body movement.

Oil pastels

Oil pastels are easily over-layered, smudged, rubbed, etc. However, their particular qualities create unique results and experiences. For the individual clearly desiring to rub a drawing medium clear through the paper this can be of great benefit, in that layer upon layer of color can be added and the product will only become richer – that is, as long as you have provided paper outside the 'self-destruct range'.

For a group of people working together over a number of sessions and who have been introduced to oil pastel, I have a 'trust game'. This activity is to present to the group a large and sturdy piece of paper. The paper is passed from one to another as they individually work on their own creations. Each person should be given an adequate amount of time with the paper so as to make the contribution they wish. Their name should be signed on the bottom, with your help if necessary. Once everyone has added to the image of color and form, the paper should be clipped to a drawing board. Then, gathering everyone around you, put turpentine on a rag and begin to rub the work. Turpentine acts upon oil pastel as upon oil paints; it is the medium for moving the pigment. Under a turpentine rag and with a little directed guidance on your part, a fascinating and beautiful group project can result. This is particularly pleasing to those persons with severe limitations to their muscle movements. Even the energy expended in one small corner of the paper by a person with a severe disability has added equally to the overall beauty of the finished product. Such group projects I try to hang where they can serve as a reminder of group cohesion and of the elements of 'magic' that we, as leaders, can put to our service. This activity usually leads to people wishing to experiment on their own drawings. I agree, as long as they will allow me to move the rag with their direction. 'Poison' is a word even the most severely limited individual understands. It is simple. You care enough for them to help them, but not to see anyone be ill or injured.

Oil pastel can also serve as a 'resist' for other media and greatly increases the opportunities for some people to experience the joys of the unexpected in the visual arts. When the person, or group, is ready to move on to experiences with paints, I first add oil pastels in mixed media work. I will speak more about this shortly. Once the individuals you are working with have experienced both chalk and oil pastels, it is advantageous to present both for exploration. As each medium responds differently to smudging, rubbing and intermixing, the results of beauty and fun can be delightful. Also you will soon be able to see how quickly certain people choose certain ways of working that provide them with the most successful route to the goal they desire to reach, even if it appears to be not far removed from play to the observer. Picasso once said: 'To draw you must close your eyes and sing.' Working with certain persons within the range of our interests gives us increased insight into how much truth is in Picasso's understanding of the uniquely tactile, sensual and direct process of drawing.

Many works in pastel are known to us, through art history books, as paintings. Such a definition is largely the result of the paint-like quality of many pastel works. It is also related to the fact that pastels are such pure pigment. As I have said before, allowing the relationship between mind and hand to be as close as possible to the drawing or painting medium has many advantages for all who have a desire to experience color. The emotions are more easily tapped because the paint-like flow of pigment on paper is so immediate.

Painting

I have already pointed out my particular desire for the use of tube watercolors. Egg cartons (of the plastic variety) or small cake tins can allow hours of unending enjoyment and exploration. Always begin by giving each person only the primary colors. By this time there has been an introduction to color mixing during our time spent with pastels. However, a new experience results the moment you put a brush into the hand or toes of someone you are working with. The paintbrush is a tool and it must be remembered that it can, for some, be a new barrier to creative activity. The brush allows new sensations but reduces the sensations of tactile immediacy with the medium. Assistance and patient, steady, guarded care must be taken, depending on the needs of the individuals with whom you are working.

I begin painting experiences by putting a bit of yellow, red and blue into spaced areas of the egg carton. We look at what happens when yellow is mixed with a bit of blue. The element of magic, or capacity to feel a power of control over a painting medium, can be, for some, the first experience with feelings of accomplishment and self-destination ever known. As I write I smile with delightful memories of the expressions on the faces of some people with whom I have worked and their incredible pride: 'I made purple! Look, it is purple.'

I help them see how the brush, loaded with pigment, gives a very intense color, and how adding water alone to the brush will produce lighter and lighter washes. A bright red can become the faintest pink hue so simply, so pleasantly. One spring as the lilacs were in bloom and a group with which I had been working had begun explorations in paints, the demonstration of washes led a young woman with a developmental disability to produce the loveliest, softly whispered interpretation of spring blooms I think I have ever seen. She was not a master artist, with all the knowledge and understanding of the medium she was working with, yet the emotion that flowed on to the paper made some of my professional colleagues' work look quite weak by comparison. She expressed the wonder of light, color, fresh new smells of the earth and the blossoms on the trees in a way I would be proud to approach in my own work.

There are many ways to use a brush: as a wash – the brush on its side, utilizing the point to draw clear distinct lines, or by using the tip of the brush dotted straight down on the paper to produce spots, leaves, parts of a flower, a person's curly hair, etc. The brush, as a result, begins to offer extensions to creative process.

Slowly I add more colors from the tube watercolors to the palette of the people I am working with. Patience is truly a virtue in working in the visual arts, for if your excitement for a person to know more media or colors exceeds good judgment, you can end up with frustrated and sometimes frightened people – some who never return to the visual arts experience.

Also, depending upon the individual or the group, you may have to limit experiences with color totally to pastel or colored pencils. This may be necessary, as I have found, when the group you are working with is very large and your support staff is small or non-existent. Painting in such situations could lead to utter frustration for all, especially as there is a probability of water jars being knocked over or paints being confused. Spilt water is spilt water, granted, yet such spills can destroy the work of many and are not worth the risk. The objective of the arts facilitator/leader is to provide creative experiences in self-exploration and it is of the greatest importance that we understand that we must consciously be aware of preventing situations which, by their nature, produce feelings of guilt or failure. If a person is angry with himself or herself or his or her own work, and purposely destroys what he or she has produced, we must accept that as their right. Group annihilation of all work within range of the running water of an overturned jar is avoidable.

In working with people with emotional disabilities, we may often see outward destruction of the work produced. The anger is directed at their product and releases or responds to the emotions expressed in the process of creating the work. Conversation, one to one, about the work and your response can often provide insights important to the success of further creative activity with that particular person. Your own analysis of such behavior depends entirely upon your training and your 'contract'.

Mixed media

After all media have been introduced and dealt with individually, then and only then do I introduce mixed media investigations. After this point all arts media will be presented for a person's choice. The desire to experiment and to have fun is basic to human nature. There need be little direction given, simply your constant availability if there are problems, and your capacity to help and to encourage excitement in the people around you to try something new.

Collage

Collage work can be very rewarding for certain people, depending upon the restrictions they personally bring to an arts session. I save magazine photos for their beautiful array of colors and other assorted papers for their textures. Tear them up before presenting them if you are aware that people will only see the imagery and not the colors. Give a sturdy piece of paper or illustration board as a back surface and, with rubber cement from the jars, allow for imagery creation from torn shapes and areas of color. To individuals with cerebral palsy, or those paralyzed in other ways with limited use of their arms, this can be a most beneficial experience.

The frustration of struggling to have color stay where one wants can be overcome with the assistance of yourself or a volunteer to wipe on the rubber cement for the people you are working with. Then as many variations of form or imagery as they desire can be explored. The fumes from rubber cement can be a problem for some people. Thus here, as in all cases, do know well the group or individual with whom you are working.

Rubber cement is pleasant to use for, once dry, the clear extra glue can simply be rubbed from the surface of the work. Some of the white nontoxic classroom glues can be used as well. However, they have one severe problem: many cause great wrinkling and here again a beautiful work becomes a sad completed work as it turns into a relief map. I imagine we have all tried the ubiquitous flour and water and we know of the discouraging crinkling and wrinkling of which I speak.

Working with music

Some people are truly frightened to begin making marks on a piece of paper. They are afraid of judgment, of ridicule and exposure. I find that the introduction of music to the atmosphere of the session is most helpful. If you are going to use music, please know what music you are choosing and exactly what you expect to be the positive results of such a choice – as some music can be an unforgivable interruption to the creative process. Certain classical music, folk music and guitar can provide an avenue of personal transformation from a state of fear to one of actually flowing with the elements of the music itself. One young woman with a developmental disability I worked with asked, as a piece of Allan Stivell's Celtic harp music finished, who it was and how the name was spelt. I wrote the name on the blackboard for all to see, and she actually signed her particular finished pastel work 'Allan Stivell'.

Partner 'trust' exercise

If you have persons who are finding it difficult to get along, who possibly live in the same group home, work in the same sheltered workshop, or are in the same permanent care unit, then possibly via an arts experience exchange some of their feelings towards one another can be dissipated. In addition, it can help those concerned to understand better, or even to appreciate more their own capacity for patience. I must, however, add a warning: please know your group well and the two particular persons whom you involve in the activity, and expect no miracles. If you are unsure, change your own 'mind frame' to make sure you see this activity as a *game* and nothing more – a game to be experienced for the fun and artistic exploration.

We all feel rather possessive about our own work. It is natural and healthy. In fact, it is what I have spent the last number of pages writing about. If you have any questions about the following activity, work through it with a fellow artist or interested party before using it with a specialized group.

The specific activity consists of pairs of people who will work together. One piece of paper is given, and conte, pencils, chalk and oil pastels are provided. The instructions are as follows. First, you, Billy, will begin. John is asked to watch and feel what might be the thoughts, color desires and mood (these descriptive terms must be adjusted according to the group with which you are working). John watches silently and observantly. Then, at your discretion, you ask Billy to give the paper to John and for Billy to observe in the same concerned way. The paper goes back and forth several times, John and Billy making their own reinterpretation of their response to the imagery already on paper. The finished product should be hung in the arts session space or the exercise repeated at another time so that the participants can each have an agreed product as a possession.

I ask the reader to remember that some distances between individuals are there for reasons. At times unknown to us, cruelties have occurred that are too inhuman for us to deal with in creative arts sessions. We must be perceptive and never ask more of an individual than he or she can give at the particular moment. Also, we must understand and show compassion towards those in our sessions who have been hurt so deeply as to be unable to respond to another individual at all. Sometimes we only know who these people are from behavioral signals, for which we must constantly have our antennae out. We are not to be judges, only to recognize that, even among 'normal' people, cruelties may be imposed by a person which make respect for that individual impossible, in fact unethical. If we can understand this fact of life, why, then, do so many arts specialists, social workers and psychologists feel that such problems do not affect those people who are described by some as handicapped, retarded, deaf, blind, and so on? Human emotion is our common denominator. If one cannot hold total respect for individuals who do not want to work with those who have hurt them, then we had better go into another field where we are not dealing with the arts and with human beings and their emotional 'backpacks', which have collected survival equipment we shall never have the privilege to know.

Group 'trust' exercise

In this activity, I always use music and involve the entire group. The activity begins with each person being given a large piece of paper. Then they choose the media they want to work with. Once everyone is set and ready to produce, I explain the rules of the game:

1   Names are put on the back of the paper and the paper is turned over. The drawing will now be placed on the surface facing you.
2   Then each person is to work along with the music I put on the tape recorder until the music stops. Once the music is stopped, then each person passes the paper on which they are working to the person on their right. Each person again begins when the music starts. Music is stopped and the papers are passed again.

This continues until all the pieces of work have moved in a full circle. Simply, choose one member of the group and watch carefully for when their paper returns to them. At this point all members will again have their original work. It is important to select lively music. 'Stage show' music seems to work the best in creating an atmosphere of gaiety and fun. There will be some individuals who always watch their drawing as it moves around. I have even had people who are less than friendly say to another, 'Don't ruin my picture.' Even though there may be a few interpersonal problems, you should keep your eyes on the exercise as it is so very valuable as a shared activity, as an exercise in sharing. The success of the game will depend on your ability to allow people to know the great pleasure in all participants sharing and in being able to take home or back to their room a piece of work that has been produced by everyone in the arts session. I have done this many times with a wide variety of people with a disability and have seen nothing but pleasure and goodwill increase among members of the group.

Music and drawing game

In this game people are again placed in pairs. Each has his or her own piece of paper upon which they are working. If the person sitting facing another decides to add a form, color or design to the other's work, they simply reach across and work on the other drawing. Again, lively, spirited music should be used, which creates a feeling of fun. There are very few times in which any negative behavior has been exhibited. If you handle the game's explanation well, it will be understood to be a game and as an experience most beneficial for all. However, some people need to be individually encouraged to touch the other's paper. We learn as human beings through such exchanges that new ideas often follow as a result of the inspiration given by another person's interpretation. Also, the opposite paper is always upside down to yours and the perspective is automatically changed as a result. The goal is to encourage trust and understanding through the exercise, which is structured in such a way as to encourage patience with another person reaching over and putting their mark upon your work. This effort to reach can be a physical extension activity as well.

One only has to be involved for a few minutes in any work to have a personal identification that says 'this is my drawing'. To relax with another person's intrusion upon our space has implications that go far beyond the art session itself. Goals such as these are a large part of the beauty of the arts as human exchange. We learn much about ourselves and other people, and the knowledge that we gain is essential for producing good art as well as for healthy relationships.

Creating pictorial images through suggested fantasy

For some individuals, if not a large majority of all people, there has been limited use of the imagination. We need, as arts facilitators, to have tricks up our sleeves to unlock creative thinking, or to remove blocks so long in place that it becomes a major part of our professional intention with certain persons.

One way I have found successful as well as most pleasurable for everyone is to select a fairy tale or other story that is rich in visual imagery. Then, giving everyone paper and a selection of media, I begin reading the story with interest and excitement. As they listen to my reading they are to produce a work that expresses the way they pictured the story or the way they felt. Images, colors and emotions, all are interpreted through each person's own perceptions. A well-chosen story can unlock many of the blocks to creative thinking. The elderly person quite often finds great imagery provoked by stories that are historical-traditional in their nature. The great richness that can be shared from having lived through so much of human history can be a beginning for awakening the creative spirit of a folk artist.

If the people with whom you are working have had little exposure to some of the great beauty of imagery provoking stories, you should not panic as they sit engrossed in the story and unable to work. The images will flow later, with such an obvious receptiveness for storytelling that you will have an indication of the likelihood of success, should the exercise be repeated.

Summary

In this chapter it has been my desire to provide an introduction to art materials and their use. I have included only a few of the many games and exploratory exchanges that can be employed. I purposely left out any of the psychologically oriented games or personal activities. My decision is related to my firm belief in the visual arts experience as a first-quality emotional experience for all people. I also have a concern for the specific intent of many such activities and the necessary psychological training that should accompany such work.

Also, I have not spent much time in dealing with the art-related activities that are known so well by everyone, for example, the gluing of macaroni in all shapes and forms to create designs, or of cracked eggshells on a surface to be painted. I know the reader can think of many more. Simply look in any elementary teacher's art directives and you have loads of such ideas. I am concerned with allowing emotional release and personal growth through the visual arts.

Your job is to provide good supplies, enthusiasm and creative inspiration. You will be needed as a keen and conscientious observer. Most difficulties can be overcome with a little help from you.

If you are fortunate enough to be working with a group of people in a situation where an exhibition of their works can be organized, that each selected as their own choice to represent them, you have the opportunity for a grand ending to what can be anything from weeks to months and sometimes years of working together. Such exhibitions should have a good accessible space and an 'opening' where others are invited and refreshments are served. This is a wonderful way to show people your appreciation for their efforts and to encourage further work and self-development through the visual arts experience. When such opportunities are not available, because of the conditions of the working situation, I have found that a finale can be accomplished through enjoying refreshments together. I give a present of pastels, paper, paints, or whatever would mean the most and be most needed. Then the highly emotional experience of having created art together does not end on a low note with simple goodbyes exchanged. You have been able to continue the inspiration.

I close with a reminder. We are working with other human beings through an emotional and highly expressive medium. We must always remain extremely humble in our interactions with others during working sessions. Openness to new experience is what we are encouraging and we too must remain open. So very much of what I have learned has been in response to what I have been taught by those whom I teach.

It is often thought that art is a form of recreation, indulged in by those who shun hardship. True artists are never at rest. Like Rodin, they labor at their work with passionate devotion, from early morning until dark. Indeed, after daylight fades, the dreaming muse begins to torment the mind until it can plunge again into manual expression.

The principles on which art is built are fundamentally the same as those of life itself. Sincerity of soul, accuracy of the outward and inward eye, constancy and patience are indispensable to any real accomplishment, be it art or merely living – perhaps the greatest art of all.[2]

Acknowledgements

For wisdom gained from working with other people I am forever grateful to Dr Dolores Armstrong and Dr Walter Hirsch. I thank them and all who, by their example, have given me such wonderful insights into the human spirit.

I thank Robert Whyte, Donna and John Harling, Sara Widness and Robert McInnis for always believing in me and my work and all the artists, writers and poets of all time, for their unending inspiration.

Lastly I thank my children, Joe, Pat, Anthony and Noelle, for enriching my life and understanding of human existence, for always keeping my viewpoints fresh and clear and for returning to me so much love.

Notes

1 F. Gettings, *You Are an Artist: A Practical Approach to Art*, New York: Hamlyn, 1966.
2 M. Hoffman, *Yesterday is Tomorrow*, New York: Crown, 1965.

Further reading

Abraham, R. (2005) *When Words Have Lost their Meaning: Alzheimer's Patients Communicate Through Art*, Westport, CT: Praeger.

Arnheim, R. (1969) *Visual Thinking*, Berkeley and Los Angeles: University of California Press.

Atack, S. (1980) *Art Activities for the Handicapped*, London: Souvenir Press.

Edwards, B. (1979) *Drawing on the Right Side of the Brain*, Los Angeles: J. P. Tarcher.

Feder, E. and Feder, B. (1981) *The Expressive Arts Therapies*, Englewood Cliffs, NJ: Prentice-Hall.

Gettings, F. (1966) *You Are an Artist: A Practical Approach to Art*, New York: Hamlyn.

Kramer, E. (1971) *Art as Therapy with Children*, New York: Schocken.

Liebmann, M. (1986) *Art Therapy for Groups*, Cambridge, MA: Brookline.

—— (ed.) (1990) *Art Therapy in Practice*, London: Jessica Kingsley Publishers.

Ludins-Katz, F. and Katz, E. (1989) *Arts and Disabilities: Establishing the Creative Art Centre for People with Disabilities*, Cambridge, MA: Brookline.

Malchiodi, C. (2003) *Handbook of Art Therapy*, New York: Guilford Press.

May, R. (1979) *The Courage to Create*, London: Bantam.

Pavey, D. (1979) *Art-Based Games*, London: Methuen.

Simon, R.M. (2005) *Self-Healing through Visual and Verbal Art Therapy*, London: Jessica Kingsley Publishers.

Ulman, E. and Dachfinger, P. (1975) *Art Therapy in Theory and Practice*, New York: Schocken.

Chapter 6

Dance

Developing self-image and self-expression through movement

Bernie Warren and Richard Coaten

All living organisms, at least once in their lives, exhibit behaviors that could be called dancing. Human beings are no exception. We are constantly pursuing movements that have repetition and rhythm and can be subdivided, by an outside observer, into movement themes or phrases. Many modern choreographers often build on these natural movement sequences to create dances that audiences pay money to watch.

The movements we make as human beings are so intricately linked with dance that learned authorities spend hours debating when an action, or series of actions, ceases to be movement and starts to enter the realm of dance. Academic discussions concerning the physiology, mechanics and aesthetics of movement are mainly irrelevant to the individual wishing to employ dance/movement in special education, rehabilitation or health care. It is important, however, to realize that dance/movement serves many very important functions for all human beings. While it is unlikely that most of us will ever perform for others in hopes of reward, money or applause, nevertheless our everyday movement sequences not only have special meaning for us but also reaffirm our being.

For all of us the body is an instrument of expression and in childhood it is through the movement of our bodies that we start to build a picture of our world. As we develop we explore our capabilities and start to learn what our bodies can do. This exploration and movement of our body parts leads to a growing awareness of our body's structure and to the growth of body image. Not only is this early corporeal exploration important to the developing self-concept of young children, but also throughout life this testing and usage of our bodies would appear to be linked to cognitive, physical and psychosocial development, particularly in the areas of health and well-being.

More important still is the link between dance/movement and emotion. The movements we initiate, the body shapes we form and the responses we present to external stimuli usually reflect our inner emotional state. The way we move, the way we stand, our gestures, all express (sometimes more accurately than the words we speak) what we feel at any given moment. In essence they express the subtext below our verbal communications. The belief in subtextual communication through movement has created the concept of dance as a mirror of the soul. This in turn has led to many referring to dance as the mother of all tongues because movement cuts across all language barriers and speaks to individuals at a primal, emotional level. For some people, particularly those born into highly technological and industrialized societies, which increasingly shun the expression of emotions, this can be very threatening. As a result emotional energy, instead of being naturally expressed, becomes pent up and is often dissipated through destructive or antisocial behavior.

At its simplest level, a dance is a statement of emotion expressed through movement. To control the statement, to make it more specific, to produce color and texture within the emotional statement, so that an observer responds, empathizes or understands, requires a great deal of training, technique and emotional integrity. This is the arduous route undertaken by the professional dancer. However, as already mentioned, at any one time we all have at least one dance within us. Often people with a disability have a great need to allow their dance to see the light of day, for both physiological and emotional reasons. Yet all too often it is these individuals who are denied the chance to explore this emotional release through dance and movement.

For people with a disability, the dance experience can be particularly valuable. For the person with a cerebral palsy, dance/movement can offer an opportunity to gain control over muscle spasms creatively. For the person who is withdrawn, the process of making a dance may allow them the opportunity to make a creative statement about themselves. For those of us making use of dance/movement in special education, rehabilitation or healthcare it is important to be aware of the positive benefits of dance/movement for gross and fine motor control, neurological functioning, circulatory stimulation, psychosocial development and so on. However, it is equally important to remember that the movements which form part of an individual's unique dance are an emotional response. It is this emotion that lifts the sequence of actions beyond the purely mechanical level of physical exercise, such as can be gained through racquetball or swimming. Dance allows an individual the chance to make a personal creative statement about their feelings through the movements they carry out. This will often have other benefits in more physiological areas, particularly for those people who have a physical disability.

The implicit benefits that can be gained through dance/movement sessions are not easily achieved. For these benefits to be gained by individuals, it is important to engender a sense of fun and personal achievement throughout the sessions. If a sense of enjoyment and personal satisfaction is lost, it is likely that the physiological and neurological benefits that can ultimately occur as a result of dance/movement sessions will also be lost: as interest, motivation and self-satisfaction will give way to boredom, repetition and alienation from being just another trained dog jumping through the same old hoops.

Practical activities

What follows is a selection of exercises, games and ideas that we have employed in our work with special client groups. The activities do not have some mystical power that can transform the neophyte into a dance/movement specialist. However, the material is enjoyable, easy to use and normally 'successful', even in the hands of individuals with little formal training in dance or movement. While some of the material is universal, and is also used by drama and music specialists in their work, the roots of all the activities are in movement.

The examples presented cover four of the basic goals a dance/movement specialist may be seeking to achieve with a particular client or group, namely: gaining greater control of isolated body parts; improving body image; achieving controlled emotional release; and becoming more socially adept. In many cases these goals are interlinked; with greater control of individual body parts in turn comes a better appreciation of the body schema and therefore, an improved body image. This knowledge, and control of the body and its extremities, in turn facilitates the channeling and releasing of emotion through movement expression.

All the activities outlined require little in the way of practical equipment. For most, a selection of percussion instruments, and/or some way of playing 'canned' music (a CD player, MP3 player or tape recorder) are all that is required. In choosing music we suggest that you select music that you like and that you know creates in you the response you wish to stimulate for individuals in your group. To this end we also suggest that you bring to each session a variety of musical styles and tempos that can encourage a wide range of movement possibilities. Certain activities may require specialized equipment and in these instances mention is made of this in the text.

As always, plan for the needs of your group. In this regard movement observation and analysis[1] (such as the rudimentary example, based on Laban Movement Analysis provided in the Appendix to this chapter) are invaluable tools for the dance/movement specialist. They give you the ability to learn very quickly how confident individuals are at relating to each other, to the material presented and to their own bodies, etc. Through careful movement observation, it is possible to gain an insight into the abilities and attitudes of participants in a relatively short space of time with little need to resort to clinical files or other sources of information.

As a final basic practical hint, we suggest that participants attending dance/movement sessions should wear loose comfortable clothing, wherever and whenever possible. However, for some people, particularly in the first few sessions, wearing 'special' clothes can be very threatening and often counterproductive. Nevertheless, so that participants can achieve the greatest range of personal movement, it is important to work towards this simple goal.

The dance/movement activities are presented here under four subheadings: warm-up, body awareness, group awareness and dances. It should be noted that this way of categorizing activities is purely a matter of convenience, as many of the activities could just as easily have been put under at least two of the other headings.

Warm-up

There are many ways to warm up a group. As with all other performing arts, a warm-up period is an essential part of each session. The warm-up is particularly important for people who rarely use their bodies, and well chosen warm-up activities will greatly reduce the chances of physical injury.

Ideally, the warm-up should meet the needs both of the group and of the activities that comprise the session. If the activities to follow are to be physically demanding, then a thorough body warm-up is necessary to avoid sprains, strains or muscle tears. If the activities are to be more contemplative, emphasizing sensitivity rather than activity, then a suitable warm-up is necessary.[2] The warm-up also provides a time for the group to become accustomed to your style and this helps with building trust, a sense of adventure and a shared energy. At a physical level, warm-ups also help to improve circulation and neuromuscular stimulation.

If at all possible, warm-up activities should provide you with an insight into the capabilities of the individuals in your group. This information may prove useful during the rest of the session. Activities such as those presented here enable you to elicit information about the basic capabilities of the group early on. For example, does everyone in the group know where their knees are? Can everyone isolate a single movement such as moving their thumb? Can they carry out more than one task at any one time? Does everyone understand 'control' words such as stop, wait, listen, etc.? Do they laugh at your jokes? If an individual fails to carry out a command, there may be a number of reasons. For example, he or she may not understand the request. He or she may not associate the word 'thumb' with the relevant body part, or may be bored with the activity or deliberately disobeying – the possibilities are almost limitless. As always try to listen with all antennas up.

Themes, ideas and movement motifs begun during the warm-up can readily be developed later on, helped by your own creative alertness which helps provide the means to *create dances* from a different place of knowing; one that neither imposes an external technique which entails learning movement and dance by imitation, nor is tied to current social and cultural ideas. Instead through observation and being in tune with both yourself and the group we create our own questions, images and material for exploration through dance.

Here are three simple warm-up activities. Unless otherwise stated, all activities are described from the point of view of the group leader.

Rob's little finger game

This is an excellent preparation for tag games or a physically demanding session, although the title itself is perhaps a little misleading. You can use this activity not only as a physical warm-up but also as a means of getting people to smile through the use of a dose of 'humor of the unexpected'.

Tell the group they are about to participate in a very strenuous activity and ask if they think they are ready to do this. Then ask the group to stretch out their right hands. After a brief pause to allow people to wonder what will happen next, tell them to wiggle their thumbs. Always ask the group to be careful, not to strain themselves. After a short wiggle tell the group to drop their right arms. As soon as they have their right arms by their sides, ask them to stretch out their left hand and wiggle that thumb. Inform them of the importance of working both sides to balance out the body energy – 'You might look lopsided if you only exercise one thumb.' Slowly increase, without stopping, the parts of the body that are being moved, adding to the thumb: fingers, wrist, elbow, shoulder on one side, and then the other thumb, fingers, wrist, elbow, shoulder on the other side, finally adding the head, neck and hips until people are moving all their body parts at the same time and hopping from one leg to the other around the room singing the national anthem. The effect is a chaotic mass of arms, legs, fingers and hips, counterpointing a rather august and nationalistic tune and almost invariably creates a light and humorous atmosphere.

This game is a good work-out for all the body. It can also become quite physically demanding. Most importantly, it can be a very valuable *diagnostic tool*.

I Am Me – a name game

This game can be played in two stages. In the first stage, the group stands in a large circle. In turns, each member of the group jumps in the air and as they land they say their name, for example, 'Bernie'. The pace of this can slowly build until as soon as one person has landed the next person starts to jump, creating a 'jumping jack wall of sound'. This leads on to the next stage, where the group moves as individuals around the room observing the following ritual. The ritual consists of a linked pattern of movements and words, for example, to make a personal statement about themselves:

Movement	Stomp	Stomp	Jump
	I	AM	SUSAN
Statements	I	FEEL	HAPPY
	I	WANT	ICE CREAM

This sequence is repeated until you feel the group has had enough. The first part of the triad is always 'I am', but the second and third parts can be varied: for example, I NEED, I HATE, I LOVE, I FEAR or whatever are the needs of your particular group. In each case the statements are linked to the movement:

Movement	Stomp	Stomp	Jump
	I	AM	JOHN
Statements	I	LOVE	SLEEPING
	I	HATE	WORK

In each case the statements are always individual personal statements.

This game can be particularly valuable in enabling people to express their emotions strongly without becoming 'spotlighted' or having the group focus on their problems, because their statements will be part of the group's 'wall of sound'.

Should you wish to bring the statements 'into the open', to be shared with the group, you can get the group back into a large circle and then ask each member of the group to cross the circle in the prescribed ritualized manner. As leader you can choose which emotions you wish each person to describe or this can be left up to members of the group. This can lead to group discussion or simply increase your store of information concerning the group.

Follow My Dance I

This is an adaptation of Follow My Leader using music and is a very enjoyable activity to follow on from an unstructured or loosely shaped beginning. Bring the group into a circle either sitting or standing so that each person has a good view of everyone else in the group. It may be helpful to play a name game immediately before starting Follow My Dance I just to jog a few memories. In the dance there is a 'dance leader' who responds to the music playing. The rest of the group then tries to copy your actions.

This leadership role is then rotated among all the members of the group. The role is passed on by making eye contact with someone in the group (for example, Sheila) and saying, 'Let's all follow Sheila.' Another way is to pass a scarf round the circle. Here, you walk round the inside of the circle holding out the scarf for the new leader to take. This encourages choice on the part of the participants. The whole group then watches and simultaneously tries to copy Sheila's actions.

In certain cases it is helpful to take control and suggest it is time to pass on the leadership role, or that an individual should continue for a little longer. This is an extremely valuable and enjoyable dance and can be used as a diagnostic tool.

An extremely important part of this dance is that it enables each member of the group to be 'spotlighted'. For a time, everyone is the centre of attention and has power over the group. There is the safety mechanism that, should this be too threatening, as soon as the person starts to feel uncomfortable they can pass the leadership on to someone else. Also, when someone has been the leader for an excessively long time, it is possible to ask him or her to pass on to someone else in the group. The time an individual wishes to lead the group is as important as the actions they do. This amount of time very often changes in response to a group meeting regularly over a long period.

It is important that you model the activity to get the group going. Remember that you must work slowly and in small stages. It is perhaps rash to overgeneralize, but simple linear staccato movements, such as stretching right hand and arm out to full extension in slow small stages, tend to be easier for most groups to follow than large elliptical or circular movements, at least in the early stages of the process. Groups can find sideways rhythmic patterns particularly difficult early on. This is perhaps a result of the mirror effect; that is, instead of copying actions we tend, in the initial stages when facing a person, to mirror them.

It is also particularly important to be aware of individual efforts, particularly when working with people with physical disabilities. For one person, simply moving an arm may be a great achievement, and negative pressure to 'copy' the exact action may be very detrimental. In contrast, for others the inability to copy may simply be laziness or lack of commitment. Coaxing may be helpful at such times and very often a slight movement made by the participant can be echoed or exaggerated slightly, drawing attention to the quality of movement or gesture. It is helpful not to intervene too early on, which can sometimes inhibit the participant by focusing on their 'inability' in contrast to their 'ability'.

The insights gained in this way can then help in the process of deciding who needs help and in what way: coaxing, pressure, stretching, etc. It is then possible to choose music suitable for Follow My Dance II or for the next session. In addition when leading it is possible to make the leader's dance include actions that stretch individual group members in a way that expands their movement vocabulary. Try to use music with a happy bounce during your first sessions of Follow My Dance I. Then try to choose music that meets the specific age and ability of the group. World music often makes a good choice. However, music can include works by a whole range of artists and styles, e.g. Van Morrison, Buena Vista Social Club, Salif Keita, Oyub Ogada, Peter Gabriel, Paul Simon, Bluegrass and klezmer, classical (piano, harp or flute), the Beatles, Sugar Hill Club Classics (hip-hop) and Chango Spasiuk (chamamé) – the list is endless.

Further examples of warm-up activities

- Find different ways to greet each other.
- Sign your name in the air; dance it as a pathway on the floor; run with it; stretch it; do it backwards.
- Walk on the out-breath, pause on the in-breath, change direction, repeat.
- Run full tilt making sure you avoid one another.
- Follow someone, allow yourself to be followed.
- Follow without being followed yourself.
- Dance with different parts of the body in contact with someone else, hands, wrists, elbows, backs.
- Draw how you feel, dance the pathways, dance someone else's pathways.
- Become fascinated by your own movements.
- Dance focusing on changing direction, levels, pathways and planes.
- Pass objects and props to one another and play with them.
- Let your head take the body on a journey.
- Repeat an action until something else happens.[3]

Body awareness

Almost all movement requires at least a limited awareness of how the body works. To a certain degree, each movement exercise helps develop an awareness of how the body moves. The activities presented here not only emphasize body movement but also help focus on body image. In addition, many of these activities allow individuals to experience the link between body image, body movement and emotional response. These practical activities represent the soma/psyche linkage that dancers know all too well and reinforce references to dance as 'emotion in motion'.

So that individuals may become aware of their full body potential, I feel it is important to help them feel comfortable with their surroundings, and gain greater awareness of the articulation of their body joints to enable them to start linking their kinesthetic actions to their internal emotions.

Electric Puppet

There are various ways of introducing this game, depending on the age and ability of the group; perhaps the most common is the idea of the electric puppet.

- Split the group into pairs and then introduce the idea of the puppet. Tell them that we will be working with a puppet that responds to a small electrical charge.
- Ask one member of each pair to be the lifeless puppet and the other to be the puppeteer.

- Introduce the concept of the 'electric baton'. A garden cane with a circumference of slightly less than the size of a dime or an English penny works well, although at first it may be worth using larger sticks, particularly with groups who have poor muscle control or kinesthetic awareness.
- Let the group know that the baton generates a small electric charge which is powerful enough to move individual parts of the inert puppet's body.
- Demonstrate how this works: e.g. when the baton touches the puppet's right arm lightly, it moves quickly away from the baton and returns slowly to its original position.
- Ask the puppets to stand as still as possible with their arms relaxed by their sides. The puppeteers then go to work to see how efficiently their puppet responds to the baton's charge.
- Always ask the puppets to close their eyes and concentrate on exactly where the electric charge touches their body, and then to move that part of the body quickly away from the charge, then smoothly and with the minimum of effort, as there is no more electricity left to power the muscles and thus the body part must work under 'gravity', back to its original position.
- After a while allow the pairs to change roles.

Despite its dramatic framework, in essence this is an exercise in body control. It can be an extremely difficult exercise for some people, as it requires a great deal of body awareness and control. Often the puppeteer starts with whole arms or legs, and moves to more specific areas, for example, little finger, big toe, and more difficult directions. It soon becomes obvious to all involved that certain movements are impossible. Also, slowly the puppet learns to move away from the stimulus – often at the beginning people move towards it. This can be reduced by asking the puppeteer to leave the electric baton where it is until the puppet moves away from it.

This game can cause problems. As a leader it is important to be aware of people who like to 'poke' or tend to work at head level. With children, particularly those with emotional problems, it may be wise, at least at first, to limit the use of the baton to the torso, legs and arms and to use an index finger as the baton. If the puppet is relaxed and focusing on the sensations of the body, it is not unusual both to sense the charge before feeling it and to achieve a meditative state.

Magic aura

It is always helpful to try to find dramatic or imaginative frameworks to use with physical activities. This often helps to suspend disbelief by stimulating the imagination so that the whole body can be totally involved. This is not a plea for individuals to be consciously thinking during kinesthetic activities as all too often this leads to cognitive blocking of feeling sensation. However, in order for the mind to be engaged, switched on if you like, individuals must want to be involved. Often a suitable dramatic framework helps to do this. This game is no exception.

Split the group into pairs. Explain that on the word 'Zing' (or other suitable word, abracadabra, shazam, etc.) a magic spell will take hold of the group. The effect of the spell is that one member will become a frozen 'statue' but the other person will have the power to free their partner. However, the power will only work if the 'healer' works slowly and goes as close as they can to their partner's body *without* touching, so they can feel the statue's body energy. If the 'healer' touches the frozen 'statue' they have to start again.

When the magic word is said the 'statue' assumes a standing star shape. This allows for a large area to be 'healed'. Ask the statues to close their eyes and both members of each pair to try to sense the body energy – to feel the aura. Once freed, the pairs reverse roles. Once both have explored the sensations and have been both 'statue' and 'healer', ask them both to keep their eyes closed during the healing process. It is often during this part of the exercise that the healer can 'see' their partner's aura,[4] even though their eyes are closed. If the pairs have a good rapport, the process can be repeated using more difficult and convoluted frozen shapes.

Again, this exercise can be particularly soothing. It requires a slow and sensitive approach by the healer and a relaxed but fixed posture of the statue. Children at first tend to want to rush through this game. Along with the obvious benefits to be gained in terms of body schema, muscle control, etc., this is a valuable sensitivity exercise, with the selection of suitable pairs often being crucial to the quality of experience that individuals receive.

Ninja

The Ninja were a breed of warrior-assassins reputed to be able to perform such superhuman feats as walking through walls, becoming invisible and breathing under water. All these feats were generated as a result of their extremely disciplined training, which emphasized mind-body co-ordination and control. This exercise is adapted from Ninja training exercises, and variants of the exercises are found in many martial arts systems.

Everyone is spread around the room with space to themselves. Inform them that the floor is made of rice paper and that great care must be taken if the rice paper is to remain intact. Then introduce the following stages one at a time, allowing the group to progress to the next stage only after mastering the basics of the previous one.

1 Point of absolute balance

- Stand ankles shoulder-width apart so an imaginary line can be drawn from the centre of the heel to the centre of the armpit.

- Turn feet out 45 degrees, knees slightly bent, hips rotated to straighten spine.
- Keep back straight – imagine a straight line drawn from the centre of the earth through the body up to the sun.
- Breathe in through nose and out through mouth.
- Weight can now be transferred easily in any direction without losing balance.

2 Forward walk

- Transfer weight slowly totally on to left leg, so that ball of right foot is last to leave floor.
- Place right foot back on floor so that weight is transferred from *heel* to *ball* to *toe* until the whole of the right foot is on the floor. The weight is then transferred totally on to the right foot as the left is removed.

This process slowly gains fluidity until the walker moves forward without consciously having to think about the movement. If 'stop' or 'freeze' is called during any of these moving exercises, individuals should be on balance and able to return to 'absolute' balance with a minimum of effort. Throughout the exercise, emphasize fluid and light movements – no jerky or heavy moves or else the rice paper will be torn.

3 Backward walk

This is the opposite of the forward walk. Transfer weight to the left leg – the ball of the right foot is still the last to leave the floor but weight is transferred back to the right leg from *toe* to *ball* to *heel*.

4 Sideways walk

This should be done as if you were walking with your back to a wall casting a four-inch shadow. Mastery of the sideways walk, done in the shadow of a wall, was one of the techniques that created the Ninja's famed invisibility. To move to the left:

- Begin in *point of absolute balance*.
- Transfer your weight to right leg.
- Lift left foot from floor, lifting foot from *heel* to *ball* to *toe*.
- Move your left foot sideways *behind* right leg (a crossing motion) and place back on floor *toe* to *ball* to *heel*.
- Keep your hips 'square' with the wall.
- Transfer weight on to left leg.

- Simultaneously, lift right foot from floor *heel* to *ball* to *toe*.
- Move your right foot *sideways in front of* left leg and place back on floor *toe* to *ball* to *heel*.
- Repeat motion.

Fluidity is achieved by simultaneously shifting weight from stationary leg as foot of moving leg starts to 'grip' the floor.

5 Half-turn jump

- On the in-breath *jump* up and turn 180 degrees.
- Breathe *out* on the return to the floor.

A very small jump is all that is needed to create the turn. Often energy is wasted trying to jump high or through not linking movement to the breath.

Once the basic movements of each component of this exercise have been mastered, then participants can be asked to keep their eyes closed and to sense where other people are in the room. Also, it is important to get participants to try to synchronize their breathing with their movements. This reduces the amount of energy expended in achieving fluidity of movement, leads to participants being more relaxed and creates a more meditative inner awareness of the body's movement. Many students, particularly those who have experience of Eastern religions and/or meditation techniques, describe this exercise as 'a moving meditation'.

Besides the reflective aspects of the exercise, this is a great way for people to gain control over locomotive muscles of the body. Once the group has gained a sense of confidence controlling the jump movements, you can add the release of explosively exhaling the word 'kiai' on the jump turn, as participants touch the floor.

Group awareness

Parachute

Very little is needed in the way of equipment for dance/movement sessions. However, a parachute (which may often be purchased at army surplus stores) is a valuable piece of equipment to have around. The qualities of the material, the feeling of group contact and the sensation of movement to be gained from working with a parachute are quite unique.

There are many different parachute games, all for different purposes. This exercise is one linked to sensation. The group stands in a circle. If there are a number of individuals in wheelchairs, start by sitting in a circle. Everybody holds on to the parachute with both hands, if this is possible. Try to work as a group, raising the parachute as high as it will go and then letting it return to the floor. Work together to try to make the rise and fall of the parachute smooth and rhythmic.

When the group has achieved this rhythmic flow, ask each person to say a word or sentence to describe what the parachute makes them feel. Ask them to say this when the parachute is at the top of its travel. This allows that individual to make eye contact with other members of the group. Then ask the group to repeat the word or sentence as the parachute returns to the floor. Sometimes the feeling described is a simple emotion, for example, happy; sometimes the feeling described is a sensation evoked by the movement of the parachute, for example, light and airy. In this way not only do participants express the sensations they feel, but they are also exposed to new vocabulary. In addition to working on linking sensation to expression, the parachute is an excellent tool for extending physical limits.

As an example, in one session I (BW) was working with a young woman who had a cerebral palsy. As a manifestation of her condition she was unable to hold up her head for more than a minute or so at a time. She became so involved in the parachute activities that she maintained focus and control over her neck muscles and her head remained erect throughout the activity. Not only this, she was able to extend the reach in her arms way beyond their normal extension. Professionals who had worked with her remarked on the fact that they had never seen her so involved in an activity and commented that she was doing things they thought she was not capable of.

Reed in the wind

This is often referred to as a trust exercise. However, it is an exercise in sensitivity. Unfortunately, all too often group leaders allow exercises such as these to become an excuse to 'scare' participants; to see if they will trust the group to let them drop almost to the floor. Instead, use this exercise to reaffirm the group and to accentuate its sensitivity, care and concern for its members.

One person (the reed) stands in the middle of a tight circle formed by the rest of the group who stand shoulder to shoulder. The reed stands eyes closed, hands by their side and ankles close together, with feet stationary, throughout the exercise.

The outer circle (the wind) place their hands gently on the reed. The 'laying on of hands' – the point where the wind touches the reed – is very important. Before any movement starts, and again after the reed's movement has stopped, there should be a time when there is a silent, non-verbal communication through the hands of the wind with the reed. The length of this communication should be dictated by the needs of the group – particularly those of the reed. At the start it is a time when the wind can reassure the reed, through touch, that they will look after him or her during the exercise.

In this exercise it is important to remain as silent as possible and *the wind should always keep their hands in contact with the reed*. Occasionally the wind may want to hum a soothing tune quietly, for example, a lullaby. It is essential that initially the movements are extremely small and made very gently and smoothly. The distance the reed is moved may be increased gradually and smoothly. After the reed has reached its maximum point of travel (this need not be much – a few inches is quite enough), it is returned slowly to the central starting position. With each new person in the middle, it is important always to begin slowly and not to fall into the trap of 'starting' from where the last reed stopped.

This is an exercise in which the entire group is able to participate. Everyone who wants to should be allowed to be the reed. If group members feel hesitant, they should be encouraged to try being the reed but they must always have the option to pass – without being made to feel guilty about it, either by the group or you. In many cases the simple 'laying on of hands' is as valuable as, if not more valuable than, the gentle swaying motion.

This exercise, carried out with a sensitive group, can practically illustrate the power of faith healers who are reputed to be able to 'cure' simply by placing their hands on people. The sense of well-being and caring generated by a supportive and sensitive group is very powerful.

Change

This is adapted from a Marian Chace exercise and can be seen as a further adaptation of Follow My Dance I. The game is based on group cohesion and following a leader as exactly as the group's capabilities allow. (Obviously, when working with a group whose individual physical disabilities are diverse, allowances must be made to acknowledge that certain movements may be impossible for particular individuals.)

The group stands, or sits, in a circle. Tell the group that you will do a repetitious action(s) that the group has to copy exactly. When everyone is synchronized, call 'change'. At this point the person on your left will be the new leader. Each time the new leader must try to subtly change the action(s) and then repeat it (them) until the group is following exactly, and then call 'change'. In this way you pass around the circle.

It is helpful to start this game without music. When the group has grasped the idea, then add music. The music that can be used is extremely varied; almost any music will do. Again this game allows individuals to be spotlighted and works towards emphasizing group identity. The group dances created in this way are often every bit as fascinating as some of the tightest show choreography – and nowhere near as expensive.

Dancing

An individual's response to an internal and/or external stimulus is extremely personal. Often there is little structure that can be imposed, for there are no easily stated rules as there are with the dance/movement games. Many dance/ movement specialists use or teach technique to their groups. For the well-trained ex-professional dancer, allowing the group to learn these techniques is certainly a legitimate option for you. However, people without this training should be extremely wary of attempting to teach 'technique'. All too often in unskilled hands it is synonymous with rote learning and as such bypasses the emotions.

All that is needed to create an urge to dance is some form of internal or external stimulus and so it is very important to have a wide range of stimuli available. For example, music, photographs and painting can all be used to create a mood or to generate a response. The choice of a particular painting for the specific needs of the group is important. Having shown the group a painting, you can allow them to create a dance from the emotions engendered by the image. This may require choice of suitable music or may be better suited by silence.

Dance In/Dance Out

This is a useful activity for groups with whom you will be working for long periods of time. It allows you a chance to see what the general mood of the group is before and/or after each session. Simply play a selection of music before the session proper begins and after it is finished. Allow the group to respond to the music in any way the music takes them. Asking them what sort of music they would like to hear at that time can be beneficial. It is very important to have a wide variety of music with you. However, after a few meetings the group will have a good idea of the range of music you carry. In later sessions ask the group to bring their own music selections with them to the dance/movement sessions.

Observation of this free-form movement activity can be used to supplement other information you have about group members. Your job is often detective work, trying to piece together a three-dimensional jigsaw full of emotion, where many of the pieces are lost or unknown. Any activity that allows you to step back and just observe provides a potential store of information in a much shorter time than most of the more directive activities. However, as a cautionary note, it is very important to beware the 'this obviously shows . . .' trap. Although certain behaviors may indicate a particular emotion or state of mind, a single observation is not sufficient to enable anyone to make a definite statement concerning one individual's capabilities. Humans are extremely complicated beings, not easily willing to oblige linear cause-and-effect hypotheses!

Feather dances

For a long time I (BW) was stumped. I kept being asked to do workshops with youngsters with severe and multiple disabilities and I felt much of my material to be unsuitable. Then my assistant, Jane Newhouse, introduced me to peacock and ostrich feathers. From that day on I have been using these feathers not just with children with severe disabilities (where they often form the bridge to my other material) but with all groups.

For this activity I usually use one of three pieces of music: Allan Stivell's 'Renaissance of the Celtic Harp', Howard Davison's 'Music from the Thunder Tree', or Deuter's 'Wind and Mountain'. Ask the group to lie, or sit, comfortably with a peacock feather in their hand. In the case of children with severe and multiple disabilities I work one to one with an 'able-bodied' person cradling and supporting them. Those unfamiliar with either the technique or the importance of cradling should read Veronica Sherborne (1990).

When the music starts ask the group to follow the eye of the peacock feather as it moves to the music. The feather often appears to have a life of its own and will take the person holding it dancing. Please note that some children and adults can be extremely disturbed by this. If so, use an ostrich feather.

With groups of children with severe disabilities, ask their supporter to work through stages. First, the feather is moved so that the eye catches the child's attention. This necessitates making very small and fluid movements. Once the child's attention has been caught, place the feather in the child's hand and manipulate the hand so that the feather moves. As the child becomes more aware that it is his body moving the feather, the manipulator slowly releases the grip on the hand until the feather is moving totally under the child's control. The children may drop the feather – if so, simply put it back in their hands.

Lastly, add a second feather, so that there is one in each hand. These three stages may be traversed quickly or may take an extremely long time and much patience on the parts of the supporters and you.

The combination of peacock and ostrich feathers allows an extension of movement; a small movement with the peacock feather creates a huge and fascinating effect for a severely restricted child; the ostrich feather, while less of an 'attention getter', has a textural quality that fascinates many. The group can be placed so they work in pairs or, in the case of more able groups, they can freely interact.

One word of warning: always be on the lookout for children who try to eat the feathers. It not only damages the feathers but can also severely injure the child. Finally, be aware of the other materials that can extend small movements of physically restricted individuals. Experimenting with different types of cloth, string, ribbons, etc. can often find the materials best suited to your group's needs.

Follow My Dance II

This is a variation on Follow My Dance I. It illustrates a way of taking a name game into a group dance and then into a partner or small group dance. It also helps participants to experience the difference between movement as exercise and movement as dance: a felt act of communication – an emotional response.

The group makes a circle. This time individuals are asked to close their eyes and have a sense of how they feel in their bodies. What follows is a sequence of instructions to be given by you to the group that are aimed at enabling participants to switch off the 'little voice' in their heads, which continually gives instructions about what to do and how to think, etc. The purpose is to allow participants to listen to messages from the body instead:

- Allow yourself to stand.
- Listen to your breath (without changing it).
- Become aware of any aches and pains.
- Allow your body to balance around a central axis.
- Feel the support of the earth.
- Imagine a cushion of air between each vertebra, how does that make you want to move?
- Your back is wide, allow it to support you.
- Imagine an electrical field of energy around your body. How wide is it?
- Say your name quietly to yourself and create a way of moving that is unique to yourself.

There are many ways of framing these questions. Explore them and find ones which work for you and for the group. Now find a shape or gesture that expresses how you feel right now or allow the shape to find you. This idea of allowing 'the shape to find you' suggests a non-directive way of working. As in 'waiting without expecting', this idea implies an allowing or waiting for a new movement idea to arise – one that is not consciously thought out or directed.

Each individual is then asked to share their shape with the rest of the group by saying their name and making the shape. The saying of the name can vary from coming at the beginning to coming at the end. After each shape and name the rest of the group echo that person's name and shape, finding a matching tone of voice and quality of movement.

At the end of this task, to help develop a movement memory in the group, you can walk round touching the shoulder of each person in turn. The rest of the group then say that person's name and repeat the movements in turn. The quality of movement, gesture and tone of voice will be very different for each person and you may wish to draw attention to any that have a special quality about them. These movements can often be developed into solo material.

Follow My Dance III

Split the group into threes or fours, and ask each group to make a dance by putting together the movements explored in Follow My Dance II in any way that feels interesting or comfortable to the group.

Each group is then asked to show their piece to the others. Another idea is to ask the audience if the dance conveys any images, thoughts or feelings for them. This can be done at the end or, better still, after each dance if there is the time.

The group may wish to incorporate this new material into developing their dance and this is the point at which the session can really develop. You may then suggest a series of ideas; or more appropriately perhaps, encourage each group to find their own way of developing what they have created. Some ideas may include:

- One group providing a sound experience for a dance group using their bodies and voices to make a sound accompaniment.
- Musical instruments could be used. Merge the dance with another group.
- Draw the dance on paper. Dance the drawing.
- Discover an emotional quality or expressiveness to the dance; dance its opposite.
- Find a moment of stillness in the dance.
- Walk with the dance. Run with the dance. Take the dance on to the floor. Play with the dance.
- The dance has an identity, give it a voice.
- Write the story of the dance and let the story inform the dance.

The ideas and possible ways to explore each dance are endless. However, your confidence in trying out new ideas and new ways of moving is dependent on your own and the group's state of creative alertness. Other art forms can be used, including poetry, music and sculpture to encourage this process of self-expression through dance.

Dance improvisation – Essences

The aim of this dance improvisation is to create a safe and comfortable environment so that individuals can make a dance that is self-directed. What is more important perhaps, it is about stilling the mind and 'climbing into the body'. This means allowing participants to turn off the self-critical little voice in the head by becoming fascinated with one's own range and quality of movement expressiveness by giving permission for individuals to dance from a more self-directed place.

Dance improvisation requires a warm-up period before starting. It also needs an ability to be confident with the elements of dance and movement, for example, changing directions, levels, planes, pathways and different dynamics, etc. Some assistance can be given by you during the dance to introduce these elements to further develop the improvisation, encouraging the imagination as well as a rich use of movement vocabulary.

In Essences, individuals visit different places in the room, find a shape or movement phrase at each place and then join them all together to create a dance. The dance created is then performed with the group.

The instructions are presented as movement ideas, images, questions and the ones given here form the essentials only. You will need to fill them out and present them in such a way as to enable the participants to feel confident and secure in their personal exploration. A safe environment needs to be established to enable participants to have 'permission' to explore the images, questions and movement tasks without feeling at risk. Imagery is presented by you and worked with by the dancer to create a satisfying and enjoyable experience.

1   *Centering*: lie on the floor. Become aware of the breath without changing it. On the out-breath release your weight into the floor. On the in-breath rest.

2   *Images of*: opening in the back, spreading, lengthening. Feeling the wholeness of the back. Opening to your tiredness, releasing, allowing.

3   *Questions about*: stilling the mind to connect with the body:

- Find a place in the room where you feel most comfortable.
- Explore that place in a way that is most comfortable for you.
- Express that place in a shape or movement phrase.
- Move to another place in the room where you feel comfortable and repeat the experience.
- Move to the first place again and explore the transition.
- Move to the second place. Discover its essence.
- Repeat the movement phrase. In what way has it changed?
- Move to a third place and repeat.
- Move to a fourth place and repeat.
- Now return to the first place.
- Move between places. Exploring the different qualities of movement.
- The essence of each place, each movement, each feeling.
- What images come to mind? Dance with the image.
- Create a movement phrase that is repeatable and made up of the four shapes or movement phrases.
- With paper and soft pastels, draw the essence of the dance on paper.
- Quickly and intuitively write any words on the drawing.
- Incorporate the image into the dance. Use the words in the dance.
- Allow the dance to be witnessed or shared with a partner or the whole group.

- Share the experience in words with a partner or with the group. Or with both.

Repeat at a different time in a different place. Enjoy the dance, creatively alert to new possibilities for self-expression, healing and renewal.[5]

The sharing can take a variety of forms in pairs, threes or in a large group. In the process of allowing this development of personal creativity, many different ways of moving are possible. It is a dialogue between stillness and movement, between a form that is understood and a form that is emerging or put another way, as a colleague used to say, not to know, but through search to find a way. There is complexity and simplicity and in the sharing of the dance these paradoxes will no doubt emerge. Your task is to enable the individuals to dance in a way that is most expressive of themselves and then to reflect on the result of that experience. The task of the participant is to have a really satisfying and enjoyable experience with comfort, ease and enjoyment the main starting points.

It is not possible in these pages to transform the movement experience into a complete written picture that will give the same result every time. If used with sensitivity, intelligence of feeling and in a spirit of adventure it is likely that Essences will encourage further self-exploration through dance.

People who have worked with Essences have commented on its ability to enable them to free up and dance from the inside/out rather than vice versa. This means dancing from a different place of knowing and understanding, a place that has brought insight and clarity as well as embodied experience. After the sharing or performance, the dance is often shared with a partner when it is possible to talk objectively and subjectively about the experience, exploring its personal relevance and meaning, giving clarity and insight.

Postscript

Dance offers individuals a path to developing a greater sensory awareness, while at the same time releasing restricting or non-aligned patterns as they appear in posture, everyday movement patterns and expressive gestures. Developing this sensory awareness enables people to begin to create their own unique dances: ones that can help to clarify, extend and define an emerging sense of self. This may in turn help to promote an independence of thought, bodily functioning, concentration, focus, and more spontaneous, less routine behavior.

The expression through dance of our unique self is a momentary fleeting embodied thing, one that cannot be fixed or easily captured in all its complexity. It can only really be sensed as a living entity and certainly not captured in print. It is a coming together of shapes, movements, thoughts and feelings, rhythms and sensations, all of which make up an emotional response, a response that brings together many seemingly disparate elements, without the use of words. There is no doubt, however, that working with dance creatively, as a way to explore space, shape, rhythm and our own bodies in movement, is a very fulfilling, enjoyable and challenging task.

Watching for those special moments of aliveness when the individual is in tune with themselves requires a creative alertness. Being creatively alert for the group means being alive to dance as a felt act of communication. However, it is also necessary to have an understanding of the overall framework within which dance/movement activity is taking place and how one's own dance group or session contributes to the overall picture. Also, keep in mind that the ideas expressed in this chapter are in no way fixed rules about what should be done. They have their history in what has gone before – movement and dance ideas that have worked in many different settings, and ones that have been worked with, changed and developed along the way. Always remember that you are working with other human beings, their emotions and their well-being, and not simply playing or performing. It is likely that during improvisations some people may encounter emotional blocks. You need to establish your own ways of helping people break through the blocks. Also it is possible that some may experience and even relive negative experiences from their past. In this case you need to establish approach(es) for immediate comfort and support to help deal with this relived experience.

Finally, dance allows individuals to gain in self-confidence and self-management by learning about their bodies, their minds and their place in the world. Dance affects everybody, from the very young to frail older people. It enlarges people's imaginations, extends their ability to communicate, increases their capacity for social action and fosters well-being. Individuals can be valued for their unique contribution and thus help to increase their own sense of self-worth. We trust that the material we have presented here, along with the suggested films and books, will provide ideas and a framework in which you may continue to expand and develop your work in dance/movement.

Appendix: movement analysis

Note: This movement analysis is based on the principles of Rudolf Laban and adapted from LUDUS Dance in Education Teachers' Pack, *The Thunder Tree*, edited by C. Thomson and B. Warren.

The body is capable of a wide range of movement, but all movement can be broken down into five basic actions. This kind of breakdown is known as a movement analysis. The five basic actions are:

- *travel*: redistribution of weight through space
- *balance*: stillness in equilibrium
- *turn*: rotation around an axis

- *jump*: launching weight into the air
- *gesture*: movement without change of weight.

Further, the body is capable of three kinds of mechanical action: *bending*, *stretching* and *twisting*. The quality of any movement can be described by four movement factors:

• *space*	high–low	near–far
• *weight*	light–strong	soft–hard
• *time*	fast–slow	sudden–sustained
• *flow*	free	bound

Actions and their movement factors can be described in many ways, as shown in Table 6.1.

As well as these elements, all movements involve one or more *parts of the body*, have a *direction*, and are executed in relation to other people or objects.

In addition to the words that describe movement actions and qualities, there are some basic descriptors, which may be useful in planning, running or describing your sessions (Table 6.2).

These ways of describing movement are fundamental to movement analysis. You can use movement analysis to help you recognize and note the movement capabilities of your group. For example, which parts of the body, if any, can they move in isolation? Can they travel? Can they balance? Can they travel, but only on the floor – that is roll, crawl – or can they travel only in a wheelchair?

Qualities drawn from movement analysis, combined with your knowledge of the individual needs and capabilities of your group, will help you to decide on your movement aims and structure effectively the content of your sessions. In addition it enables you to describe and record an individual's behavior in movement terms, and to detail the changes that occur in your sessions over time.

Table 6.1 How you move

Actions			Qualities		
hop	rock	stab	gentle	wide	lingering
skip	crawl	stroke	weak	small	dashing
step	slither	cut	heavy	tall	hurrying
run	twizzle	pinch	firm	thin	
bounce	wiggle	throw	long	fat	
leap	shake	catch	short	flat	
fall	carry	hold	angular	stiff	
stand	push	release	spiky	floppy	
rise	pull	wave	bendy	delicate	
roll	kick	flutter	curved	floating	
see-saw	punch	tense	rounded	flicking	

Table 6.2 Basic descriptors

Body parts	Directions	Relationships
What you move	*Where you move*	*How or with whom*
whole body	up	with
head	down	against
neck	in	together
shoulders	out	copying
arms	backwards	contrasting
elbows	forwards	in pairs
wrists	in front	in threes, fours . . .
hands	behind	in groups
fingers	left	following
back	right	leading
hips	into the middle	joining
bottom	out to the side	leaving
tummy	straight	passing
legs	sideways	taking turns
knees	zig-zag	containing/enclosing
ankles	circle	
feet	spiral	
toes		
eyes		
mouth		
nose		

Acknowledgements

I (RC) wish to thank the following professional colleagues for their work, their vision and for the influence they have had on my own work in this field: Mary Fulkerson, Wolfgang Stange, Hilda Holger, Joanna Harris, Marcia Leventhal, Penny Greenland, Janice Parker, Gabrielle Parker, Steve Paxton, Alison McMorland, Carola Gross, Jasmine Pasch, Gerry Hunt, Bonnie Meekums, Klaas Overzee, Christina McDonald and Peter Brinson.

I would also like to acknowledge the ongoing support and friendship of Miranda Tufnell who continues to inspire and influence the development of dance and movement for health and well-being in the UK.

I (BW) wish to thank the following professional colleagues, some of whom I am lucky enough to count as my friends, for their work and vision and for the influence they have had on my own work in this field: Veronica Sherborne, Keith Yon, Kedzie Penfield, Walli Meir, Steph Record, Veronica Lewis, Jane Newhouse, Helen Payne; and particularly Lesley Hutchison and Chris Thomson for their support during my time with LUDUS Dance Company, and Sensei O'Tani who awakened me to the way of the circle. However, my greatest thanks go to Dr George Mager and The 50/50 Theatre

Company for showing me not only the power of the discipline and art of dance, but also the effect this art form can have on the lives of people with disabilities.

Notes

1 There are a number of formal and informal methods of analyzing movements. For further information see North (1972), Bartenieff (1980) or Kestenberg (1999).
2 For example see exercises presented in Chapter 3.
3 Repetition is a key idea for allowing movement material to develop in an organic way. The movement has some connection with what has gone before and a state of creative alertness allows the movement potential of that moment to be developed.
4 There can be a number of explanations why the healers see their partner's aura. Some require a leap of faith, a belief in the existence of body energy fields. Other more pragmatic explanations rest on the concept of feeling body heat and creating a mind's-eye, heat-outlined picture of their partner.
5 If the reader wants to take this work further, then the publications of Fulkerson (1977) and Tufnell and Crickmay (1990, 2004) should prove very helpful in suggesting imagery and ideas for finding the inner dancer.

Further reading

Bartenieff, I. (1980) *Body Movement – Coping with the Environment*, New York: Gordon and Breach.

Bernstein, P.L. (1979) *Eight Theoretical Approaches in Dance-Movement Therapy*, Dubuque and Toronto: Kendall/Hunt.

—— (1981) *Theory and Method in Dance Movement Therapy*, 3rd edn, Dubuque and Toronto: Kendall/Hunt.

Caplow-Lindner, E. (1979) *Therapeutic Dance/Movement*, London: Human Sciences Press [expressive activities for older adults].

Fulkerson, M. (1977) *Language of the Axis*, Dartington: Dartington College of Arts, Theatre Papers, 1st Series no. 12.

Garnet, E. (1982) *Movement is Life*, Princeton: Princeton Book Co. [a holistic approach to exercise for older adults].

Greenland, P. (1987) *Dance – A Non-Verbal Approach (A Handbook for Leaders)*, Leeds: Jabadao, Centre for Movement Learning and Health.

—— (ed.) (2000) *What Dancers Do that other Health Workers Don't*, Leeds: Jabadao, Centre for Movement Learning and Health.

Halprin, D. (2003) *The Expressive Body in Life, Art, and Therapy: Working with Movement, Metaphor, and Meaning*, London: Jessica Kingsley Publishers.

Hanna, J.L. (1979) *To Dance is Human – A Theory-of Non-Verbal Communication*, Austin, TX: University of Texas Press.

—— (2006) *Dancing for Health: Conquering and Preventing Stress*, Lanham, MD: AltaMira Press.

Harris, J.G. (1988) *A Practicum for Dance Therapy*, London: ADMT Publications, Springfield Hospital.

Hartley, L. (1984) *Body Mind Centring*, London: ADMT Publications, Springfield Hospital.

Innes A. and Hatfield, K. (2001) *Healing Arts Therapies and Person-Centred Dementia Care*, Bradford: University of Bradford, Bradford Dementia Group Good Practice Guides.

Keleman, S. (1985) *Emotional Anatomy*, Thousand Oaks, CA: Center Press.

Kestenberg, J. (1999) *The Meaning of Movement – Developmental and Clinical Perspectives of the Kestenberg Movement Profile*, Amsterdam: Gordon and Breach.

Lamb, W. and Watson, E. (1987) *Body Code: The Meaning in Movement*, Princeton: Princeton Book Co.

Lange, R. (1975) *The Nature of Dance – An Anthropological Perspective*, Plymouth: Macdonald and Evans.

Lerman, L. (1980) *Teaching Dance to Senior Adults*, Springfield, IL: Thomas.

Levete, G. (1982) *No Handicap to Dance*, London: Souvenir Press.

Levy, F. (1988) *Dance Movement Therapy. A Healing Art*, Virginia: American Alliance for Health, Physical Education, Recreation and Dance.

North, M. (1972) *Personality Assessment through Movement*, London: Macdonald and Evans.

Pasch, J. (1984) *Creative Dance with People with Learning Difficulties*, London: ADMT Publications, Springfield Hospital.

Payne, H. (1984) *Responding with Dance*, London: ADMT Publications, Springfield Hospital.

—— (2006) *Dance Movement Therapy: Theory, Research and Practice*, (2nd edn), London: Routledge.

Sherborne, V. (1990) *Developmental Movement for Children*, Cambridge: Cambridge University Press.

Torbett, M. (1980) *Follow Me*, New York: Prentice-Hall.

Tufnell, M. and Crickmay, C. (1990) *Body, Space, Image*, London: Virago.

—— (2004) *A Widening Field – Journeys in Body and Imagination*, Alton: Dance Books.

Videos

American Dance-Movement Therapy Association (1984) *Dance Therapy – the Power of Movement*, Berkeley: University of California.

Bernstein, P.L. (1975) *To Move is to Be Alive: A Developmental Approach in Dance-Movement Therapy*, Pittsburgh: Pittsburgh Guidance Center.

Corfield, L. (2000) *The Thinking Body: The Legacy of Mabel Todd Explained*, Piermont, NY: Teachers' Video Workshop.

Jabadao (1987) *Dance – A Non-Verbal Approach*, Leeds: Jabadao Centre for Movement Learning and Health.

Jabadao (1987) *Dancing for Celebration*, Leeds: Jabadao Centre for Movement Learning and Health.

Sherborne, V. (1976) *A Sense of Movement*, Ipswich: Concorde Films.

—— (1982) *Building Bridges*, Ipswich: Concorde Films.

—— (1990) *Developmental Movement for Children*, Cambridge: Cambridge University Press.

Chapter 7

Expanding human potential through music

Keith Yon

Why is music of such value to me that I feel others could similarly benefit? Simply, music lifts me: my feelings, thinking and spirit are extended beyond the strictures of ordinariness, paradoxically by taking me physically inwards to my body centre. Having a centre to hold on to allows me to move between moods which are normally judged as opposites, e.g. happiness and sadness, the one to be hoped for and the other avoided. In view of the fact that feeling is the source of action, it cannot be so undervalued, especially for those who find it unmanageable. Rather, the body should exercise its means to accommodate all feelings with the ability for transcending those that prove unpleasant.

My personal experience of feelings is like inner movement, self-understanding, continuously fluid. Words, on the other hand, seem like articulated sounds trying to make objective sense, first to myself, then for sharing. Music, with its sounds faithfully reproducing both sustained and articulated movement, and its language, which uses the elements of words, i.e. feeling vowel and articulating consonant, is, rationally speaking, 'nonsense'. But, on the principle that animals sing, whereas humans may speak – speech being heightened singing – music provides an interim state allowing feelings to be revealed that may not be defined in words.

Immobility of body, mind, feelings or spirit can constitute handicap; but seeing that these aspects of an individual may be interrelated, the immobility, for example, of body and mind, may be remedied or at least alleviated through the potential of mobility in feelings or spirit. Physical, emotional, intellectual or spiritual preferences of musical experience evolve from personal need. I would like everybody to experience what happens to me in music: the spaciousness of Monteverdi, the self-statement of Bach, the form of Mozart, the sense of time transcended by Schumann, the vibrant silences of Webern, the jolt out of complacency by Stravinsky; and to confront, as in many modern compositions, the relationship between music and life: music or noise, animate or inanimate sound. But being involved in response to satisfying personal neuroses, musical taste must, in the educational interests of allowing others to function as individuals, be questioned in favor of underlying principles, directly related to the fundamental concern of individuality. This concern is to function within the pace, spaces and forms of society, which may be directly allied to the elements of music: rhythm, tune and texture. An infant exploring forms in space and time builds imaginative resources: an elderly individual is a treasury of images that only need forms, time and space to be realized.

Musical form, not limited by narrative, may take the imagination beyond its normal expectation and give the individual a greater satisfaction from having structured a period of time creatively. With my groups I try to induce a sense of extended form by means of the format of the sessions themselves, both (a) of the individual sessions, and (b) as stages within an extended program.

Individual sessions

That each session is experienced as a journey or story is crucial: all cultural groups use stories to reaffirm themselves. A story is a central event, an overall build-up, climax and release, sustained on a succession of subsidiary events, each smaller versions of the larger. So the journey through the session progresses by stages of build-ups, climaxes and releases, through which the leader, like the storyteller acting beyond their normal body and voice, attempts to sustain a sense of overall caring.

It is worth making regular weekly visits to map an inmate's time in an institution. These may be invigorated into a 'landscape' by exploring time, space and forms; rhythm, tune and textures.

In a north London school in which racially opposed groups had no time or space for each other, I found that by placing the rival Greek and Turkish or black and white groups side by side, they avoided confrontation and could acknowledge at least the presence of the others. Having been encouraged to sing or listen to chosen songs, interleaving the lines of one group with those of the other, they had to experience silences alternating with sounds. The silences were initially antagonistic but, gradually affected by the music, could acquire a semblance of coexistence. The change in the children's normal spaces and sense of time produced a musical form more relevant to their needs.

Play with spaces, time and forms proved effective in other seemingly remedial situations, e.g. actors having to sing, musicians to speak, visual artists to move and dancers to make sounds. Over the years this has extended to communication therapy with second language casualties, mentally ill patients and prisoners, arriving at my present concerns, which involve exploring expressive alternatives with people with a disability.

Extended programs

The length of the program must be agreed. Even if the group is unable to comprehend fully a time span of eight or ten weeks, I still perform a ritual, from halfway through, of a weekly countdown, so that at the end they may not feel suddenly abandoned: the parting is prepared and mutual. Arts experience aiming to help accommodate pain should avoid inflicting it. The final session cannot be the climax of the program, but a time to release myself gently from their environment.

A class of intelligent teenagers with a physical disability, conscious of their social prowess and the regard of their 'non-disabled' peers, found my sessions 'mad', and in order to be able to undertake the session, which presumably they wanted to, had to ritualize every meeting by protesting against what I asked of them. Responsibility for their 'madness' being removed on to me allowed them, within the secret of their play space, to enjoy themselves and transcend their disability with impressive ingenuity and individuality.

The parameters of our relationship have also to be recognized. As leaders we aim to set up an ambience of acceptance, and to provide a microcosm of society for individuals to test their personal and social expressive skills. But, in response to particular situations, we may need to limit our parameters to providing only as much time and space as those with whom we are working might be able to manage. In extreme situations, as helpers, we may need to become barely more than their physical parameters. Actual body contact will allow us to become interpreters of their containment or expression. Within any learning situation, fluidity between the roles of helper, therapist and leader allows the artist which is in all of us to be revealed: to contest confinements of body, society or sanity.

Practical activities

My work model is a matrix, one axis of which is a continuum from handicap to non-handicap, and the other from individual to group. The individual who cannot move within this matrix, in any sense, seems to me to be handicapped. Essentially my work involves expression – gradual rather than sudden, considered rather than reflex, but I have had to become more concerned for finding inner resources through music: increasing an individual's capacity for feeling to the extent that they are motivated to find, rather than be taught, their most effective means of expression. My role as reassurer, then catalyst, changes to reflector to help individuals evaluate their experiences.

Throughout this chapter I make reference to several key ideas regarding both forms and structures. I make great use of the circle within my sessions. Circles allow for both containment and for the possibility of a group member to become an individual within the group, by moving into the circle to perform. It also provides the possibility for each participant to become a leader and possibly to be imitated by the group.

Rudimentary musical experience can be described as the difference between:

- *duplet* pulses, i.e. two even beats, e.g. X X, and
- *triplet* pulses, i.e. two uneven pulses, e.g. long-short, *X* X, or short-long, X *X*; or three beats, e.g. X X X.

I make extensive reference to these two forms for transforming modes of communication in speech:

- *duplet*, giving information, generally controlled pulse stresses, as opposed to
- *triplet*, expressing feeling, expansive pulse stresses: a pulse = two or three beats, a stress = two or three syllables.

To give a 'physical' example of each form: running = duplet, skipping = triplet.

Alex, aged 19, who normally walked fast, noticing little, became excited by his self- and environment awareness, being held back by a strong wind. Similarly, changing duplet into triplet pulse to each step made him more open.

Nigel, aged 29, though possessing an extensive repertoire of tunes which he hummed, only grunted isolated sounds. By encouraging the grunt rebound 'uh-uh' for a two-syllable word (e.g. Figure 7.1a), then extending to three (e.g. Figure 7.1b), I could use the third sound of the triplet as the first sound of a new stress (e.g. Figure 7.1c).

An initial sound, sign or mark may be comparatively easily prompted. The problem is encouraging the individual to react to it to make the second: keeping him alive during the gap.

I also use semicircle formations. This opening of the circle longways is a crucial learning experience. It is important as a midway point, comparable to the body opening from self-contained sphere to other-aware erect, by way of 'demi', half-open and enclosed: animal alert, martial artist.

The area of play, that is, the space within which to behave beyond the norm, may be defined by instruments, chairs, etc. Low benches proved useful as a 'catwalk' into a 'circus' from the changing rooms, then angled to define a more manageable space within a large room.

How this all works in practice is best demonstrated in the format of a typical session of mime:

- Greeting
- Body exercise

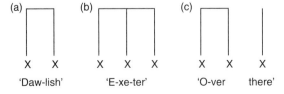

Figure 7.1 Duplet and triplet pulses.

- Sound play
- Reflection.

Greeting

The group, including myself, is seated in a circle on the floor, if possible. Some people may need assistance from a helper who can act as a physical and vocal extension and/or interpreter.

Hello

A simple song is used to greet each member: 'Hello Sue, Hello Hamish', etc. 'Hello' sung allows the 'lo' to be suspended as long as is necessary to gain the nominee's attention, which is then confirmed by naming: 'Helloooooooo – Jim!' The suspension of the sound may be enlivened by repeating the 'hello' as a sustained and articulated phrase.

When it is possible for the list of names to be sung without suspending the 'lo', that is, on one breath, an overall intention is set up. But it is more musical and structurally beneficial to phrase the names in groups of three or four similar to actions within actions, as in a story. The group, by pointing to each person in turn being named, might gain in concentration and focus, particularly in the case of those people unable to create sound.

Absent

Having celebrated those who are present, it is sensitive to remember those who are absent (Figure 7.2). The absence of individuals from the group can be used as an occasion to acknowledge sadness and thus to extend concerns beyond immediate confines, raising the status of those present.

Framing

The group members, in turn, name themselves, so that each name may stand out individually. However, the name needs to be framed, either by the vulnerability of a pause (providing an opportunity to manage silence) or by the

Figure 7.2 Absence acknowledgement.

group repeating the syllables of the name, and clapping them (keeping them lifted in silence and providing an immediate memory exercise), as shown in Figure 7.3, resulting in an exciting rhythm.

Joe   X   Helena   X   X   X   Herman   X   X   Dot   X, etc.

Figure 7.3 Framing.

Gestures

Each individual sings his or her name accompanied by hand or facial gestures, which are imitated by the group either after or simultaneously with the singer: e.g. laughing *at* oneself, *with* the group is socially healthy. Simultaneity, e.g. mirror-image exercise, helps envisaging oneself removed; imitation from the side when touch or confrontation is impossible.

Good morning signed

This is a more elaborate song accompanied by signing (Figure 7.4a) after which a contrasting coda is shouted, clapped and stamped (Figure 7.4b): the rhythm of a football (soccer) chant.

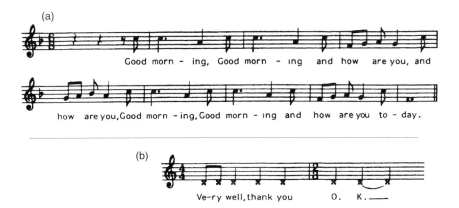

Figure 7.4 Good morning signed.

Parrot-fashion learning is justified here because a football chant is social currency; it gives a sense of belonging (chorus: David Ward). Gesture or signing, paradoxically by taking pressure off the eyes and releasing tension from upper body, allows fuller eye contact.

'Oh what a beautiful morning'

This and similar popular songs may be sung to get body and voice moving together, swaying from side to side:

> Oh what a beautiful morning, oh what a beautiful day
> LEFT   RIGHT   LEFT   RIGHT   LEFT   RIGHT
>
> I have a beautiful feeling, everything's going my way.
> LEFT   RIGHT   LEFT   RIGHT   LEFT   RIGHT

Use familiarity with communal songs to balance rawer, cruder sounds of creativity. Though still the containing stage of the session, expressive elements may be introduced through slight modification of regular rhythm, suspended double beat to allow extended reaching, i.e. opposition of left and right sides (Figure 7.5).

Reaching arms and extending vowel approximation yawning: maximum longways stretch, anus to soft palate; and sideways, hand to hand, the most lifted sensation in the body which, sustained, is the basis of singing.

With some disturbed groups, repetition of familiar songs might be the extent of the session, i.e. confirming manageable space and working within it. However, a creative dimension (listening, play and formalizing) is possible in exercising qualities of: loud–soft, far–near; song-dances exploring small–large circles; fast–slow, e.g. song sung at double and triple speeds; using major-minor keys to transform moods.

Events

Songs need sometimes to be improvised to cover exigencies, e.g. a birthday, a cold, a hurt finger, new glasses, an intrusion, a visitor, etc. Use a simple song structure such as 'Who has, Who has, Who has come into the room?'

Rocking forwards and backwards

This song accompanies forwards–backwards rocking, first in duplet pulse (Figure 7.6).

Then rocking in triplet pulse (Figure 7.7), obsessive rocking, reflex motion, being accepted then extended: pausing long enough to allow the body to curl into itself enclosed in self-communication, humming an extra layer of

Figure 7.5 Rhythm modification.

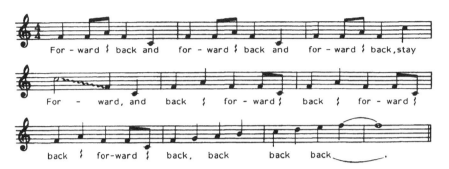

Figure 7.6 Forwards–backwards rocking in duplet pulse.

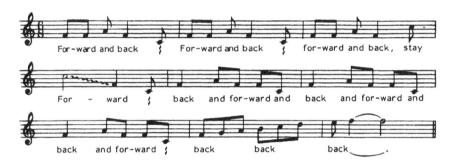

Figure 7.7 Forwards–backwards rocking in triplet pulse.

'smell'; allowing the body to fall backwards and straighten out, retaining self-assurance of curled-up sphere. If some people with disabilities are unable to rock on their own, work in pairs (with one person cradling the other) to feed in the duplet and the triplet pulses.

Rocking sideways

Sideways rocking movement allows 'limitless' reaching (Figure 7.8). Long lines of pairs can become ships, shipwrecks, underwater movement and sounds.

Figure 7.8 Rocking sideways.

The moment of overbalance in reaching is related to a suspended beat, of duplet becoming triplet (Figure 7.9).

Figure 7.9 Duplet becoming triplet.

Pull the boat, push the boat

This is a modification of a favorite action song (Figure 7.10): exercising seesaw for two-way action of communication; distinguish 'push and be pushed' or 'pull and be pulled' from 'push and pull'. Reach–recoil reflex action of individuals who compulsively put objects in mouth extended to considered action.

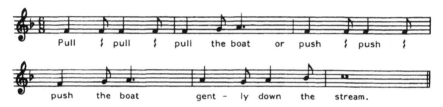

Figure 7.10 Pull the boat, push the boat.

Body exercise

Individuals of limited or no vocal means need to experience song in their silent bodies (as a self-recognizing container and expresser of feelings, i.e. self-communication prior to other communication). The musical lift comes through the feet, if standing, or the bottom, if seated.

Silent song

Sing and dance a song, then dance the song:

- without singing it outwardly,
- without using the arms,
- without using the body or feet. Hear the song in silence.

Humming

The group practices humming – 'Mmmmm' – while curling themselves up. Then, while stretching themselves out, they articulate the sound: 'Mememe', extending the vowel and possibly rising to the octave above. This is similar to singers tuning up: 'M' inward lip movement; teeth kept apart for free jaw.

Figure 7.11 Toe song.

Toe song

This song accompanies massaging appropriate parts of the body. It can provide the important sensation of simple syncopation between pulses on 'big' (or 'little', 'pink', 'brown', etc.), challenging rigidity of pulses: principle applies to time between striking instrument; motivation; compare vowel between consonants (Figure 7.11).

The last verse may be 'Oh there were ten fingers, etc.', in which case the word 'reached' may reach up the eight steps of the scale, with the hands trying to touch the sky and the body coming erect. Then the cadence, instead of falling, remains open in a flourish of sound, after which the silent body tries to maintain the sense of flourish.

Contrast this with walking on pointed toes, 'lordly', and smooth heels, 'peasant', which exercises high and low body centers producing different qualities of sound, catering for individuals of different dispositions. Also try this exercise in syncopated clapping:

<pre>
               clap   clap   clap   clap
duplet –
          step   step   step   step

               clap clap   clap clap   clap clap   clap clap
triplet –
          step   step   step   step
</pre>

Body blues

The sad quality of this song is effective at a containing, turning inwards stage of a session (Figure 7.12). The song sequence of *upwards*, heels – knees – back – fingers, and *downwards*, sides – bottom, makes a satisfying arc.

Tarzan song

This is a sequence of vocal sounds, duplicating those experienced slapping the body cavities:

Foot///:Calf///:Knee///:Thigh///:Belly///:Chest///:Neck///:Mouth (Yodel)

Oh my heels are worn_ down.   Oh   my heels   are

worn_ down.   They've been   travelling too long, _____ and they're

worn_ down.   Lord   have mer - cy—   on my_ heels.

Figure 7.12 Body blues.

An alternative arrival at the top of the body is to roll the head around, humming in gentle triplet. This should ideally be experienced in the fast group-regulated version only after individual exploration of cavities' resonances.

Rockets

Humming drones, as if engines starting up, accompany hands massaging the thighs downwards to the knee, where they lift off; sounds duplicate their 'flight' to its apex, then sparkle, as 'fireworks', in a sustained cadenza, the hands, at length, returning to the knee-base and the voice to its drone. This can create a warming at the body centre. The sense of centre is reaffirmed from tension drawn downwards before lifting.

Breath

Whether vocal or silent, individuals may exercise the three basic types of breathing: (1) breathe in and hold the breath till bursting; (2) breathe in and out regularly to counts, e.g. one in, one out, two in, two out, etc.; (3) breathe out for as long as possible.

1 Held breath blocking tension in the muscle here exercised in fun normally to be avoided; uncontrolled release of energy in aggressive reflex action may be transformed into considered expression, e.g. expletives – sentences, grunts – songs, kicks – dance steps, hitting – gestures.
2 Both shallow and deep breathing need exercise; avoid percussive in/out motion, raising tension: instead exercising rolling abdominal movement, i.e. inwards and upwards for exhalation and outwards and downwards for inhalation.

3   Extending breath to spread thoughts and feelings out; self – prior to other – recognition.

Sentence

Build a song based on repeated parts of a sentence, e.g.:

(a) 'Today . . .'
(b) 'Today I am . . .'
(c) 'Today I am feeling . . .'
(d) 'Today I am feeling very tired . . .'
(e) 'Today I am feeling very tired because I got up late.'

The principle of sentence is a thing (noun) activated (verb); also sentence structure is based on Who, What happened, When, Where, How and Why; and uses polyrhythm of speech stresses, i.e. mixture of two and three; the essential rhythmic expression in undemonstrative cultures.

Each phrase may be repeated until assimilated by the group, the breath between exaggerated with the lengthening phrases. Full breath release avoids frustration build-up.

Interlude

During the first part of the session the group should have experienced sounds ranging from very loud to very soft, indicating the parameters within which they may be expressive in the second part. The overall intention so far has been to treat the body as an instrument: as a group member, tuning it up first to contain feelings, through close body contact; then for expression: individuals start to develop a secure physical base for creating sounds which allows them to venture beyond their bodily confines. An expression echoed by at least one other voice is the basis of communication. Therefore, like an instrument, the body-voice has to be sympathetically 'toned' to respond effectively and appropriately.

Individuals concerned only to express themselves may be as wayward as suits their purpose. But when intent upon communicating, be it with an audience of one or many, they have to accept the necessity for agreed structures, e.g. the conductor's beat, being in tune, being in step and, in social dance, the agreed feet patterns (over which real communication is played through eye and upper body contact, etc.). This is how music is normally experienced and taught: the leader presenting models based on accepted musical products within which individuals may choose to conform or rebel.

In contrast to this structured practice, music may be taught organically, beginning with the crude materials of sounds which, through a process of exploration, become realized in individual forms. The dilemma of whether the finished production of a piece of music is more beneficial than the process undergone producing it, a topic which occupies so much pedagogic discussion, is in practice dispelled. Process is product in a state of transformation, whereas product is process suspended. Whether structured or organic, the means for helping individuals to create are only as effective as the leader employing them. Ultimately I may communicate only the habit of conviction and motivation, i.e. what keeps me in one piece and what moves me to action: stillness and action. It is salutary to remember that infants reveal in their rudimentary language an intuitive sense of symmetry: 'da-da,' 'ma-ma,' etc. (The sequence of sound rebound couplet, i.e. 'uh-uh,' 'ga-ga,' 'da-da,' 'ma-ma' and 'ba-ba' trace infant development from amorphous to self-identification.) Musical form is simply the dynamic of knowing that a sound will be repeated, and being surprised when it is.

The relationship between process and product is crucial when working with people with a disability who cannot manage the sharing of social 'products', i.e. cannot communicate, and who, to ensure that their frustration may be alleviated, need to be provided with alternatives, forms of expression evolved from individual rudimentary sounds. It is essential for people with a disability to experience something of the repertoire of music and songs to increase their sense of belonging in their society. These received forms, articulated intervals, structured rhythms, etc., which are the elements of 'proper' music, some people may find difficult to accommodate, but through play they may in time assimilate them into their vocabulary.

It must be remembered that the musical sounds normally heard are articulated, i.e. played on keyed or fretted instruments, or are formal speech syllables: the gaps between, being sufficient to cause disquiet or excess tension, are likely to be abhorred by individuals lacking the technique for managing discomfort. Therefore it is essential to fortify the ability to accommodate stimuli by having the experience of more readily acceptable sounds, e.g. unbroken, melismatic intervals, which abound in folksongs, jazz and Eastern music: a swanee (slide) whistle should be part of every leader's equipment.

Even more fundamental is the experience gained from playing with free sound, i.e. unstructured rhythms, microtonal intervals and noise: humming, grunts, expletives, banging, etc. It is not uncommon to find individuals, not only those people with a disability, for whom the sensation of noise beating *at* their bodies (therefore requiring no response) is more to their liking than the spaces of rhythm and interval, which demand exposure of feelings. Transforming noise into music is finding the lifting quality of sound. Sound being an extension of the body must also be three-dimensional (depth, vertical, lateral) and must reproduce the elements of the most immediate form of contact which it displaces: smell–touch:

1 *Depth.* Animal sounds evolved to establish territory, clothing the body in vibration like an extra *texture* of skin: purring, humming, hardly more

than a more intense layer of reassuring smell; by this means the body may choose either to isolate or express itself.

2 *Vertical.* Changes in vibration produce notes of different intervals i.e. *tune:* the change from one vibration to another, producing a feeling of suspension in the spaces between the intervals. Lack of interval, however microtonal, is noise.

3 *Lateral.* Sound may travel where the body, for either physical or social reasons, may not: suspending itself in time, either sustained or kept lifted on articulating pulses, i.e. *rhythm*, which has the potential to behave with the dual characteristics of touch:

(a) as if handling, giving information, the one-way traffic of expression, favoring the control of duplet pulses;

(b) as if caressing, the two-way action of communication, sharing feelings, warmth oscillating in the space between bodies, favoring the expansive propensity of triplet pulses. The spaces between the pulses allow the body to be controlled or to soar; over-insistence on the pulse of rigidity of beat is tantamount to noise. (A lawnmower, moved by muscular effort, makes sound phrases nearer to music than the mechanical rigidity of repeated beats from one driven by a motor.) Rhythmic patterns seem to be the property of the primitive and young, whereas sustained melody seems to satisfy more mature natures.

The following sections isolate the elements of music in an order which is perhaps more accessible to people with a disability: rhythm, tune, texture. They attempt to provide: first, scope for both structured and organic processes of creativity, which is to say, forms as the bases rather than the ideals of exploration; second, rudiments for developing from accommodation to assimilation and finally, group and individual involvement. Throughout, the essentials of creativity should be kept to the fore:

- Listening going into oneself: is it sound or silence?
- Play – sorting things out: is it noise (inanimate sound) or music?
- Formalizing – moving into expression or action: is it relevant, animated?

Where I have thought it helpful, I have related the elements of music to other media. Because I firmly support the notion that instrumental sounds should be related to the body-voice, I shall continue to limit examples to the voice, hoping that their application to music generally is obvious.

Sound play

Rhythm

This section explores the lateral aspect of music; breath or sound phrases conveyed over a period of time, either sustained (1 to 4) or articulated by pulses (5 to 11), allowing choice of being secure on the pulses or expansive between them. A breath phrase (a potential step, gesture or sound phrase) may be sustained or broken up, i.e. articulated with a build-up of excitement towards the phrase climax in proportion to the relationship of pulses. However, mechanically regular pulses or beats spell musical death, even within rhythmic patterns of social dance; a triplet should not be based on three even beats, but rather on the principles of the suspended duplet.

Tennis

Pairs face each other throwing sounds across to each other, tracing the 'flight of the ball' with their hands and voices: transforming antagonism to co-operation; an essential 'developmental stage' for most groups.

Ball of string

In a circle, individuals pass round a ball of string, humming and changing pitch as the string changes hands. When the string is substituted by sound being 'handed' around, the changing notes may be sung by the group, or individuals may hold on to their notes, building a block of sound. The changing notes may simply 'climb' the scale: 1 to 8 for the diatonic, and 1 to 5 for the pentatonic.

Star points

A piece of string is passed across the circle preferably of an odd number above five, to any but a neighbor. When the string is returned to its beginning the points of a star will have been created. If the group is numbered consecutively, the passage of the string, picked out on the numbered keys of, say, a xylophone, will make a 'star tune' to which words may be added, for example, to describe direction: 'to George . . . to Val', etc.

The string is best passed through the spokes of chairs, allowing the 'star' to be placed near the floor providing 'hopscotch' spaces, each space a different note. Then, if moved up and down the spokes, the flat, two-dimensional figure becomes three-dimensional, among the shapes of which individuals may crawl, tracing the lines of string in sustained and changing notes. This is a two- to three-dimensional exercise in body image, essential for individuals who feel they are always on display.

Star radials

One end of a large ball of string is secured to the floor in the centre of the circle. Each group member in turn is responsible for creating a radial, pointing in the direction he or she wishes their radial to go, and sustaining a note or gesture for the length he or she wishes the radial to be as the leader moves the string from centre until the sound terminates, i.e. the radial reaches its 'point'. The string is secured to the floor and returned to the centre for the next group member to create a radial.

Support music

The group sits in a semicircle and its members make sounds to accompany individuals in turn traveling to a spot that may be defined by a large card on the floor. Different textures of sound may be explored to parallel the walking, which build in intensity as the traveler nears his or her goal. When he or she steps on to the card, the accompanying group sustains a sound for as long as he or she chooses to remain on it: then they accompany his or her return journey. Distinction needs to be made between sounds that: (a) duplicate each step; (b) more profitably for extending halting walk, lift the gap between steps (syncopation), i.e. downwards action of step lifts body.

Tile-dance chorus

Individuals choose a sequence of colored floor tiles as a step pattern to be repeated as a dance chorus, e.g. 'Blue tile, blue tile, red tile, yellow; who is now a clever fellow?' Between the choruses individuals may improvise free steps and sounds.

Stepping stones

The 'banks of a river' are defined on the floor and individuals, in actuality and in sound, try to cross in one go. The river is widened until stepping stones – large pieces of card – are required to facilitate crossing. Travelers, accompanied by group chorus, may either:

- linger on each stone, to admire or reflect on the 'landscape' of sounds, the quality of which is different on each 'stone', or
- move across with urgency, which will result in regular steps and the syncopated lift taking precedence over the step (creating a 'communication dilemma' whether to advance or reflect).

On reaching the other 'bank', the traveler, accompanied by the group, releases the tension built up in the crossing, in a cadenza of triumphant sound, particularly after the second mode of crossing.

Football chant

Four cards are equally spaced in line on the floor. The leader maintains a regular pulse, singing and/or clicking fingers. The group, in single file, travel along the cards singing in time with the pulse, each beginning when the one before has completed the line, resulting in a continuous line of sound. Another set of four cards is added (Figure 7.13a), card 3 of each set is halved (Figure 7.13b), card 1 of set 2 is halved (Figure 7.13c), then the cards of set 2 are rearranged (Figure 7.13d), resulting in the rhythm of another popular British football (soccer) chant. Individuals may arrange a sequence of beats and half-beats for the others to attempt, either traveling, as described above, or clapping.

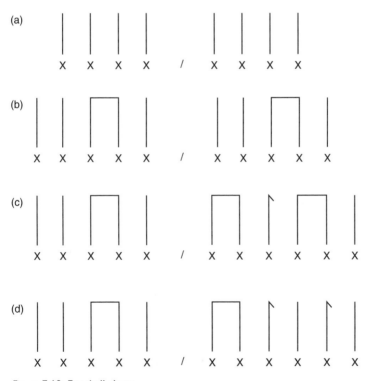

Figure 7.13 Football chant.

Court dances

Step to a piece of music in 4/4 time, alternating left and right feet or sides of the body on the first beats of successive bars, which will result in the rhythms that formed the basis of court and social dances.

Sounds structured and free and silent

The group moves, claps and/or sings a repeated pattern of four beats. Experience of rhythms is better through sideways movement, i.e. opposition, rather than clapping:

- structured – on the beat for the four beats
- free – over a period of four beats
- silent – for the duration of four beats. Repeat.

The free section will be anarchic. The leader will have to indicate the beginning and end of the silent section. Experiencing the 'electricity' in the silence after the free section reveals an individual's sense of control. Managing the contrast of feelings is dependent, ideally, on an ability to maintain a sense of centre, or for fast readjustment afterwards.

Groups of more able individuals have, individually, chosen difficult repeated patterns, e.g. 5 on the beat, 3 free and 11 silent, which when performed together resulted in a fascinating chorus choreography.

Subdivision

A regular pulse is set up in foot tapping, above which the voice and hands subdivide, exercising duplet, i.e. half-, quarter- or eighth-beats, and triplet, i.e. third- or sixth-beats, as much as possible playing off the main beats: syncopation.

That the presentation of this section might suggest a progression from individual to group rhythms is not to be interpreted as group member superseding individual. The progression could as easily be reversed from structured to free rhythm.

Tune

This section exercises the vertical aspect of music: the pitch of interval, just as the important rhythmic sensation is time suspended between the pulses, so is the experience of space within the interval, i.e. the change of vibration from one note to the next, intrinsic to music.

Plainsong

The group sustains a drone, above which individuals 'take flight' in sounds, words and hand gestures, contrasting free play of long and short notes with structured regular rhythms and coming to rest on the drone. To assist individuals who have limited sounds, the leader may have to pick up the pitch of the note and gesture and bring them to earth. The principle behind unaccompanied song or plainsong is that the drone is understood.

Chords

The group sustains a note and feels the changes in the body as chords are changed below it, preferably sustained on the organ or accordion, first slowly then quickened. Chord changes may be gradual, for example:

- I–III or VI, i.e. two notes in common
- I–IV or V, i.e. one note in common
- I–II or VII, i.e. no notes in common.

Songs may be selected with these principles in mind, e.g. (a) Beatles songs; (b) almost any song; (c) 'Drunken Sailor'. Predominance of IIV-V chords, progression one note in common, is related to minimum of sustaining 'touch'. People with a disability might prefer the security of two notes in common.

Major and minor

The group sings a song, in major and minor, and the leader inserts suitable verses in the opposite mode, accommodating change of mood.

Blocks of sound

The leader conducts the group, which sustains notes, changing them as he or she indicates. Or the leader may play them on the organ or accordion by superimposing as a listening exercise.

Neil, aged 16, having defined his territory on the piano with toys and spit, banged relentlessly on two adjacent white notes, i.e. a minor second nearest to noise on the piano requiring limited response.

I tried to join in playing the same notes further down the piano, i.e. less vibration, and grouping in two and three, i.e. opening space, without success.

Moving his hands one note, i.e. two white notes with black note between, i.e. a major second, presumably because of increased interval space, caused him to pause. Through gradual play he managed to assimilate this sound.

I would have liked to develop this principle working down the intervals of the harmonic scale, i.e. minor third, major third, fourth and fifth, but we lost contact.

Support music

After standing on a card, accompanied by a chorus, an individual may have the choice of two, three or four cards (of different colors) to step on to, to each of which the group sings a different (generalized) pitch, e.g. high or low, very high or very low, according to his signing. Or a group of five people sit at the piano: very low, low, middle, high, very high, and the leader-conductor, facing them, 'conducts' them.

Soccer chant

The original four cards may be 'pitched' (Figure 7.14a) resulting in the final chant rhythm as in Figure 7.14b. This is an example of perfect intervals, essential components to vocabulary.

Grunting

Exercise grunting at different pitches. Each group member grunts a note and indicates its pitch in the air, which is repeated by the group. Grunts may be repeated singly at first; then grouped in twos, threes or fours; finally as a whole sequence, phrased in twos, threes or fours. Related to building group sentences, one word each, or group stories, one action each.

Articulated intervals

Certain musical intervals, e.g. octave, fifth and minor third, are common in normal communication, and may be effectively exercised in isolation. Limiting the pitch may be compensated by inventive use of rhythm and texture.

Figure 7.14 Soccer chant.

Octave

Play with the sound of the octave, ascending and descending, by leap and step.

Organum

Sing songs, some verses of which the leader sings or accompanies the fifth below.

Thumb fifths

Using hand signs, thumb up = 5 and thumb down = 1, the leader improvises rhythmic patterns, for example:

```
 5 5  5  5   5
1   1  1  1 1  1, etc.
```

for the group to imitate simultaneously, which creates great fun. Decrease in waiting for group to catch up, indication of reflex and involvement; hand signs based on tetrachord: upper of scale a fifth above lower half.

Minor third

Play calling games utilizing the natural calling sound of the falling minor third.

Within the interval

The group sings a song, but dwells on each word or note for as long as it takes them to be fully involved in it. Then gradually the speed is quickened to normal but still intent upon keeping wholly involved. Take note that some people may be too slow or too deep to 'keep up'.

Keening

Improvise a 'lament' by sustaining a note and ornamenting above and below it, sliding from note to note, with hand gestures to help. Perfect intervals ornamented, e.g. 8 by +7, 5 by −6, 4 by +3 and 1 by −2, produce wild, sensual, 'archaic' mode, opposite to ascetic, Dorian mode: 8 −7 +6 5 4 −3 +2 1, favored in the West; range between 'archaic' and Dorian has greater subtlety than polarization of major and minor.

Ornamented folksongs

Sing a folksong and ornament it lavishly with melisma (a group of notes sung to one syllable), being aware whether the ornaments are melodic or harmonic.

Textures

Texture is the 'depth' element of sound against a background of silence. However, terms such as 'high', 'low', etc. may not be helpful: a blind pianist describing how he learnt part playing used terms like 'forward', 'back'.

Tactile objects

Play with the textures and shapes of visual objects, lingering over a quality as long as is desired, looking at it from different angles and height and trying to translate them into sounds.

Percussive and sustained songs

Individuals stand near to slung cymbals to feel the effect of sound on their bodies, and respond to the different effects of banged and rolled sound (a percussive jolt accommodated by gradually increasing tremolo).

Piano quintet

A group – of five at the most – sits in front of a piano, which has its front removed and the sustaining pedal depressed or is totally stripped down to the strings, to allow the different qualities of plucked or strummed string sounds to affect their bodies.

Opposites

Explore materials of opposite qualities of texture, e.g. sharp–blunt, hard–soft, cold–warm, heavy–light, oily–gritty, rough–smooth, angular–curved, etc. Try to reproduce these qualities in movement and sounds: sustained–articulated, smooth–percussive, direct–indirect, etc., exercising slow–fast changes between qualities.

The opposite qualities of sound–silence may have been related to the negative–positive cutouts and remnants for a 'lilypond'. Although given limited space here, the experience of listening is in some situations more relevant than activity.

The elements

The floor may be divided into four areas: 'water', 'air', 'earth' and 'sky', which dictate the qualities of sound that individuals may make as they pass through them.

Stereophonic sound

Groups of different sizes are placed around a room and make sounds producing stereophonic effects, concentrating particularly on feeling the silence between, and choosing between 'nice' and 'nasty' sounds with which to reply, i.e. individual experience of consonance and dissonance.

Calling

Pairs and groups play with sounds of calling from far–near, related to the size of appropriate gestures, big–small. Confusing loud–near, soft–big, etc. causes great fun. Alternatively, the use of signing, supplementing speech, alleviates tension.

Mirrors

Pairs face each other and move towards and away, attempting to make simultaneous sounds and gestures.

Sound images

Make up sound images based on textures and qualities (rather than shapes) of, for example, wind, walking, tree, etc., or of characters, for example, compounds of heavy, symmetrical, short, indirect, percussive, etc., which are repeated as refrains during the recitation of a story by the leader. Try allowing words to be sustained in near-singing to hold attention.

Vowels

Explore rudimentary animal sounds, for example 'AH' – contented, 'EE' – screaming, and 'OO' – pouting. Then modify them as human sounds, e.g. 'EH' – half-scream, and 'OH' – half-pout: constituting the structure of the five basic or cardinal vowels. Include continental 'U' = 'OO' + 'EE', and 'Ø' + 'EH' to exercise facial muscles.

'Big bang'

The whole group, each with one sound, possibly played on piano or instrument, together make a loud noise and repeat their notes, individually increasing the length of silence between. This will need to be conducted by the leader from a prepared 'score', possibly on graph paper. This is an exercise in managing silences, sustaining climax: of chance composition.

Name chorus

In a circle, the group sing their names, with choices of:

* high or low pitch, keeping to a regular pulse
* long or short duration, each individual coming in immediately the one before has finished
* immediate or delayed entry, as soon as the individual before has opened his mouth to utter, resulting in a chorus of banked sounds and silences.

Reflection

The climax of the session will have been the creation of a piece of music. Each individual and the group will have to some degree presented a bit of themselves and will probably be feeling excited and exposed. This is similar to the post-climax in Greek drama for teaching morality. However, just as children may tear up drawings after creating them, so they need time to come to terms after revealing themselves in sound. They will need to be taken back to normality. Try to include time before and after sessions to take the group from and return to norm; providing an opportunity for them to take something from the session, it is to be hoped, to help enrich their lives.

To help some groups of children with physical disabilities be more aware of floor exercise influencing their normal lives I kept them in their chairs, extending their activities until they felt they needed to move to the floor. Being returned, they could recapture what they had done, particularly if there was the visual record of a 'map' of their wanderings (marked in individual colors) translated into songs and stories. With other groups, exercises were repeated in different positions, e.g. on the floor, half-erect and fully erect, or sitting, standing and moving, to reinforce their value.

Memory

The leader recalls the events of the session, probably as a link for the following week, as a story (exercising sense of structure; story taking listeners out of themselves following a narrative and reflecting on the events) in recitative, encouraging moments of group participation, e.g. recalling in sounds the ways they had moved, songs from stories or to cover events, the weather, etc.

Grounding

Sing songs of individual choice, gradually reducing the level of activity and sound to humming and silence.

Postscript

Throughout, rather than emphasizing the specifics of musical language or appreciation of musical form, I have concentrated on integrating a sense of form into the body by experience to find a 'grammar' common to the arts, as an aid towards managing the morass of stimuli in life: a sentence is a thing (noun) enlivened (verb); a tune is a string of sounds animated by rhythm. Familiarity with this process of 'animation' may help to enliven the individual for whom the symbols of life have become stuck, including that of oneself as a cipher. Coming to terms with oneself as an individual functioning within society may be helped by the experience of singing or playing in a group:

- the same thing at the same time: *tune, organum*
- the same thing at different times: *canon, counterpoint*
- different things at the same time: *harmony*
- different things at different times: ?

The form of a song or symphony is essentially a journey in which feelings are transformed. For many their source of transformation, awareness of possibilities, is restricted to television soap opera, which is limited both in the spaces of the imagination and length of involvement.

Acknowledgements

I am extremely indebted to the Carnegie UK Trust who generously funded the project based at Dartington College of Arts, Devon: 'The Arts in the Education of Handicapped Children and Young People', which made it possible for me: to study communication from the other side of normal; to work with Bruce Kent, who was so generous in sharing experiences relating visual art to movement and music, and David Ward, from whose music-making with children with a very wide range of disabilities I learnt much about the physicality of music and whose books are compulsory reading for anyone interested in this area of work; and to meet the many teachers, therapists, helpers and artists questioning the boundary between handicapped and non-handicapped people. Special reference must be made to Veronica Sherborne for the illuminating experience of her movement workshops from which many of the body exercises in this writing are adaptations for group and chorus work.

Further reading

Alvin, J. (1975) *Music Therapy*, New York: Basic Books.
Bailey, P. (1965) *They Can Make Music*, Oxford: Oxford University Press.
Feder, E. and Feder, B. (1981) *The Expressive Arts Therapies*, Sarasota, FL: Feder Publications.

Gaston, E.T. (ed.), (1968) *Music in Therapy*, London: Macmillan.

Kenny, C. (1995) *Listening, Playing, Creating: Essays on the Power of Sound*, Albany, NY: SUNY Press.

Michel, D.E. (1976) *Music Therapy: An Introduction to Therapy and Special Education through Music*, Springfield, IL: Charles C. Thomas.

Nordoff, P. and Robbins, C. (1965) *Music Therapy for Handicapped Children*, New York: Steiner Publications.

Sherborne, V. (1990) *Developmental Movement for Children*, Cambridge: Cambridge University Press.

Ward, D. (1973) *Music for Slow Learners*, Oxford: Oxford University Press.

Chapter 8

Drama

Using the imagination as a stepping stone for personal growth

Bernie Warren

For many people drama is something that happens on a stage which separates the performers from the audience, and establishes for the people watching that the people presenting events are actors. Yet this presentation of imagined acts on a stage is simply one facet of dramatic activity and although it is perhaps the most generally accepted view of what drama is, it is not necessarily the most important. It is this misconception in many people's minds, that drama is only a presentation on a stage and thus the sole property of skilled and talented individuals, which has created blocks for individuals seeking to achieve their full creative potential, and in some cases even prevents their imaginations from coming into play at all. It is against this often self-imposed wall that professionals in the fields of developmental drama, personal creativity and drama therapy have been chipping away for more than 40 years.

The origins of drama are to be found in storytelling and in ritual. In most cases, spontaneous actions precede ritual. In the creation of ritual these spontaneous actions, which are seen to have meaning for the well-being of the group, become transformed into a symbolic act. It now becomes essential for the original spontaneous actions to be carried out in a set order and with a particular style. This specific pattern is believed to be essential to the ritual 'working' and, as a result, spontaneity is lost. This is a similar process to the one most people have, consciously or unconsciously, pursued with their own creativity. They have lost contact with the source of their spontaneity and have fallen back on external frameworks that impose boundaries on their imagination and, more disastrously, often totally remove any emotional reaction and substitute it with conscious control or predetermined outcomes.

Drama is an example of human interaction and rarely, if ever, occurs in isolation. It is concerned with human beings communicating with one another: verbally, physically and emotionally. Most importantly, this dramatic interaction is part of our everyday lives. Many role theorists have pointed out that we are constantly shifting roles. Earlier in this book (p.34), Rob Watling elaborates on the way in which context and function affect traditional material. In a similar way the roles we take are influenced by their context – that is, *where* we are, *who* we are talking to, etc. – and their function.

Thus the roles we take are often dictated by circumstances beyond our control.

Perhaps the most important external influences on our often unconscious role playing are the people with whom we interact. In everyday interactions it is not just *what* we say, but *how* we say it that conveys not only our meaning but also our feelings. Preceding every action there is thought, sometimes subconscious, which in turn is inextricably linked to our imagination. Our every action, nuance of inflection and gesture is recorded, sometimes subliminally, by the people with whom we communicate. They then calibrate their actions and the roles they take accordingly. I believe that the essence of drama is encapsulated in this process.

Courtney (1980) suggests drama is about the process whereby 'imaginative thought becomes action' – in word or deed – and is particularly concerned with the way that this 'dramatic action' affects other people's actions. In essence drama is the communication of our imagination, in a way that affects our interactions with others, whether this be on stage or in our daily lives.

Daily, one of our biggest problems is communicating what we mean. Every one of us spends a large part of our day talking at but not necessarily communicating with others. I use the analogy of human beings as transceivers each with our own 'radio station', created by, among other things, our previous experience, our vocabulary and our genetic make-up. We each transmit on a 'single wavelength' whose tone, quality and intensity are influenced to an extent by our choice of language and our relationship to the listener and the context in which we interact. However, while we have the capacity to receive an incoming 'signal' on almost any wavelength, frequently we are not listening because we are too busy working on what we are going to say next. As a result, we miss the point or lose the feeling of what the person talking to us is saying.

This process relates to all human communications. As I sit writing these words, displaced both in time and space from you reading them, I am struggling to find those words that will best convey my meaning to you. I am well aware that what I write, on the basis of my language system and world map, will have to be interpreted by you and that every reader will have a widely differing, unique background. So, as I write, I call on my imagination, trying to be aware of who will be reading these words, what their backgrounds are and what, if any, common ground they share. I am at the beginnings of the dramatic process. I am struggling to communicate and my imagination is *affecting* my actions. I am searching for the mode by which as many readers can hear me as possible, and in the process I have to review the roles I have taken to transmit my meaning in my past.

Drama is concerned with interpersonal communication. Many people have difficulty communicating. Much of this results from an inability to change roles or respond to an alteration in external circumstances. This lack of role flexibility[1] may be a result of a number of interrelated factors, for example, poor language use, inadequate motor skills, emotional blocks, poor social skills, etc. These factors often conspire to maintain an individual's inability to respond to external changes.

Through drama, individuals are not only being allowed to use their imaginations, but can also be encouraged to enjoy using them. Through games, improvisations and theatre scripts, different roles[2] can be taken. It is through this role play that individuals can start to imagine what it is like to be someone else. These imaginative leaps can, through enactment and discussion of well-known job roles (for example, teacher, farmer, lawyer, police officer, etc.), engender a greater understanding of social roles, or through similar enactment and discussion of more personal material lead to a greater awareness of one's self and one's relationship to family, friends and past life.

It is through dramatic process, by playing other roles and engaging our imaginations and emotions, that we can increase our role flexibility, develop our powers of communication and learn to interact acceptably in the society in which we live.

Practical activities

All the material presented here is 'track tested' and requires little or no equipment. I have divided the material into three sections: name games, awakening the imagination and creating character(s). Unless otherwise stated, the games are presented from the perspective of the leader.

Name games

In the beginning an individual's name is perhaps the most important thing they bring into a room. For some of the people I work with their name is the only thing they can share with the group and some find even this too much for them. Our name is our identity. It tells others who we are and reaffirms our own existence. Name games allow the group to get to know one another and establish a sense of group spirit.

I generally play a name game at the beginning of each session, just to re-establish the group. This is particularly important if the group meets once a week or less. Name games also allow each individual to be spotlighted, that is, for a short time individual participants are the centre of attention. Activities that spotlight need to be set up so that they are non-threatening and supportive, so that those involved may gain a positive reinforcement of self-image and feel secure within the group's limelight.

A name game sets the tone of 'we as a group are here and we all have names, personalities, feelings; we are all individuals'.

Simple name game(s)

Initially this game and its many variations are best played sitting in a circle. Start by saying your name. Then ask each person to say their own name in turn around the circle. First go to your right and then to your left, all the way round the circle.

A variation is for the leader to walk around the inside of the circle, stopping in front of each group member and saying 'My name's Bernie, and what's your name?' On the reply, e.g. 'My name's Susan', you and Susan shake hands. This continues until the leader has been introduced to the entire group.[3]

Mr (or Ms) Engine

Mr Engine is a variation on shaking hands. It is a children's game I learnt from Bert Amies that is full of sound, ritual and enjoyment. The group sits in a circle with the leader standing in the centre. The leader is the engine of the train – known as 'Mr or Ms Engine'.

As the engine moves it makes steam train noises, e.g. 'Choo choo choo choo, Choo choo choo choo.' When the engine comes to a halt in front of one of the group members, it goes 'Woo woo', making an action as if pulling on a lever. There then follows a ritual exchange. The engine starts 'Hello, little girl.' Hopefully the girl replies 'Hello, Mr Engine.' Leader then says 'What's your name?' The girl replies, 'My name is Sue.' Leader to rest of group, 'Her name is Sue.' To Sue he says, 'Would you like to join my train, Sue?' She replies (hopefully), 'Yes, please.' At this point Sue 'joins the train' by standing behind the engine and putting her arms around Mr Engine's waist or on Mr Engine's shoulders.

Slowly, the number of 'cars' behind Mr Engine increases, each linking around the waist of the car in front. When the engine has cars added, the name of the new person is said by each member of the train with the last car saying that name to the rest of the group. So if the train with two cars stops in front of Brian, the ritual goes like this: engine to first car, 'His name is Brian.' First car to second car, 'His name is Brian (pause). Would you like to join our train, Brian?' In this way the person's name is passed down the train and the greater the number of cars the train has, the more times the name is said.

This repetition of the person's name acts as a form of spotlighting and the extended repetition in some ways compensates for being one of the last cars to join the train. However, it is very important that the last people to join are made to feel part of the group.

The structure of the game allows for full group involvement at all stages of its development. There are ritual chants with the entire group accompanying the leader on the 'Choo choo choo choo, Choo choo choo choo' and on the 'Woo Woo, Woo Woo'. The group members can physically become the moving train and when the whole group is part of the train, a song can be sung as the train moves around the room, in and out of the furniture. One of my favored songs is 'Chattanooga Choo Choo'.

This is a great game to get people involved, out of their chairs and moving. If you have the luxury of volunteers,[4] try to intersperse them between the people who might need assistance. Occasionally people will refuse to join the train, but a little gentle persuasion is often all that is needed. In the case of someone obstinately refusing to join the train, try *not* to spend undue time attempting to coax them because you risk losing the attention of other members of the group. After moving as a unit, the train can uncouple one car at a time. Again this can be accompanied by a song or a group chant. This game is a good way of separating and mixing group members.

Dracula

This is one of my favorite and most theatrical[5] games. It is also one that is asked for repeatedly by groups of all ages and abilities. Over the years this game has changed quite considerably, mainly as a result of the groups who have played it.

At the start of the game the group sits in a circle with the leader standing in the middle. I ask the group about vampires and Dracula. After a very brief discussion, I tell them that I am going to be Dracula, one of the 'undead', and that they are all in the land of the living. I tell them that Dracula can return to the land of the living only if he can find a victim to take his place. Dracula does this by means of an 'instant blood exchange' through placing his fangs (Dracula's index fingers) at the back of the victim's neck. The victim then becomes the new Dracula. Sometimes I tell them that Dracula's spirit is always in need of a new host body to avoid the ravages of time – this adds to the blood exchange idea.

However, Dracula doesn't have it easy! As Dracula walks towards his victims, finger fangs outstretched, the intended victim makes the sign of the cross (by crossing index fingers). As soon as the sign of the cross is made, the rest of the group shouts the victim's name. If they are successful and call the victim's name before Dracula touches his neck, then Dracula must go in search of another victim. If Dracula gets there first, then the victim and Dracula change places and the group has a new Dracula.

Once the group has the general idea of how to play the game, extra rules can be added. Here are some examples:

(a) Dracula can be given a 'handicap', for example, he has to walk with a limp, take baby steps, close one eye, count to three in front of the victim, etc.
(b) Victims have to direct their 'cross' at *one* member of the group who then has to call the victim's name.

(c) Adding to (b), if that one member of the group is too slow, it is he, not Dracula's victim, who becomes the new Dracula.

This is a great game for generating eye contact, group feeling and emotional response. Some important points to watch: young children can occasionally be scared by Dracula; always play a simple name game before Dracula; beware of violent Draculas (poking in the back of the neck can hurt!); be prepared to allow Dracula to 'suck blood' from the victim's knees, particularly important for Draculas who use wheelchairs.

My final point about Dracula concerns equipment. I play this game with the added extra of a cape – Dracula's cape – a black one with a scarlet red inner lining. This has really added to the game. It allows Dracula to gain added movement by using the cape's material, it seems to enable the more reticent individuals to 'become' Dracula and it allows for a social exchange between Dracula and victim. At the point of transformation when Dracula has caught a victim, the old Dracula helps the new Dracula on with the cape before sitting down as a member of the land of the living. This Transylvanian valet service is often one of the comic highlights of the game.

Tarzan

This is another one of my favorite and most asked for games. It is often the first name game I play with a new group. I always tell a story before the game, about Tarzan swinging through the jungle and filling it with the sound of his own name. The story can take a number of turns and has a number of explanations for the famous Tarzan call with the explanation changing to meet the needs of the group I am working with.

The basic game is as follows. Go round the circle and ask each person's name. Then I tell the Tarzan story and say that we are going to fill the room with the sound of our names. Then go round the circle, stopping at each group member, who says their name. This is then echoed by the rest of the group shouting that name while beating their chests. This goes all the way round the circle until everyone's name has filled the room, and finally we all beat our chests and shout the Tarzan call.

This is a great game for spotlighting individuals. Even the shyest person's face lights up when they hear the entire group shouting their name and that sound filling the room.

These are but a few examples from the huge array of simple and dramatic name games available in the literature. Often a group will have special, favorite name games. These may be ones you have introduced or, more likely, ones they have adapted or created.

Awakening the imagination

Many of the people we work with have been actively discouraged from using their imaginations. Programs that emphasize socially acceptable behaviors and the facing of reality – in the programmer's terms – cause the often fertile imaginations of individuals in our groups to atrophy. I am not suggesting that individuals should not be helped to face the realities of our often inhumane and alienating industrialized society: what I am suggesting is that there are many ways in which this can be achieved. One of these is through the individual's imagination. I feel that in order to help them grasp a sense of the socially accepted norms of reality, we must first gain a sense of how they imagine the world, and attempt to see the world through their eyes so that we do not always transfer or project our world view on to them. Our understanding of their perceptions of the world, gained through imaginative exercises, can provide a framework in which to initiate a change to more socially acceptable behavior. The first three games deal with awakening and engaging the senses, and the others in this section focus on the act of creating *something from nothing*, and on the imagination taking a concrete object and transforming it into something else.

Keeper of the keys

A variation on a traditional children's game. I tell the group a story about a pirate who amasses great wealth and keeps this in his house. However, the pirate is often away from his home and needs someone to guard his house and treasure. He is told of a blind person whose hearing is so acute they can hear a pin drop in a crowded room. After an embellished preamble, one of the group sits on a chair in the centre of the circle, closes their eyes and becomes the Guardian of the Treasure. The rest of the group is seated in a circle around the Guardian. In front of the Guardian are the keys to the treasure; for children this is often described as a huge store of candy or chocolate. The rest of the group tries, one at a time, to take the keys without being heard. When the Guardian hears a noise he or she points in the direction of the noise saying, 'Get out of this house.' If the would-be-thief is pointed at, he or she has to go back to their seat. If the thief captures the keys without being spotted, he or she becomes the new Guardian.

Added complications can be to give the Guardian a gun (extended index finger) the verbal taunt now becomes 'Get out of this house, bang!' This adds the dramatic element of a theatrical death. The thief can be required to get the keys from under the Guardian's nose and back to the thief's seat; or a group of two or three thieves can work as a team to get the keys from the Guardian (this can be very unsettling for the person playing the Guardian and should not be tried early on).

This game is extremely good for accentuating auditory skills. It is also an exercise in control for the thief, who must try not to be heard, and for the rest of the group who must remain quiet and still.

There is a tendency for Guardians not to keep their eyes totally closed. However, I am reluctant to use a blindfold. My own experience is that many individuals are scared by wearing a blindfold. The return to trust – trusting the individual to keep his or her eyes closed – requires patience and a liberal dose of turning a blind eye in the initial stages. Slowly, individuals will be less scared of closing their eyes and will become totally engaged in the game. Pushing and cajoling them to close their eyes will probably only aggravate the problem.

Male or female?

This game is a regular favorite. I have found it particularly good when working with groups of long-stay institutionalized people, especially seniors, as it seems to provide that essential element of acceptable human contact so often lacking from these people's lives.

The group sits in a circle with one member of the group sitting in the middle. The person in the middle has his or her eyes closed. One at a time other members of the group go and gently touch the person in the centre, who then has to guess whether he or she was touched by a man or a woman. I never force anyone either to sit in the centre or to get up and touch the person sitting there. I let the game continue until everyone who wants to has had a go.

This game provides a fascinating experience. When you are in the middle it is extremely difficult to discern if the touch is that of a man or a woman. However, it does force you to be aware of other factors, for example, pressure, warmth, sound – particularly breathing and smell. After a while, when working with a group over a long period of time, I can generally pick out exactly who is touching me by the sounds they make coming towards me, their breathing pattern, the way they touch me and so on. As an observer, the ways that people approach the person in the middle and then make physical contact can be particularly informative concerning the dynamics of the group. Often, individuals hide their feelings behind the words they use to communicate. In this exercise these feelings are made concrete, often in very subtle ways.

This activity can also be used as part of work on sex roles and stereotypes. Often, when working with teenagers, a discussion is an essential close to this activity. Other groups, particularly those involving people with developmental disabilities, often turn this game into a competition and some individuals get bitterly disappointed if they guess incorrectly. This disappointment needs to be dissipated either through group support or a 'success' in another activity, or whatever means is appropriate to that individual in your group.

This is generally one of the first physical contact activities I use with a group as it gives me a rough gauge of how individuals in the group respond to being touched. It also gives a pointer to who will or will not work well together. This activity can lead into more directed activities dealing with emotion and physical contact.

The magic box

I often carry with me a large trunk. On the outside, painted in large letters, are the words 'Bernie's Magic Box'. This box has a practical purpose, as it enables me to carry with me all the equipment I ever use – tape recorder, tapes, parachute, etc. However, it has another far more important function and that is to serve as a focus for group members' imaginations.

The magic box is an extremely simple tool. It is one of those timeless dramatic activities. Stanislavski used a version of the magic box for training actors, and many noted drama specialists have some form of magic box exercise. In essence the magic box is a projective exercise. All I ask as leader is 'What do you think is in the box?' The group then responds by projecting from their imaginations what they think is in the box. The responses of the group can then be directed or shaped by the leader in a number of ways.

First, I generally employ a *free association* approach – where I simply allow the group to come up with as many ideas as possible. When using this approach I try not to make judgments, although I do make mental notes of who said what. Also, I attempt to provide an environment that allows the group to imagine as many things to be inside the box as they want to tell me about.

Sometimes I am slightly more directive, taking a *theme-based* approach. Here I tell the group there is food or treasure or unusual objects inside the box. This is an approach I take with youngsters with developmental disabilities. I still allow the group to freewheel, but within a given framework. This can provide the necessary grounding for individuals who are 'paralyzed' by a completely open-ended task.

Sometimes I break with a freewheeling or free-association approach and take a *question-based* approach. Here, as soon as an individual has a particular idea about what is in the box, I ask questions related to the object they have described. For example, if they have suggested there is a purse in the box, I might ask 'What color is it?' 'How large is it?' 'Is it soft?' 'Does it have writing on the outside?' As a result of these questions, often a clear picture of this object can be created in a very short space of time.

Once the group has created objects, there are a number of ways of working with the ideas. Here are two basic approaches. Having created a variety of objects to be found in the box, take the 'imagined' objects from the box one at a time and pass them round the group. Get the group to take the time to feel each object's texture, weight, etc. At some point I might ask one of the group to describe the object to the rest of the group.

Another technique is to use two or three objects that the group created which might link together. For example, one group told me that in the box, among other things, were a bloody hand, a sword and a dragon's tooth. I then asked the group to tell me how the objects got there. In this way, from the objects a group creates, a story can evolve, which can then be 'acted out'. The magic box then, in common with other activities described in this section, allows the group to use its collective experience as the basis for the dramatic activity. I will pursue these ideas through description of other activities in this chapter. The magic box can also be used to reinforce the magical qualities of objects that are taken out of it, such as the magic newspaper.

Magic newspaper

This is one of my 'old faithfuls', which I use at some point in my work with every group. This game is both a starting point for mime and a diagnostic tool. I produce from my magic box the magic newspaper. I tell the group that this may look like an ordinary newspaper, but it is in fact magic. At this point most of the group is, to say the least, skeptical. I say that the magic of the newspaper is that, by working with it, the paper can become anything you want and that, without telling anyone, the group will immediately know what it is. I then create a telescope, someone in the group says 'telescope', I reply, 'See, magic works every time' and we're off. I might then show a few more examples of the newspaper's power and then the paper is passed around the circle. Each person has a chance to work with the 'magic'. The only rule is that you cannot pass twice. So if you cannot think or make something first time round, you must do something the next time.

The way that individuals respond to the magic newspaper is fascinating and it is for me, as already mentioned, a very valuable diagnostic tool. From the way individuals use the paper I can gain information that enables me to make observations about the way that each person's imagination functions. In general terms, there are three basic ways of working with the magic news-paper – moving from the concrete to the abstract use of imagination. First, people work at a concrete level. The focus is on *making* the newspaper into something. Here the paper has to be an actual representation, for example, a hat, an airplane or a newspaper. What work the individual does with the paper is related to origami. Further along, people reach a stage where they are less concerned about what the object looks like and more concerned about how to use it. The focus is on *using* the newspaper as something, for example, a paintbrush, a baseball bat or fishing rod. This marks a mid-point between the concrete and the abstract uses of the newspaper. At the most abstract level, the focus is on the newspaper being *part of* a larger imaginative picture, for example, the newspaper is the lead for a dog being taken for a walk. The focus is now on the dog *not* on the lead. The shift of focus on the newspaper is from making into, to using as, to being part of something – it is a shift from the concrete to the abstract use of imagination. The way each individual uses the paper can serve as a guide to the level at which other imaginative exercises might best be started.

Although the way in which people use the newspaper is a clue to the way in which they use their imaginations, it is by no means a direct cause-and-effect relationship. People who are able to function at the highest abstract level are often intimidated during the first sessions of the magic newspaper and appear to function only at a concrete level. Also, some people appear to be functioning at a higher, more abstract level than would at first be expected. There may also be some who can only copy others. All of these pieces of information should be made note of and used to help fill out the three-dimensional jigsaws that are the individuals within your group. No single piece alone can complete the picture but every little piece of information helps.

Magic Clay

This is an extension of the magic newspaper. Again it can be a starting point for mime work. I was first introduced to this exercise early on in my training as part of a mime workshop. The workshop leaders introduced this as an exercise which allowed the mime to 'produce' objects on stage with a minimum of fuss and effort. Magic Clay is my reworking of that simple exercise.

I tell the group that I have a ball of magic clay and that when I work with it I can create objects. I then stretch the clay, drawing it out and shaping it, perhaps into a bouquet of flowers that I then present to someone in the group. When we have completed our transaction, I mould the clay back into a ball and pass it to the person next to me. The clay is passed around the circle with each person consciously creating something, using and demonstrating it so that the group understands, and returning it to the shape of a ball. In this stage of the exercise the ball is being consciously shaped and manipulated by the group member holding it.

Another way of using the magic clay is to ask the individuals holding it to close their eyes and let the clay move them. The skeptics among my readers will argue that something that does not exist cannot move the individual not holding it. In a sense they are right, yet what is being asked is for the person holding the clay to try to suspend the cerebral override that we all employ in almost any task and let the subconscious take over. The need is to do, without thinking about what to do. The results can be fascinating. I ask individuals to describe their experiences as they are happening, telling the rest of the group what they experienced (the colors, shapes, weight, textures, etc.) when working with the clay. I always emphasize that there is no need to describe or label what has been created, as the end of the process does not have to be something known or tangible.

When the individual lets go of conscious control of the clay, the emotions and the feelings take over. There must be no criticism or judgment of the creation – this is not a work of art, this is a work of emotion, color and form. The effect of the experience on the individual varies immensely, depending on their emotional state and the degree to which they allow themselves to go with the clay. In most cases, people describe it as a relaxing, refreshing and pleasant experience. For others it can act as a stimulus to open the floodgates for troublesome or unresolved experience. It is essential that you are aware of this possibility and timetable Magic Clay so that there is always time to explore anything that comes up as a result of the exercise and you do not simply close the session with the activity. This activity integrates well with various visual arts techniques, for example, 'painting' the experience with the clay.

Tennis–elbow–foot game

The group sits in a circle. The idea is to throw a soft ball from one person to another. As the ball is thrown, the thrower says a word, for example 'tennis'. The catcher must then respond with the first word that comes into their head, for example 'elbow', simultaneously throwing the ball to another person as they do so. The game is based on an instant response to the word that went before. There should be no time to pre-plan because you never know what word you will have to respond to. If there is a break in continuity or if someone pauses before responding, blocking has almost certainly occurred.

This is an extremely interesting and often entertaining game. It is an excellent exercise to work against blocking and as such to promote spontaneity and creativity. It forms a good springboard for storytelling exercises. It can give valuable clues about individuals within the group in much the same way as the magic box. When working with people with a developmental disability or young children it is often best to start with a theme, such as colors. So the task would then be to say the first color that you think of. Again, it is important to cross-reference information. For example, if a child is stuck with the response 'yellow', certain questions need to be answered. Do they also repeatedly choose yellow in art work? Do they describe their house as yellow? If they do, why? Is it the only color they know? Some more deep-seated reason? It is important to gain as much first-hand information as possible, but it is also important to cross-refer experiences with the other professionals who work with that individual.

Earlier in this volume I have made reference to the importance of the contract between the leader and the group. If the contract is a 'therapeutic' one, then the leader will probably want to make note of the *pattern, repetition* and *blocking* of responses. This information in combination with that gained from other activities and sources, may lead to an 'intervention' or 'strategy for change'.

In the context above the *pattern is* the sequence of words exchanged between group members, for example, 'on top', 'underneath', 'blanket', 'bed'.

Repetition is where an individual is stuck with a particular word or limited response, for example, 'purple', or only using words related to touch. *Blocking* is what occurs when an individual is unable to respond to a particular word or topic, such as 'love'.

The reasons for the patterns, repetition or blocking can be many. One aberration that should be considered when looking at the pattern is whether individuals were responding to the penultimate word. This happens when the game is being played fast and the group members are new to each other.

Repetition is usually an individual problem and may simply be a language deficiency. This is particularly likely for people with developmental disabilities. However, with a more 'verbal' group the repetition *may* be psychological in origin.

Blocking is far more complicated and highlights the problem posed by evaluating the group's responses. Certain words or topics, for example, sexuality, may be blocked for a number of individual or collective reasons. One of the most obvious is that individuals feel a lack of trust and confidence in other members of the group. The reasons for this lack of trust may be a key to the direction a strategy for change should take.

In general terms, it is unusual for a group of post-pubescent people *not* to mention sex – covertly or overtly – at some point in the game. However, with adolescents, given a supportive and creative environment, the pattern may be predominantly concerned with sex. This can lead to very interesting discussions after the game.

Guided Fantasy

The term 'guided fantasy' is one that is used loosely to describe a leader relating a pertinent tale, anecdote or similar stimulus to an individual or groups. At its simplest, the guided fantasy has been the stock in trade of all good storytellers since humankind first started telling stories. At its central core is the need to engage individuals in the events of the story. Therefore, there is a need to choose material that is specific not only to the group's needs but also to their way of viewing the world.

Traditional material (myths, legends, song, etc.), with its store of wisdom and knowledge may often be a suitable starting point for a guided fantasy. The way a story or stimulus is used by a leader can take a number of directions, with the direction often being dictated by the nature of the intended outcome of the exercise.

In a guided fantasy the leader's role can be directive or non-directive, and the participants may be actively or passively involved. In a *non-directive* approach the leader simply provides a loose framework – suggestions to stimulate the imagination. In a *directive* approach the leader makes statements that give step-by-step instructions – literally guiding the imagination. These styles are often mixed, so that statements such as 'You walk down the road and come to a big house. You walk up to the front door' may be inter-spersed with questions: 'What color is the door?' 'Is the door open?' The leader may even leave the end totally open for individuals to supply the conclusion that satisfies their needs.

The participants in a guided fantasy may be *passive*; that is relaxed, lying on the floor, eyes closed. The leader may use terms such as 'imagine you are looking at a large cinema screen' – suggesting that the story is happening there and then on the screen, or reference may be made to an environment: 'You are in a garden full of flowers – brightly colored, beautiful, sweet-smelling – take time to smell the flowers, feel their texture, look at the colors.' The emphasis may then be placed on action or sensation or both.

In a guided fantasy where the participants are *active,* they do what the story suggests. Thus, if the story calls for the heroine to ride into town, the participants act as if they were riding into town. If it calls for the heroine to pick a magical flower, the participants act as if they are picking that flower. When participants are active, they are like actors responding to the instruc-tions in the script – they are wide awake and respond in their own creative way within the restrictions imposed by the script.

Sometimes a guided fantasy may be both active and non-directive. When used with a group this is often referred to as a community exercise. Guided fantasy, as with so many other creative activities, is often a stepping stone to the discussion it creates as a result of participants being engaged in the activity. This discussion is often as important as the activity that preceded it.

Creating character(s)

The creation of characters, through both storytelling and the act of becoming someone else, is the natural extension of awakening the imagination. It is this dramatic awakening, the linking of words to emotion that also forms the backbone for many of the verbal forms of individualized counseling and therapy. In the act of suspending conscious control, in the removing of those blocks that prevent us from being truly creative, we regain contact with the raw emotions, past experiences and inspiration that are the source of the personal creative statement – the *unique creative thumbprint* that only we as individuals can make. These blocks are the death of personal creativity. We all have them and we all employ them. They allow us to hide behind a wall. They also act as barriers to social performers acting on the stage of everyday life, fully creating the roles that allow them truly to communicate.

In my work I have identified what I believe to be three major blocks to being spontaneous and creative. I feel they are present in all of us and are in many ways a necessary defense in certain social situations. However, they are often more apparent in people who have limited role flexibility and communi-cation skills. I call the three major blocks 'the wall', 'the censor' and 'playing the crowd'.

1   *The wall.* Here, conscious control is so great and people are so desperately trying to be creative that they cannot do anything. A common response is 'I had many ideas but when it was my turn to do something, my mind went blank.'

2   *The censor.* Here, people are able to do something but it is feeble, half-hearted. If questioned, common responses are 'I thought that was what you wanted' or, what is more important, 'I didn't know what others would think.'

3   *Playing the crowd.* Here, the exhibited behavior is of someone frantically creating. It is, however, surface behavior – attention seeking. The individual will use any means of being the centre of the group's attention. At the extreme, there is no censoring behavior. Often 'taboo' subjects are played up, with emphasis on cheap laughs and crowd reinforcement.

In exercises or games where the awakened imagination develops a story and later creates characters, these three blocks are particularly prevalent. The skilled leader can make use of the blocks, first, by making note of them and later, often in the same session, providing material that allows a chance for the individual to overcome them.

The characters created and the stories they tell often provide a three-dimensional map of where individuals have come from, where they are going to and, sometimes, where they stopped along the way. The construction of the sentences, the inflection used, and the body posture assumed are every bit as important as the content. The leader must be all eyes and ears, sensing the subtext of what is said both in and out of character. In carefully listening to, observing and developing the events during the session, the leader is able not only to establish a creative environment, but also to help individuals regain contact with themselves and thus start to increase role flexibility and communication skills.

To be continued (group storytelling)

This is an excellent way to create a script or story that has significance for the group. The story created can be recorded by means of a tape recorder. It can then be written down and used as a stimulus for other activities, and can be used as a guided fantasy, a theatre script or a starting point for developing reading and writing skills.[6]

The group sits in a circle. The leader starts a story going, for example, 'Once upon a time in a large city lived a large cat called Tikka.' This first sentence is then built on, a section at a time, by each member of the circle, one at a time, contributing to the story – a word, a phrase, a sentence or whatever seems appropriate. Slowly the group introduces new characters and situations, which develop the action. The focus may shift dramatically as a result of characters and situations introduced by the group. What is important is that each group member is actively involved in creating the story – it is an expression of their shared, collective experiences and imaginations.

To spice up the activity, with a group who have had experience in creating their own stories, I take a soft ball and ask individuals, when they have added their section to the story, to throw the ball to someone else. This makes contributions more spontaneous because you never know when it will be your turn.

Another variation is to have someone in the centre acting out the story as it is being created. I have a rule that they can sit back in the circle at any time and choose who will replace them. Again, you never know when it will be your turn to be in the centre of the circle. The 'actor' often decides to swap with a 'storyteller' when the addition to the story is difficult for them to perform. This forces the 'storyteller' to take their own medicine, normally to the great amusement of the rest of the group.

It is important that less verbal people are allowed to contribute at their own level. For some people with a developmental disability this may require the leader asking questions, some of which a court of law might view as leading the witness, so that each individual can participate. Other individuals may require the leader to intervene to prevent one person controlling the story for an extended time. This person is an obvious candidate to be 'the actor' when the time comes to act out the story.

Liar's tag

The group sits in a circle. The leader starts miming an action, such as brushing his teeth. Number two, the person on his left, asks 'What are you doing?' The leader then has to lie, for example: 'I'm riding my bike.' Number two must then mime riding a bike. Number three then asks number two 'What are you doing?' The reply might be 'I'm taking a bath.' Number three must then mime taking a bath, and so on.

The person performing the action must tell the questioner a lie, and the questioner must then act out that lie. Again, this is an excellent game for most groups. For some groups with slower than average cognitive skills, the leader must be patient and allow time for the group to work at their own pace and within their own limitations.

I'm sorry I must be leaving

This is a standard acting improvisation that is often a riot to watch. I start a scene with one person in a given situation, such as watching television, a second person enters and chooses his character, and a scene starts to develop through improvisation. At some point in the scene a third person joins the action. At this point the first person must find a legitimate excuse to leave the scene.

Each time a new 'actor' joins the scene the first person in the scene must leave. Thus, when number four joins the scene, number two must leave and when number five joins, then number three must leave, and so on. The effect is a continuously changing non-stop scene with each new actor choosing his character and how he will react to the people left on stage.

A variation on I'm Sorry I Must Be Leaving is to start number one with an action, for example, washing windows. When number two comes in, he takes number one's action but changes it slightly into something else, such as grooming a horse. Number one and number two then interact by number one joining in number two's activity until number three joins the action. Number one must now find an excuse to leave and number two must find a way of joining in number three's actions. Thus number three might now be conducting an orchestra so number two might pick up a violin and be conducted. It is important for the development of the game that *the last person in is always in control of the scene.*

Again there is a fast-changing, free-flowing improvisation being played out for the audience. This is an excellent game with almost any group. Obviously, for groups whose cognitive skills are slower than average, the game moves more slowly and may need more direction from the leader, but having played the game a couple of times, people slowly gain an awareness of the rules and create some fascinating scenes and scene changes.

Who owned the bag?

This is a projective exercise and has many similarities to the Magic Box. I bring in a battered and aged bag. I have two I use regularly. One is an old-fashioned leather briefcase and the other is a hold-all made from alligator hide. I tell the group that it is a very old bag and has had many owners. I then ask the group to tell me who owned the bag. When someone tells me they know who owned the bag, I ask them to tell me about the owner. Normally the first piece of information concerns the owner's job, for example, 'It was owned by a doctor.' Once the group member has started to tell me about the owner, I start asking questions, for example, 'What's the owner's name?' 'How old is he?' 'How tall?' 'What color is his hair?' 'How much does he weigh?' Slowly, the person is building a physical picture of the bag's owner. Then I can start asking questions about the owner's lifestyle, the sort of house he lives in, his favorite foods, etc. Once I have done this with one person, then the group can be involved in asking subsequent informants about other owners of the bag.

In using a simple stimulus, an old bag, as a focal point, the group is able to create characters. These characters can be used in other exercises. Owners of the bag can act out the exchange of the bag from one to another. Scenes can be played with the bag's owner as the central character. The character can be used in a situation that is yet unresolved by his or her creator, and so on.

The leader can always ask questions about the bag's owner that may help the person describing him. If the description is very concrete, questions relating to emotion can be asked, such as 'How does he feel about his job?' If the description is very abstract, the leader can ask questions that 'anchor' the group member, for example, 'What size of shoes does he wear?'

It is important to let the group member describing the bag's owner know that they are always right. They cannot say 'I think he is five feet six inches' for they are creating the character. The way the individual creates the character, the points they describe, the ones they avoid, particularly those dealing with the character's emotions, can be very valuable clues to completing the three-dimensional jigsaws I have spoken about throughout this chapter.

Postscript

As mentioned elsewhere it should be stressed that the games and ideas presented here are starting points for therapeutic work, they are not the work itself. This requires many years of training, something that can neither be substituted by nor conveyed in a book.

However, in this chapter I have described some of the ways in which drama can be used with people to awaken the imagination and create characters. I have tried to emphasize throughout the close link between imagination and dramatic action. Many groups are thought of as being incapable, unable to take part, and yet my experience is that in almost all cases this belief is unfounded. There are many with whom the process is a long, hard one but when the results occur, when someone is able to allow their imaginative thoughts to become action, to participate in dramatic activity, the wait and the effort all seem worthwhile.

In working with any group, the only real limits to an individual's taking part in dramatic activities are time, patience and the limits of the leader's imagination. It is within the power of the human imagination to overcome mental restrictions, physical limitations and emotional barriers and, in so doing, truly to move mountains.

Acknowledgements

I wish to thank all the professional colleagues and friends for their advice, encouragement and inspiration over the years and my students who have taught me more than they will know; and above all my first mentor, the late Bert Amies MBE, who is the single most important influence on my way of working and my current profession.

Notes

1 Role flexibility can be seen as both a change of 'social role', e.g. from husband to teacher to shopper to father to son, etc., but also it can be seen in terms of a change

in 'social status' – dominant, equal or subordinate. In any set social role we may be required to change status not only frequently but also rapidly during interactions with others. Role flexibility is not only an essential skill for actors, but also invaluable in facilitating everyday communication. See Johnstone (1981) for a different perspective on status interactions in relation to theatre.

2 Role and character are frequently used interchangeably in the literature. However, when I speak of role play, I am referring to improvised dramas created by the meeting and interaction of set role types, for example, student and teacher, traffic cop and motorist. The responses of the types are left to the imaginations of the individuals playing the role, but are based on experience and their general perceptions of that social role. However, the more information that is given about the role, for example, name, age, favorite color, gender, marital status, occupation of parents, etc., the closer one gets to a character with a known past history and probable emotional responses to any given situation. The greater the detail, the more the individual must respond 'as if' they were that character. This is, in essence, the basis of naturalistic acting.

3 You cannot wash your hands too often. Wash with soap under warm water for as long as it takes you to sing the 'ABC Song'. If water and soap are not available, use a hand sanitizer.

4 Extra helpers, whether volunteers or paid aides, can be a great help, but they can also be a pain in the – ! Often, so much time is spent helping the helpers understand a particular way of working, or an individual's specific needs, that the moment is lost. However, sensitive or well-trained helpers who support those in greatest need without becoming too obtrusive can make the leader's job so much simpler. Volunteer help is essential when working with individuals with profound disabilities. Much of my time is spent recruiting and educating voluntary help from janitors and kitchen staff as well as the more obvious professional colleagues and students.

5 When a player enters the circle, they enter a space where anything can happen. When they become Dracula they transform the other players into both participants in and spectators of the dramatic action. The game involves a costumed player creating a character that involves the emotions of all other participants. As such, this game demonstrates many of the quintessential elements of theatre.

6 From the recording of the group's story a storybook can be produced. This book can be used for people to read from. It can also be produced with large script and lots of space between each word to allow the person to copy the word. This is not new educational practice, but the material the person is learning from has been created by them and this can affect the motivation to learn. Good results have been achieved using this method with adolescents from inner city areas who are streetwise but 'learning disabled'.

Further reading

Boal, A. (1992) *Games for Actors and Non-Actors*, London: Routledge.

Courtney, R. (1980) *The Dramatic Curriculum*, London: Heineman.

Emunah, R. (1995) *Acting for Real: Drama Therapy Process, Technique, and Performance*, New York: Brunner/Mazel.

Gordon, D. (1978) *Therapeutic Metaphor*, Cuperdine, CA: Meta.

Grainger, R. (1990) *Drama and Healing*, London: Jessica Kingsley Publishers.

Jennings, S. (1973) *Remedial Drama*, London: Pitman.

—— (1997) *Creative Drama in Groupwork*, Bicester: Winslow Press.

—— (2006) *The Handbook of Dramatherapy*, London: Routledge.

Johnstone, K. (1981) *Impro*, London: Eyre Methuen.

Landy, R. (1986) *Drama Therapy*, Springfield, IL: Charles C. Thomas.

Shaw, A., Perks, W. and Stevens, C.J. (1981) *Perspectives: Drama and Theatre by, with and for Handicapped Individuals*, Washington, DC: ATA.

Spolin, V. (1963) *Improvisations for the Theatre*, Evanston, IL: Northwestern University Press.

Warren, B. (1996) *Drama Games: Drama and Group Activities for Leaders Working with People of all Ages and Abilities*, North York, Ontario: Captus Press.

Way, B. (1969) *Development Through Drama*, London: Longman.

Films

Breaking Free (1981), directed by Chris Noonan.

Feeling Good Feeling Proud (1981), directed by Richard Heus.

Chapter 9

Storymaking and storytelling

Weaving the fabric that creates our lives

Cheryl Neill

Introduction

There are really only two kinds of stories: those that we tell to others and those that someone else tells to us. While all stories are true (in the sense that all are a reflection of different states of the human mind), they are also metaphors for life experience; for they are mirrors in which we see facets of ourselves. Good stories, like our dreams, are full of symbolic images where different aspects of the psyche are highlighted. Our subconscious often recognizes these symbols while our conscious mind does not.

When working with people in healthcare, rehabilitation or special education settings, traditional methods of healing and therapy can be greatly enhanced by storytelling and storymaking. Many of these individuals have a preconception of the world, a rigid set of unconscious 'truths' which can stop them from moving forward. The unconscious mind is very difficult to reach by rational argument alone.

A reason for this is that opinions and views of reality are extremely well guarded by what William James referred to as the 'sentiment of rationality'. This is the feeling of 'rightness' given to an opinion that then becomes the only one accepted as rational. Although other opinions and explanations may exist, the one chosen is the best liked and defended against all others. Since it is best liked, it is rational. Here is a simple example: 'I am overweight because my mother overfed me as a child.' Other obvious arguments could be put forward such as I just like to eat, but because I like my argument I will rationalize it and defend it.

This is what happens to some individuals who believe that the way they view the world and their behavior is the only 'rational' way of seeing or behaving. Arguing against such a view usually only causes them to cling more stubbornly to their opinion. In fact, this 'sentiment of rationality' is very resistant to logic and rational talk.

Herein lies the value of stories. Stories do not tackle these barriers head on; they circumvent them by appealing directly to the unconscious. Stories are also non-threatening since on the surface they seem non-invasive. After all, at any point in a story, listeners can decide that the story is not about them! Even when the conscious mind has made such a decision, the unconscious side may not agree.

Stories work on two main levels. One level appeals to the intellectual, rational, left side of the brain that absorbs the plot and the spoken language, dream imagery and symbols. This side is not interested in moralistic principles and rational arguments. It is also not swayed by interpretive language, rather it has an instinctive vocabulary and is the least guarded against new ways of seeing or outside help. This phenomenon and other aspects of story will be examined in this chapter, as well as how to choose, prepare and tell stories to others.

The beginning of story

One spring I was working with a group of 11-, 12- and 13-year-olds in a storytelling session. I had just finished a tale that described the great Greek pantheon of gods – the one that speaks of the birth of Athena from Zeus's head and gives details of the magical hall of the deities on Mount Olympus. I had no sooner finished when a young man, a serious thoughtful boy, spoke up.

'Now that makes sense to me,' he said excitedly, 'a god to look after different areas of the world.'

'What do you mean?' I queried, knowing somehow where this was leading.

'Well,' he answered enthusiastically, 'how can one god look after the whole world and the universe too? I've always thought that there was something wrong with that! It makes much more sense that there are lots of gods – each of them having their own specialty – wind, sun, grass, animals – you know?'

'Yes, yes,' chorused others in the group. 'That does make a lot more sense. It's too big a job for one god.'

The discussion went on a while longer and I thought of the phone calls from disturbed parents I would be receiving as a result. To my surprise (and relief) this didn't happen, but still I was struck by the struggle of these modern children, this enlightened progeny acquainted with 'new science', computers and cellular phones, trying to understand, to make sense of their 2000-year-old mythology. It reminded me of a quotation that came from the Gnostic period: 'The trouble with Yahweh [god] is he thinks he's god.' Obviously, these children had come to the same conclusion.

One might not think that in today's modern world anyone is much concerned with these spiritual matters, but it has been my experience, working in storytelling sessions with both children and adults alike, that symbolic material, myths and legends in particular are not only firm favorites but seem to feed a real need, especially as people feel more and more cut off from nature, society and self.

Participants in my storytelling classes consistently choose to tell American

Indian and Eastern myths when given the assignment to prepare a story of their choice to tell for others. Given the wealth of folkloric material available to them, I found this curious. Then I realized that there was something about these particular stories that grabs both teller and listener. In both traditions there are many spirit gods, some not quite anthropomorphized, others in animal guise. There is a wonderful respect for nature. These are in high contrast to our own heritage that stresses the superiority of man over beast, sees a singular god as being outside the world and mankind and favors the taming of nature rather than the nurturing of it. A totally different civilization and way of living are experienced when the informing myth presents nature as 'fallen' (as in the Garden of Eden story) or seen as a manifestation of divine presence on earth.

It seems that in these trying times, for people who are struggling to reconcile lifestyle with spiritual concerns, storymaking and storytelling that include some mythological material which points to the revelation of divinity in nature may help individuals to find a path that puts them in accord with their surroundings.

The goal of all mythologies is to instruct the members of a given society on their role throughout life; to put people in accord with the nature of life, death and the universe. The basic motivating factors that govern the behavior of human beings have not changed since early times. The life crises of birth, initiation, marriage, separation and death are the same ones that have been faced by humanity since time immemorial and these are still the main motivational forces today in all societies, despite historic modifications and differing social systems.[1]

Mythology helps individuals to identify not with particular isolated incidents but with the universal images that transcend time and place them in accord with all those who have gone before and all those who will follow. These rites continue to elevate the ordinary individual to the status of warrior, bride, widow or priest. These roles (and the accompanying rituals such as weddings and wakes) are manifestations of the archetypes of myth. By participating in the ritual, we are participating in the myth.

Down through the ages the custodians of the traditional, instructive material of myth and legend have been the storytellers. They have held positions of great awe and reverence and were counted upon to remember the past and reveal the future. They were often thought, as in the case of the shamanic traditions found in many places in the world (including the American Indian and Inuit in North America), to walk amongst the very gods and to have power over life and death.[2]

In all cases, in primitive times, the storyteller was not an ordinary individual and the stories were not told for entertainment but for instructional and transformational purposes. Myths were definitely not created by ordinary folk. Their stories refer to psychological insights governed by natural environmental factors. The images of virgin births, great floods and resurrections are found in most mythological traditions and seem to be examples of what Jung refers to as a collective unconscious. Keep in mind that these are symbolic images and not to be taken as literal fact. To concretize the symbol is to lose its message. Mythology is a picture language and its goal is to transcend history and to let the mind open to the great mysteries of life and the universe.

Mythic symbolism was disguised in many pieces of literature. T. S. Eliot's *The Wasteland* (a reworking of the Grail legends from the twelfth century), Robert Browning's *Childe Roland to the Dark Tower Came* (towers are found in all mythic traditions, usually representing the central axis of the world) and James Joyce's *Ulysses* (a familiar mythic frame to express 'modern' and personal feelings) are all examples of archetypal images disguised as profane literature. There are hundreds more pieces that could be categorized in this vein. Even today, our novels and films abound with symbolic imagery – the search for paradise, the 'perfect' man or woman, the hero's quest, slaying the monster and life after death.

We can see that mythology still plays a dominant role in our lives and material that is rich in symbolism needs to be sought out and rediscovered. The question is, why do we need to tell these stories when television and film can do it for us?

First, a story told orally allows listeners to imagine the hero, the monster, the tower, in their own way. The symbolic figures will be painted according to the needs of the individual. How disappointed I remember feeling when the filmed version of a beloved tale did not match my own imagined one.

Second, there is a personalized feeling one receives when listening to a real person tell a story. There is a human connection, a thread sustained by eye contact and motivated by the audience's mood or reaction to the material.

Third, there can be audience participation. In the old days most of the stories were known by heart and the crowd was encouraged to join in on key phrases or on parts that were sung.

Fourth, many stories are meant to be shared orally and do not lend themselves well to the visual medium. I am thinking of those where gods are represented or supernatural events occur. Sometimes the special effects of film are so special that the symbolism is lost in favor of the effect.

Personally (as more and more people are channeled into sitting in front of computer screens), I feel the need for the oral tradition becomes almost imperative. Many of our children see more of teachers than they do of parents, and new technology is making even this human contact less and less possible.

Storytelling has fallen on hard times and it will take great effort to restore it to its rightful place. When trying to resurrect the art, we must search for material that will hold meaning for today's audiences. The wonderful thing about most mythic stories is that they distance listeners from themselves and allow the symbols to work on the unconscious level. The listener identifies with the hero or heroine and can learn vicariously from the triumph over great obstacles and hardships that are experienced or the tragic ending that some characters face.

Choosing stories

Choosing stories is one of the most challenging tasks facing a teller. This is particularly true if the objective of the telling is work in special education, rehabilitation or healthcare settings on personal development or self-healing. I will endeavor to help identify some meaty material and its uses in the next section.

Teaching stories

There exists in almost every tradition a body of instructional material known as 'teaching stories'. These have existed in both oral and written form for thousands of years. Examples that the reader may already be familiar with are Sufi, Zen and many Christian and Hasidic stories. These works are not to be confused with parables or fables, which although instructional in nature tend to be more openly didactic with moralistic principles and values. True teaching stories do not preach. Their distinctive feature is that (although appearing to be simply entertaining) their inner content stays with you long after the story is done. Also, in some cases, the listener may not even be aware of external significance at all, until an event in their lives parallels the story in some way.

For this reason, using teaching stories tends to be a little like learning the procedures for fire safety. We review what to do, and this information is stored in order to be prepared in case a fire breaks out. However, fires do not happen every day. The knowledge of fire safety stays dormant in the brain until the need for it arises. The same applies to teaching stories. When something in life triggers its memory it gives insight into human behavior and thought, and often points past the individual human act to a greater and deeper truth. They may be thought of as a kind of pattern of human response. We can hold them up against our own lives and get some sense of what fits and what does not. Most teaching stories are very 'lean'. They do not make superfluous points or add unnecessary characters. They are pure protein for the inner mind, no fat, no cholesterol.

It is not the goal of teaching stories to give rational explanations for human behavior. There is also no right way of interpreting these stories, no right answers. When working with a group, comments on the story should be confined to personal interpretations only – there should not be any commenting on other people's comments. All individual reactions are valid for the person who has them; all interpretations or feelings true. It is often interesting to help participants in these sessions to look for patterns in their responses.

For instance, similar reactions to similar characters or behavior in a number of stories may point to the way in which the participant holds the world. The more opposed the reaction is, the more certain we can be that we have struck an important note.

It sounds as though teaching stories are extremely powerful tools. The job then is to identify teaching stories from other kinds of material.

Finding the story

First, there are books that are labeled teaching stories. Good libraries and bookstores can be helpful to find them.

Second, look for traditional material; this includes myths, legends and folktales. Generally speaking, the older the tale, the richer the inner content. If it were not so the tale would not have survived for so long. A good example of the kind of material that works well on both outer and inner contents is the trickster tales of various traditions. Coyote, for instance, in North American Indian legends is a trickster character. He is portrayed as a powerful, godlike figure one moment and a sniveling coward the next. The same kind of figure is also found in the Turkish stories of Nasreddin (there are various spellings). He also appears at different times as both a wise man and a fool or as a teacher or a student. Two other popular trickster characters are Loki of the Norse mythology and Jack of the Appalachian mountains in the United States. Perhaps in all of these characters we find the dualism within ourselves and this is the reason why these stories have remained so popular.

Another source for teaching stories is folktales. Not all are as rich as some of the above material. However, some stories do strike a chord. You can identify such a story if it stays with you after a few readings. Again, look for stories that do not preach but seem to speak of some inner truth.

Myths

Of course myths come under the heading of teaching stories as well. Some of these stories can be quite gruesome (witness many of the Greek myths as an example). However, in most cases there is a certain satisfaction in the fact that the characters in myth who show distinctive character flaws (greed, vanity or disobedience) receive what they deserve. These stories can spark great debate over whether the punishment meted out was too severe or not. It is interesting that in the Greek tradition, as well as in many stories from the Christian faith, obedience is the main factor for punishment in the story. This is contrary to other traditions, such as Celtic, Norse and Germanic myths where disobedience often helps the character to grow in wisdom or strength.

Think of stories where there is a door that must not be opened at all cost. Yet the hero is placed in the position where the door must be opened in order for the kingdom to be saved or the elixir to be retrieved from evil hands.

Telling a variety of myths from many traditions is a good way to find out with what basic belief system we identify.

Legends

When speaking of legends, I am referring to stories that are usually based on historical figures in specific time periods. These characters are larger than life – the figures have been endowed with almost superhuman qualities and are able to transcend ordinary human possibilities. Again they are essentially tutorial in nature and most often contain the same symbols as myths. The Grail legends of Sir Gawain and the Green Knight, King Arthur and Lancelot come to mind; also, tales of Robin Hood. It seems to matter little if the ultimate conclusion of the story shows the hero gaining a kingdom, a princess or some other reward. The final success is the culmination of a spiritual quest in which the individual (Robin Hood, for instance) against great odds (the Sheriff of Nottingham and his men) earns a sense of himself in terms of self-integration, wisdom and spiritual realization (Robin becomes a man and takes his rightful place as leader of his people).

All these sources are good ones for meaty stories. The reader is encouraged to discover material from a variety of traditions and to choose from as wide a selection of stories as possible. Once you begin reading you will find that even some newspaper stories parallel the teaching stories you have been reading and are also excellent to use. Sometimes the line between life and art is indeed a very fine one.

Simple folk and fairy tales

Some of the same symbols contained in myths and legends can be found in simple folk and fairy tales. These stories are told primarily for entertainment and are not purposely designed to instruct the individual on matters of living with the order of nature, society and the universe. Most of the tales end happily and were the pastimes of simple folk whiling away the days and nights long ago. Nevertheless, one can still discern mythological motifs within them. An example would be a character venturing deep into the forest who suddenly hears a voice or meets a 'helper' sometimes disguised as a bird or animal who points the way out of the woods.

These stories are now primarily for children and can be looked upon as a form of children's mythology. Many of the tales are about initiation into adulthood expressed by killing dragons, crossing dangerous thresholds or getting past a place where one is stuck in childhood (Snow White is an example of this – the little girl goes to sleep until the prince comes and awakens her womanhood).

Since these tales are not looked upon as real events (Little Red Riding Hood is not a 'real' girl for instance) the symbols inherent in the material are able to do their work and can leave important subliminal messages for the psyche.

Many tales contain vestiges of primitive beliefs and customs. Supernatural tales, tales of animal magic and those fairies, gnomes and giants were all once contained in the myths of the past. There are timeless images that we recognize: the young man going off to seek his fortune, the little girl pondering life while tossing a golden ball, the mother waiting for news of a son called to war, all these and more speak of the eternal cycle of life and of concerns that swirl in the deep waters of human memory.

Readers will find their own favorites. One can recognize a good story for telling when it calls to you repeatedly. These are the ones that need telling as, if they call to you, you can be sure they will appeal to others as well.

Telling teaching stories

As a rule, teaching stories should be repeated as faithfully to the original as possible. This is because the wording has been mulled over and perfected countless times to maximize impact. Try to stay with the vocabulary that is used and avoid improvising new situations or dialogue for the characters.

Another distinct difference between telling teaching stories and regular stories is that teaching stories should be told with as little personal inflection, emphasis or judgment on the part of the teller as possible. The teaching story is told slowly so that the listeners are encouraged to work on personal insights without relying on the teller for clues. This takes a little getting used to as most of us want to make our tales lively and full of personality. This will work against the material in this case.

A cautionary note about these particular stories is not to tell too many in one session. They were originally designed to be told one at a time so that there would be ample time for reflection. I would suggest using only one or perhaps two in an hour session.

Home stories

As mentioned before, there are two types of story, 'theirs' (teaching stories) and 'ours' (home stories). There are those carried in the myths, legends and folktales of a given society and those that are familial – told to us by parents and relatives. It is the latter 'home stories', a term coined by Barton,[3] that we will deal with here.

Home stories form a substantial body of largely unconscious material that provides the framework for what we may recognize as personal identity. These are made up of an interwoven set of stories, rituals, customs and rites that shape our world view, often causing this view to be held uncritically, and give a sense of meaning and direction to our lives. These informing myths, as Sam Keen calls them, have the power to propel individuals forward with confidence in their ability and a healthy perspective on their place in the world or they can stifle feelings of self-worth and leave people feeling power-less to change their fate. Home stories can give the illusion of 'no choice' for what is simply a judgment call.

We begin to receive these messages as children. Our ideas on self-worth, race, color and creed are all part of this body of knowledge. We learn whom to recognize as the good guys (our family, our country, our church), who are enemies (foreign leaders, politicians, big business), what is right (look before crossing the street, eat everything on your plate, love your mother), what is wrong (hitting, communism), who to fear (the boss, the law), and whom to imitate (daddy or mom). This information is absorbed and stored away in our unconscious and is called upon when important decisions need to be made. Statements such as 'That is the way it is' or 'You can't change things' or 'Welcome to the real world' are a reflection of such a perspective on the world. So is 'It's not like it was in the good old days.'

Of course the truths of one family may not be shared by others. Dys-functional families, for instance, often share an inherited view of reality that would seem abnormal to most. This view is very difficult to overcome in the face of other 'normal' situations since reality is always shaped more on an unconscious level than a conscious one. The illusion of 'that's the way it is' is very strong and difficult to change.

As well as these family truths there are also the larger societal ones that help to form a larger accepted view of the world. Ours, in the Western trad-ition, assumes that values such as free enterprise, democracy and competition are fundamentally right. This largely unconscious assumption promotes both obedience and action without discrimination within this framework.

Thus status quo and time-worn 'truths' become sacred, almost holy. It can be seen that, unless there is a radical forced change to lifestyle, such as a world war or depression, society will stick to the proven path, even when change can be shown to be needed. (A good example of this is the struggle to revamp the educational system – a large segment of the population is still clinging to the 'back to basics' movement.) Marshall McLuhan refers to the phenomenon as 'a walk into the future while looking through a rear view mirror'. This picture is further complicated by the media of television and film.

People are bombarded psychologically by ideals. Fashion is dictated by soap operas and rock stars, eating habits by commercials. Heroes may be created and villains exposed. Sometimes, as in the case of dealings with foreign countries, people may be convinced that foreign leaders are the essence of evil one week and our trusted partner in the global village the next. This picture, obviously, can be very muddy and confusing to people struggling to find their identity and role in society.

Consider also the names of our main streets: everywhere we see examples of famous historical conquerors, generals, politicians and statesmen. Our informing myth of competition and hierarchy is very clear. There are very few poets, painters, musicians or storytellers on this list. One can understand the disillusionment in many young people when it begins to dawn on them that the great North American dream of fame, money and power is but an illusion for most and they are left awash in a sea of media-induced wants and needs.

It becomes increasingly clear as we reflect on the above, that stories (particularly those of childhood) need to be put into a kind of perspective in order to be dealt with objectively. For as Bernie Warren suggests: 'From the day we are born our lives are enmeshed in story. The way we talk about ourselves and the way that others talk about us creates the story of our lives.' James Hillman stresses the great significance of story awareness in childhood:

> To have had stories of any sort in childhood puts a person into a basic recognition of, and familiarity with, the legitimate reality of story per se. It is something given with life, with speech and communications, and not something later that comes with learning and literature. Coming early in life it is already a perspective on life. One integrates life as story because one has stories in the back of the mind (unconscious) as containers for organising events into meaningful experiences. The stories are means of finding oneself in events that might not otherwise make psychological sense at all.[4]

So childhood conceptions are brought forward into adulthood and operate within our daily lives. I have been concerned, as an instructor of storytelling and storymaking, with uncovering these lost or buried pieces of the puzzle. In order to deal better with external struggles, it is often very helpful to understand the internal ones. This can bring new meaning to the term 'know thyself'.

The activities that I use to uncover lost stories are designed to shed light on otherwise forgotten material and the new or rediscovered insights to be helpful, eye-opening and often produce a feeling of nostalgia, empowerment and well-being.

Techniques for learning and sharing stories

We have previously discussed the telling of teaching stories, which has a separate technique from most other material. The next section concentrates on looking at the components of most other stories and gives some exercises to help develop skills to tell them.

General characteristics of story

Shape

All stories (with the exception of some North American Indian myths which have no real ending per se) have three basic sections: the beginning, the middle and the end. Each has a specific function or goal.

The first section or 'act' establishes the setting for the story, introduces the main character, outlines the situation that propels the main character into action and sets up the outer motivation of the hero/heroine – what is to be achieved by the end of the story. The second section builds the obstacles, impasses or conflicts that the main character must overcome. It is also the section where character development takes place. The last section contains the highest moment or climax of the story. The ending should also resolve whether or not the hero/heroine has met the objectives set out in section one.

Roughly speaking, the first section takes up about one quarter of the story, the middle section about half and the ending about one quarter. If you are telling a ten-minute story, then two minutes would be spent on the objectives of section one, six minutes on section two and two minutes on section three. A visual image of this is shown below:

1   2   3

Establish   Build tension and characters   Resolve

Conflict

All stories have problems, conflicts or hurdles that the main character must face. Each of these must be made to seem greater and more difficult than the previous one. If the teller makes the first obstacle as overwhelming as the last, most difficult hurdle, without any break in the tension, the other obstacles become a land of anticlimax. The idea is to make each challenge a little more insurmountable than the last so that the tension of whether or not the main characters will reach their objective is maintained. This is represented in Figure 9.1.

Figure 9.1 Storytelling techniques.

Pacing

The momentum of the story must build steadily as the main character progresses towards the climax (usually the last most difficult obstacle of all). The pace must accelerate. This is done in two ways.

First, the gaps between hurdles or conflicts must become shorter and shorter. There is consequently less time for the listeners to 'catch their breath' ('catching breath' is very important and discussed later).

Second, there should be an increase in the speed of delivery and an increase in the intensity of the voice. This is sometimes accompanied by a shortening of sentences which gives the illusion that the story is going faster.

Now, in order to maximize the impact of the final climax it is absolutely imperative that the listeners understand what is going on in the story. It is disastrous to have to stop and explain how the hero/heroine got into the mess in the first place. If this happens, it is usually because not enough attention was given to section one. The accelerated pace will not be maintained if explanations are necessary at a crucial moment so be sure to emphasize the story set up and tell it slowly and carefully.

Creating highs and lows

A story told from beginning to end in a highly emotional tone will leave the listener emotionally uninvolved. This is because there is only so much emotional investment a person can give at a stretch. Highly emotional moments must be balanced by ones with less emotional impact so that the audience has a chance to take a breath. Failure to do this creates a situation of overstimulation where the audience becomes desensitized and emotionally distanced from the story. A plot where there is non-stop violence, for instance, becomes monotonous, even boring, if there is no break in the action. Think of each intense moment as needing a set-up, a punch and a breather. The idea is to maximize each emotional segment and ensure the listener's emotional involvement. A roller coaster is a good image to remember here.

The finale

The climax of the story is that scene, usually found in the third section, where the hero/heroine meets the greatest obstacle. It is the highest emotional point of the story. It must be unambiguous to the listener. The hero/heroine either succeeds in achieving the goal or does not. Many novice tellers writing their own stories spend a great deal of time developing the storyline up to the highest climactic moment but fail to provide a satisfactory ending because the main motivation of the hero/heroine has been left unresolved. The audience must know at the onset what the character visibly or physically hopes to achieve or accomplish and this must be resolved satisfactorily and decisively at the end. This does not mean that all endings must be happy ones, it means that the audience needs to be clear as to whether the character met the objectives put forth at the beginning of the story.

Credibility

All stories have a kind of rule structure that must be adhered to in order for them to be believable or logical. Even stories of gods with superpowers have limitations within their unique universe. The teller must make sure that the world where their characters reside appears to have a plausible structure. A character cannot be dead one minute and alive the next, as an example, unless it is clearly spelled out that this is possible within the boundaries of the character's world.

Characters must talk and act within the limits of their powers and abilities and situations must appear logical. There must be compelling reasons why characters act as they do or the listener will disengage from the story or not stay in emotional accord with the character. This is why it is critical to outline the setting and the abilities of the characters early in the story. Remember, even Superman has his weakness and this is what makes him an engaging and sympathetic hero.

The story in pictures

I find it helpful to see the story as a series of snapshots. I make a set of pictures in my mind that gives me the order of the scenes. Then it is quite easy to flesh out the action around each picture. I also list words or phrases that I associate with each picture or episode and create an outline for each story, creating enough to jog the memory. The idea is to keep this outline short so that remembering it does not become more of a chore than learning the story. I most emphatically suggest that with the exception of teaching stories the teller *does not memorize* the story. Memorizing can be disastrous since a forgotten line or phrase can make the mind go completely blank leaving the teller truly at a loss for words. The teller should also be free to add details to the story, as previously shown. This is what makes storytelling such an appealing form. The story is new each time the teller begins.

However, I do suggest that the first line be memorized (just to get the teller started with confidence) and also the last line (many tellers find it difficult to end a story satisfactorily). In this way, the teller is able to bring both personality, style and response to the audience, to bear on the body of the tale.

Physicalizing the story

One interesting way of practicing a story is to work on it as though it were a physical exercise. The objective of the following exercises, based on Laban's[5] principles for understanding the quality and range of the body's movement, is to make the storyteller as fluent and flexible in the use of body and voice as possible. Laban's techniques, which involve looking at human movement along the continuums of time, space, force and flow, are widely used for the training of dancers and theatre students. Below are some adaptations of these exercises to help tellers visualize the motion found within the story.

Time

All stories happen within a certain time frame. As an example, a story may take place over the space of several hours, days or years. The story has a specific entry point where we meet the hero/heroine and a specific destination or ending point.

We want to maximize impact in certain sections (the hurdles or conflicts referred to previously) as we go along, and we also want the plot to move at an accelerated pace as the hero/heroine meets the final climax and proceeds to the final moments of the story. Try the following exercises and keep in mind a story you are presently working on.

1   Walk at a normal pace around the room. Notice that your heartbeat is steady and regular. Your body should feel relaxed, unhurried. Increase the pace slightly and notice the feeling even this slight step up in momentum gives the body. Build up speed until you are moving as fast as you can without running. Notice the tension in your arms and upper body.

2   Now stop and start with quick, sudden bursts (it is a good idea to have one participant use a drum beat to indicate the stopping and starting). What sensation do you now feel in the body? What effect does this type of pace have on your heartbeat?

3   Return to normal pace and then slowly decrease your movement until you are going at the slowest possible pace without stopping. What kind of feeling are you now experiencing?

Keeping these exercises in mind it can be seen that combinations of a sustained or increased pace in your story possibly using intermittent pauses or slowing down can dramatically affect the body's involuntary response to it.

Try doing the same exercises vocalizing a nonsense syllable like 'aah' as you move. As your pace increases let the volume of your voice become more intense.

This kind of variation is what the storyteller is trying for within the story. Remember that the teller's body language, the signs that this is a stressful moment, is 'read' by the audience and is as important as the words themselves. As for when to use a sustained or increased pace refer back to the section on the shape of a story.

Space

Another concept directly related to that of time is that of space. All stories take up a certain amount of space. Some move along directly to the point with a sparse amount of extraneous detail as though in a rather narrow band and others tend to meander, picking up threads of other characters, using detailed descriptions of settings or objects and sometimes recounting asides or adjunct stories about the main characters that may add to our understanding of their motives or actions.

In order to physicalize this try the following exercises. It is always up to the teller which technique will be used. No matter which one is chosen, both need to be well under control:

1   Pick a point in the room. Focus on it ignoring all other objects around it. Go there directly without losing sight of your objective. Do not let anything else catch your interest.
2   Now, try going across the room to a new point. This time, however, allow your eyes to be caught by different objects or colors. Focus on this for a little while, even moving towards the new focus before returning to your objective. Take your time and don't feel that you are being rushed.

Some stories, those with a moral, for instance, often have a very narrow focus both in the meaning itself and the language used to propel the story. It is like the first exercise which is very controlled and purposeful. Some other tales, such as those from the Irish tradition, are the opposite. The story seems to meander off the point now and then as we learn more about the 'root to Paddy's problems', for instance, or as details are added in order to keep the story from advancing too quickly. Do not be fooled into thinking that the meandering technique is an excuse just to improvise instead of planning the story carefully. Just as you would have to map out the route you took in the second exercise in order to repeat it, the storyteller too must carefully plan all asides or added information. Any extraneous material must be designed to add to the impact of the story. Both techniques take practice. Remember that too much meandering can obscure the hero's motivation and the point of the story can become lost.

Force

Every story needs to be considered in terms of force. By this I mean the impact of the story on the listener. Is it subtle and light, like the touch of a feather, or blunt and heavy? Much of the control of this has to do with the teller's body language and use of voice. Is the teller conveying the tension in the story by lightening their own voice and muscles or is the body and voice in neutral? To get an idea of the difference try this:

1   Tighten your muscles slowly to the slow beat of a drum. As the drummer increases the pace, tighten more. When the drummer produces one final loud beat, crumple to the floor allowing the tension to flow from your body. This is how the set-up, punch and breather mentioned previously works. The set-up includes an increase in tension in both body and voice. The tension and intensity of voice rises to a peak or climax and then decreases once the climactic moment is passed so that the listeners are allowed to rest. Remember the roller coaster ride!

2   Move around the room now as if gravity were of no concern. Picture yourself physically rising up on each step. Think of the air in your lungs and arteries turning to helium. It rises up through the top of your head to escape. If you give sound to this you will probably notice the sound is centered in your head somewhere behind the eyes. There are stories where a far-away feeling is needed either for characterization purposes or as a way for the teller to speak in a detached manner. Visualizing this exercise may be helpful while telling in order to recreate this feeling of lightness both for yourself and the audience.

3   Explore strong, firm, slashing motions. Move around the room taking great strides. Notice your body's commitment to each stroke and the abrupt end to each movement. Add sounds to the strokes. Try to see where this technique might be used to enhance the movement of a story. How could it be used in a fast-paced action story with lots of excitement, for instance?

Flow

The last of the four areas to explore is that of flow. This element is very much connected to the qualities of space and force and time. I like to think of flow as the kind of control the teller exercises on the other aspects above. Consider these two polar opposites.

1   *Bound flow.* Remember the exercise of crossing the room directly, without distraction? Try this same exercise but imagine you are doing so while balancing a tray of very expensive glasses filled with champagne. Even though your ultimate focus remains the same and the time it takes to cross is roughly equal, the control of the body is very different. Without the tray, it is quite relaxed as you cross, arms swinging at your sides perhaps. As soon as the tray is added, tension is also added.

2   *Free flow.* Contrast the first exercise with this. Try turning the body, slowly at first, in a circling motion. Increase the speed until you feel the impetus of the outward pull on the body. When the energy is at its peak, allow the movement to run out until it is spent or is stopped by something else (such as the wall or if you spin downward the floor). In free

flow, the movement is not controlled as in bound flow. Try adding sound to these two exercises.

The teller must decide which kind of story they are telling. Does it need the teller to appear very controlled from beginning to end or would a seemingly more improvised style (as though the story has a momentum of its own) be better? I like to think of the first one as a kind of precision march and the second as a dance. Generally, myths and many folktales require the first while fantasy stories and humorous stories, especially with chase scenes, require the second.

All four elements are important, particularly with novice tellers. Vocalizing the exercises is also very good, since many people are timid about using the range of their own voices. Exercises help to break down these barriers in an acceptable format where no one is being put on the spot.

Gesture

A further area that I would like to mention is the teller's use of gestures. The teller must bring to life all of the characters, the setting and plot and theme for each story. Gestures must be used to enhance the story and should not detract from it. Nervous groping at buttons, tapping of feet or pacing and fidgeting while telling can draw so much attention that the actual story is lost. Be aware of body language and the use of the hands. Let gestures arise naturally from the story. Some tellers are more animated than others. This should not be stifled but should be under control.

These are a few of the components that make for a successful storytelling experience. These can be mastered by the reader and then shared with their own groups of inexperienced tellers. The main caution is to go slowly and enjoy the reactions that occur when a story is well told. Each success will encourage the teller to risk longer and longer stories and with a little practice a fairly extensive repertoire can be built up. Storytelling is an art but with a little dedication it is accessible to everyone.

> Bow bended, my story's ended;
> If you don't like it, you may mend it.
> (Old ending for fairy tale)

Techniques for sharing home stories

One of the great causes of difficulties for people today, I feel, is brought about by our emphasis on becoming something other than what we already are. It seems that we are never good enough, smart enough, rich enough, beautiful enough or happy enough. There always is more that we must do or be in order to attain personal fulfillment. Consequently, the value of our lives as they are, the experiences we have had, are often viewed as rather dull, or at best not terribly significant. Countless times I have asked beginning story-telling groups, particularly teenage and young adults, to share a little about themselves only to receive the 'my life is really dull' or 'nothing exciting has ever happened to me' or 'I have nothing to tell' response. This seems to me to be extremely significant. How can one find meaning in one's life if one doesn't see anything of significance or value in it?

One of the great importances of sharing home stories is to bring to light the experiences that shape us and to *give them significance* and hence mean-ing. Home stories also promote, as shown previously, a new understanding of these stories as the foundation of a unique view of the world, our own personal sense of reality.

Beginnings

When beginning with a group about to examine home stories, I try to estab-lish a trust level and intimacy that will allow for more personal material to be shared. I do this in two ways: first, by sharing one or two of my own personal stories, usually in a lighthearted vein to show that even the leader is human; second, by encouraging participants to share details about themselves that, while very low key and non-threatening in detail bring about a personal knowledge of each member. The following activity, popular with many storytelling animators, is a good one to begin with.

I am

We all receive a name at birth and this is a great place to start telling home stories. Perhaps we are called after Uncle Herbert, our mother's favorite brother, or the doctor who delivered us. Maybe our name means 'strength' or 'steadfast' or 'one who loves horses' in another language. It could be that a middle name is a former last name of a grandmother or great-grandmother. Finding out about and sharing information about names and family gives all members of the group both something in common and something unique to share with others

There is something very special about knowing personal details about some-one. It seems that by sharing, a bond is established. Perhaps this is because we only share information about ourselves with those who are meaningful to us in some way. The following activities lay a foundation of acceptance and belonging for later work:

1   To stimulate interest and to help those who have no access to such infor-mation, bring in books of name definitions – both given and surnames. Allow time for research and informal sharing. Later, let each person relate what they learned or already know about their names to a partner.

This may be further increased to groups of four, each person telling about their partner, rather than about themselves.

2   Individuals may also bring in a family heirloom or an object that holds significance of some kind for their family. Again, these may be shared with a partner or in small groups (no more than five).

3   A third activity is to try to find out a little about their family history – the country of origin, for instance, or an anecdote about a grandparent. (Remember that we are keeping it simple at this point, no need to write a lengthy tale or make it perfect. We are only trying to build a sense of sharing within the group.)

In all cases keep these little beginning story fragments short and confine the sharing to one to four people. Whole-group sharing can be very intimidating to first-time tellers, especially those who feel isolated or powerless in their daily lives.

Now, there may be some members of the group who do not have (or cannot share for some reason) any history of their names or family or find it difficult to talk about themselves at all. Perhaps their background is so troubled that they need to develop confidence to face it themselves. In these and all cases, participants should not be pushed to share information if they are not ready to do so. In these first activities it is sometimes enough for some just to look up their name origins in the book and to share the information. The more accepting the animator is of the individual's freedom to choose what is to be shared, the sooner these participants will feel safe enough to reveal more details about themselves.

My house

One of my favorite means of uncovering details of stories to do with the past is based on an activity I discovered in a book called *Telling Your Story* by Sam Keen and Anne Fox. This involves giving each person a very large piece of squared paper and asking them to draw a floor plan (the inside) of the very first house they clearly remember living in. It should include doors, windows, closets and cupboards. They are encouraged to remember the kind of furniture, wallpaper and floor coverings that were in this house, as well as any other details that made the house special. Many people also include the garden and garage if they were there as well. Here are some questions that will stimulate memories while doing this activity:

1   What was your favorite room? Why?
2   Did you have a favorite hiding place?
3   What room if any was off limits?
4   What window gave the best view?
5   What room do you associate with family activities?

6   Did you have a best friend? Where did you play?

Each person writes down snatches of ideas as they spring up right on the paper after the floor plan is complete. This activity may take one session or may be worked on over a series depending on the interest of the group. The result is a rich supply of story fragments that may be shared in small groups or with the group as a whole. Some of these may be developed into a longer story for sharing as well.

I have seen participants become so absorbed in this 'house collage' that they actually research pieces of wallpaper and textures of materials on sofas and chairs and bring in samples to accompany their drawings. Others cut facsimiles from old catalogues and paste them in place. No matter how it is rendered, this activity always sparks a wealth of personal stories and it is gratifying to watch as some hidden or obscure memory suddenly surfaces and a group member eagerly shares an insight into the past.

Schooldays

Most of us have both good and bad memories of schooldays and these tend to be quite vivid as they represent the first dealings with outside authority figures, new exciting experiences, fears and frustrations and formal routine. Much of who we turn out to be and how we view education in general stems from this time.

Some of the attitudes of older participants can also be clearly related to this period. 'If it was good enough for me, it's good enough for my child', or conversely 'I hated school. I want my children to enjoy it.' Some see it as a kind of initiation that must be endured in order to reach adulthood: 'I got the strap lots of times when I was in school, but I survived it.'

I like to bring people back to their earliest recollections of school. With some groups, I use the same technique as in the house activity, having them create a map of their school, their route home, favorite game to play on the way to and from school, etc. A floor plan of one particular schoolroom is also an interesting place to begin, as is a physical description of a teacher who stands out in their minds in some way (either because they were exceptionally mean or exceptionally nice). Here are some questions to help focus the group:

1   Do you remember the first time you were in trouble at school?
2   Who was your favorite teacher?
3   Who was the meanest teacher?
4   Did you ever skip school in favor of another activity?
5   What games did you play during free time?
6   Who was your best friend?
7   Were you ever picked on by others? Did you ever pick on anyone else?
8   What rules do you remember from this time?

There is usually a great deal of discussion around this topic and these story fragments are once again very rich in detail. Some people elect to write those memories down in a kind of diary and these in turn often trigger other remembrances as well (such as vacation times, after-school activities and field trips).

Heroes and villains, friends and enemies

Many of those figures whom we consider to be heroic or villainous are a consequence of a kind of societal consensus as we have seen. Still, it is often quite revealing to go back and look at who was held up to us by our family as either a pillar of society or as an example of evil. We may often gain insight into our value system, beliefs and prejudices (either conscious or unconscious) by examining our past:

1 Who did your parents hold as examples of good citizens?
2 Who did they discourage or forbid you to play with?
3 What causes or ideas were championed in your house?
4 Do you remember any incidents that involved prejudice of some kind?
5 What behavior was frowned upon (either by members of the family or by neighbors, friends, etc.)?
6 Who was your hero/heroine?
7 What qualities did you admire in them?
8 Does this still hold true today?
9 Who was your best friend?
10 Who was your enemy? Why?

There are many topics under home stories that could be examined in the above manner. These include religion, fantasies and dreams, fears (superstitions, strange events, first public performance, first time away from home, etc.), initiations (first dates, dares, forbidden places) and deaths (pets, relatives).

When dealing with home stories, it is not really important that they are told the right way. The emphasis in fact is in the discovery process and on the personal insight that comes from uncovering the hidden story. It will be less inhibiting to both the teller and the listener if the structure for sharing the tales remains loose and above all non-judgmental in format. The stories should be allowed to flow freely for their own sake.

Sometimes tales of surprising clarity and quality are brought forth and, of course, these are a welcome gift. But it is the spirit of the tales that binds the group, leaving everyone with a sense of discovery and insight into the complex forms of human nature and behavior.

Stories just for fun

We have seen that stories have great power. They point to connections between the past and the present and can inform us of our innermost feelings, fears and hopes. But what about telling just for the fun of it? This is probably the best reason of all to share stories! Here are some of the activities that I have used in my own sessions for no other reason than to share them.

The tall tale

A tale is an exaggerated story that is intended to make the listener laugh. A good way to give novice tellers the idea of how a tale might grow out of proportion is as follows. Ask three volunteers to leave the room. Have the rest of the group seated in a circle and tell the following little story:

> Once there was a man who was not used to country living who came to visit a cowboy way out west. One day he was out for a walk when he came upon a snake pinned down by a boulder that had rolled off a cliff. He released the rattler (for it was a rattlesnake) and won its eternal gratitude. It followed him like a pet dog everywhere he went and even slept at the foot of his bed at night.
>
> One night, the man awoke with a start, feeling something was wrong. The snake was missing from its accustomed place. The man went out to the kitchen, feeling a draft from that direction. Sure enough, the window was open and there was the snake with its body tightly wrapped around a burglar, with its tail hanging out the window, rattling for help!

Ask one volunteer to come back into the room. Let someone who just heard the story retell it. The first volunteer then retells it to the second volunteer who has been brought back into the room and then the second repeats the story to the third volunteer. The third volunteer tells the story a final time to the group. It is interesting to notice:

- how different each version is from the last and whether details are altered
- the choice of words each teller uses
- whether the teller uses a dialect to embellish the story
- if the punchline stays the same in successive tellings.

Liar, Liar, Pants on Fire

This activity encourages the participants to really exaggerate the details of their stories. The idea is to take a perfectly normal activity such as getting up in the morning or eating lunch and to exaggerate it all out of proportion.

I usually ask the participant to recount either that morning's activities, something that has happened to them recently or something they saw happening to someone else. There is no particular order to the tellings. Each volunteer begins where the last person left off, trying to connect the story in some way to the previous one.

For example, if the last tale was about a really bad start to the day, the next teller could begin by saying, 'Hah! you think that was a bad morning? Listen to this' and then tell the tale. In this way, the tellings become a kind of collective, flowing from one story to the next.

The tellers should also be encouraged to have a reason for telling the story. For instance, it might be to make the audience feel sorry for them or to make them laugh or to make them believe they have superhuman qualities!

Superman, Wonder Woman

Ask the group to tell what attributes they associate with superheroes. Share these informally in round-robin fashion. Each person should now imagine a superhero of personal choice and 'become' that person. He or she may be in disguise during the day as an ordinary individual, but at night or in times of crisis turns into . . .

Give them one of the following situations to build the story around (they could also make up their own if they wish):

1   There are thieves breaking into a bank in the middle of the night. Tell how you foil their plans.
2   There is a damsel in distress. She is floating down a fast-flowing river on a log. There is a waterfall around the next curve. Tell how you bring her to safety.
3   There is a giant earthquake or volcano eruption and the government call on you to stop it. Tell how you save the day.

I knew her when

Recite the following little poem:

> There was a maid on Scrabble Hill
> And if not dead she lives there still
> She never drank, she never lied,
> She never laughed, she never cried.

Ask participants in small groups of three or four to do the following activities:

1   Write down what they know about the maid. These are facts they can glean from the poem.

2 Write down what questions they might have that are not answered in the poem.

3 Write down who might know the answers to their questions (i.e. neighbors, relatives, friends, etc.).

4 Now ask one person in each group to become the person they would most like to question. Let the rest be reporters, historians, police officers or someone else who might be interested in the maid. Let each group have about five or six minutes to question their 'witness', then elect one person to report their findings to the group.

5 Each group can then prepare a group telling of what they think is the real story behind the poem of the maid. They should do this in a round-robin fashion where each person tells a portion of the completed tale. These tales are then shared with the whole group.

It is fun to work with existing dialogue, script or printed material and then to find the hidden story lurking just underneath the surface. The same technique works well with portions of novels. I try to take a section from a book that leaves lots of questions unanswered. It can be right at the beginning of the story or at the climax. There is no right or wrong of course. The participants are free to tell the story based on the story fragment in their own way. It is often interesting to go back and read the original book to see the author's version.

Postscript

Throughout this chapter on storymaking and storytelling I have tried to show the great value, even the need, of sharing stories, both our own and those of others. We live in interesting times where technological advancements and artificial intelligence make it difficult sometimes to remember our humanity. Through the reawakening of the inner mind, through storytelling, we participate in our common heritage and come to sense the fundamental mysteries of being, in which we all share. The activation of our imaginative life, the life that is inside, is one of the most challenging tasks open to us, both personally and professionally. If our technology is an expression of our intelligence, then our stories are an expression of our soul. The balance lies somewhere between.

Notes

1 M. Eliade, *The Myth of the Eternal Return*, Princeton, NJ: Princeton University Press, 1974, p. 5.
2 M. Eliade, *Images and Symbols*, Princeton, NJ: Princeton University Press, 1991, p. 26.
3 B. Barton, *Tell Me Another*, Markham, Ontario: Pembroke Publishers Ltd, 1986.
4 J. Hillman, 'A note on story', *Parabola* 4(4), 1989, 43.
5 R. Laban, *Modern Educational Dance*, London: MacDonald and Evans, 1975.

Further reading

Anderson, H.C. (1861) *Danish Fairy Legends and Tales* (trans. C. Peachey), London: Henry G. Bohn.

Arkhurst, J.C. (1964) *The Adventure of Spider: West African Folk Tales*, Boston: Little Brown.

Barton, B. (1986) *Tell Me Another*, Markham, Ontario: Pembroke.

Bettelheim, B. (1989) *The Uses of Enchantment*, New York: Random House.

Campbell, J. (1949) *The Hero With a Thousand Faces*, New York: Princeton University Press.

Campbell, J. (1990) *The Hero's Journey*, New York: Harper and Row.

Chase, R. (1943) *The Jack Tales*, Cambridge, MA: Houghton Mifflin.

Crimmens, P. (2006) *Drama Therapy and Storymaking in Special Education*, London: Jessica Kingsley Publishers.

Curtis, N. (1907) *The Indian's Book: An Offering by the American Indians of Indian Lore, Musical and Narrative to Form a Record of the Songs and Legends of Their Race*, New York: Harper and Brothers.

Eliade, M. (1974) *The Myth of the Eternal Return*, Princeton, NJ: Princeton University Press.

—— (1991) *Images and Symbols*, Princeton, NJ: Princeton University Press.

Erdoes, R. and Ortiz, A. (1984) *American Indian Myths and Legends*, New York: Pantheon.

Feldmann, S. (1965) *The Storytelling Store: Myths and Tales of the American Indian*, New York: Dell.

Gersie, A. and King, N. (1990) *Storymaking in Education and Therapy*, London: Jessica Kingsley Publishers.

Grimm, J. and Grimm, W. (1972) *The Complete Grimm's Fairy Tales*, New York: Pantheon.

Hamilton, E. (1942) *Mythology*, Boston: Little Brown.

Hillman, J. (1989) 'A Note on Story', *Parabola*, 4(4): 43.

Keen S. and Fox, A. (1989) *Telling Your Story*, Los Angeles: Tarcher.

Laban, R. (1975) *Modern Educational Dance*, London: MacDonald and Evans.

Opie, I. and Opie, P. (1974) *The Classic Fairy Tales*, Oxford: Oxford University Press.

Perrault, C. (1957) *Fairy Tales of Charles Perrault* (trans. G. Brereton), Harmondsworth: Penguin.

Ransome, A. (1968) *Old Peter's Russian Tales*, London: Thomas Nelson.

Rasmussen, K. (1921) *Eskimo Folk Tales* (ed. and trans. W. Worster), London: Glyldendal.

Rosen, B. (1988) *And None of It Was Nonsense*, Richmond Hill, Ontario: Scholastic Tab.

Sawyer, R. (1970) *The Way of the Storyteller*, New York: Penguin.

Shah, I. (1979) *World Tales*, New York: Harcourt Brace Jovanovitch.

Shedlock, M.L. (1951) *The Art of the Storyteller*, New York: Dover.

Wilson, B.K. (1989) *Scottish Folktales and Legends*, New York: Oxford University Press.

Zipes, J. (1983) *Fairy Tales and the Art of Subversion*, New York: Weldman.

Chapter 10

Creating community

Ensemble performance using masks, puppets and theatre

Wende Welch

Anyone who has ever worked in the theatre will say that the experience is anything but private. Creating theatre involves many people working together, ultimately to communicate something to someone else. Theatre cannot exist for and of itself; it is only complete when it is performed for an audience. It depends on human interaction.

In this way, theatre can be seen as a microcosm of life itself. Just as we weave in and out of the events, crises and victories that occur in our lives, so too does the theatre artist. The agents of these events comprise the many relationships we are constantly building, maintaining or destroying throughout life's journey. Though the relationships between characters in a play may seem contrived, this should not lead us to believe that they are any less valid than our real life relationships.

The appeal of the theatre lies in the desire to witness and experience the mystery of human survival in extraordinary circumstances. The actors commit to the playing of their parts for an audience who wants to see them succeed. The pursuit of human achievement, reaching and perhaps surpassing one's potential, offers the participant and the spectator an opportunity to unite and celebrate the joy of life. In this way, theatre demands a sense of community for its success. It requires the joint effort of individuals coming together to pursue a common goal.

The arts serve this purpose by enabling an individual – or group of individuals – to express themselves, to communicate their ideas through whatever medium they choose. Providing the opportunity for this self-expression places responsibility on the community to expose individuals to the various forms of art. The chance for individuals to enrich their lives through artistic endeavors not only stimulates personal growth but also builds confidence through a sense of achievement. The result is a community that benefits from such capable and functioning members.

Theatre is a medium that can be used to create an environment where integration can occur.[1] The collaborative nature of theatre lends itself to the exploration of artistic expression as a collective. This is what many theatre artists refer to as ensemble. Ensemble means together. The spirit of ensemble implies an unselfish support for the others with whom one works in harmony. The strength of a group is only as strong as its individuals. When integrating persons with disabilities into a theatrical environment, I have found that creating an ensemble proves both a necessity and a boon for all involved.[2] Under such circumstances, the combined efforts and talents of the collective ideally balance out to involve as well as serve the immediate needs of each individual within the group.

Ensemble theatre can be used effectively in an integrated setting as an aid to increased self-expression, and therefore self-awareness. In addition, imagine how such exploration might affect the individual's involvement in the greater community in which they live.

Mask and puppetry

Masks and puppets can be any inanimate object brought to life through human effort before an audience.[3] They both belong to a family of theatre animation that has existed for centuries in many different cultures. The dramatic function of mask and puppetry is not unlike any other performing art form. Essentially, it strives for communication between performer and audience: the actor, musician, dancer, singer or puppeteer shares something with the spectator, who in turn responds, thus reinforcing the will of the performer to communicate. This creates a constant cycle of exchange that unites the performer and audience. The success of a performance depends on the degree to which both performer and audience are willing to accept and commit to this interaction. The result is a shared human experience on many levels: intellectually, physically, spiritually and emotionally.

However, where some performing art forms might achieve this experience based on a subjective approach, mask and puppetry choose an objective presentation to fulfill the same function. For example, an actor playing a character in a play will elicit a different response from each audience member simply because human beings see other human beings differently. Their responses to the actor's appearance, the sound of his or her voice, the way he or she uses his or her body, and how he or she makes use of these to play the character will naturally vary according to personal taste. However, a mask or a puppet has one expression. It intends to capture the essence of an emotion or character trait. The audience immediately distinguishes the good character from the evil character. Mask and puppetry operate on less sophisticated principles, thereby making the theatrical convention easier to accept. This is directly responsible for the success of mask and puppetry with both children and adults.

The art of mask and puppetry mirrors that of the theatre, but adds another level. Discovering the reality of the inanimate object – the mask or the puppet – goes beyond using only one's body and voice to communicate with an audience. The performer must develop a relationship with the mask or puppet to breathe life into it. This should not be mistaken for hiding behind the mask or puppet, using it as a crutch, transferring the responsibility for any action or thought on to the object itself. It is up to the performer to explore fully the potential of the mask or puppet: what is it capable of doing, feeling and saying? The answers to these questions lie in the ability of the performer to objectify the emotion of the character. Only then will the mask or puppet speak and delight its audience; when bond between actor and mask or puppeteer and puppet is an organic one, and therefore imperceptible.

Theatre with mask and puppetry can aid in building a sense of ensemble in an integrated setting. The first step involves learning to relate to an inanimate object. For those with certain developmental disabilities, this may come easier than having to relate to another human being. For others with severe physical disabilities, such interaction may only be possible with the help of other members of the group. Through playing, relationships begin to form as communication occurs between the individuals and the masks or puppets. Discovering the character of the mask or puppet requires the individual to explore imaginative ways of using their body and voice. This may lead to increased self-awareness and the confidence to express oneself. In an integrated group setting, participation fluctuates between doing, helping and observing. A sense of ensemble grows as individuals begin to trust and support one another. All of this work must ultimately serve the final step – the performance. Such a challenge rewards each individual with pride in their achievement. The discovery and realization of the individual's contribution to the whole has involved the group in reaffirming the need to create community.

Workshops

The following are suggested activities designed to warm up the individual's voice and body, in preparation for the creative work to follow. The warm-up should be a group activity, as a sense of ensemble must be implemented from the beginning. In an integrated group setting, all workshop activities may require assigning individuals to assist those with a disability. In such cases, the focus of the exercises becomes an investigation of how to help one another to perform the given task together.

Voice[4]

When warming up the voice, try to incorporate exercises that stimulate the body as well as the mind. For our purposes in the theatre, and specifically with mask and puppetry, emphasis should be placed on breath support, amplification of sound using the various vocal resonators, and the articulation of thoughts and feelings organically. The voice is inside the body. We release it when we feel the need to express ourselves.

Breath support begins with an awareness of the body. Ideally, the skeleton acts against gravity to support the body, relieving the muscles of that duty, leaving them free for movement. When this occurs, the breathing musculature responds freely, providing a more efficient support for the voice. Try rolling up and down the spine. Roll the head, shoulders and arms; raising and releasing arms, elbows and wrists – all with an increased awareness of the breath moving freely in the body.

Allow those with limited physical capabilities to work within their own range of movement. If they require assistance, encourage one or two other members of the group to help guide that individual through the exercises by gently moving the head, shoulders, arms and wrists for them. Working together in this way should only be attempted with the consent of the individual and if there is no risk of jeopardizing their physical condition. Avoid rolling down the spine. Similar results can be arrived at by having someone cradle the back of the individual's head and jaw in their hands, while another supports the upper arms. Gently lift the head and arms straight up, allowing the spine to hang and the muscles around it to relax. Note increased awareness and freedom of the breathing muscles.

Humming provides a gentle means for waking up the resonators in the body, face and head. Feel the voice rumble, buzz or ping in various parts of the body while collecting vibrations on the lips. Then open the mouth and release the sound. Use vivid images that excite the mind and involve the voice and body in play: animals, insects, vehicles, industrial noise, carnival sounds, etc. Encourage interaction during these exercises.

Articulation implies clear speech. However 'correct' pronunciation won't move an audience without clear thought behind it. This point proves doubly vital for mask and puppetry, where articulation governs the animation of the mask or puppet. Effective communication through a mask or puppet requires precise speech and movement. Developing a sense of rhythm can help achieve this. Singing, preferably accompanied by some movement or dance, offers a comprehensive warm-up and unites the group. Here, you may choose to divide the group into smaller groups of twos, threes or fours, creating a less awkward and crowded environment for the sake of integrating with those individuals with a physical disability or those who have a visual disability. Singing in rounds offers an ideal warm-up for an integrated group and could prove a less threatening activity for those with developmental disabilities who need extra encouragement.

Body

A gentle stretch should precede and follow any physical activity. Animating a mask or a puppet for the first time may painfully awaken muscles one never dreamed one had. Pay particular attention to the neck, shoulders, arms, wrists, hands, fingers, waist, lower back and calves. Again, offer physical assistance to those who ask for it, within their range of movement capability.

The following simple playground game is a thorough actor's warm-up in disguise. It sharpens listening and memorization skills, stimulates the body to respond to changing circumstances, builds concentration, hand–eye coordination and physical stamina – and is fun!

Water babies[5]

For this a soft ball, approximately 10 cm in diameter, is required. In a circle, each individual in the group calls out a number, beginning with one. This number becomes theirs for the game and they will need to remember it, as well as those of the others. (If you chose to use this game in an orientation session, you may wish to substitute names for numbers.) To begin the game, one individual stands in the centre of the circle, throws the ball straight up into the air, and calls out a number (not their own). The individual whose number was called must now catch the ball. If they catch it, they throw the ball back into the air, calling out a new number. If they miss it, they must first retrieve the ball and then call 'freeze'. When someone has missed the ball, the others in the group must flee to the perimeter of the defined play area before that individual calls 'freeze'.

Once 'freeze' is called, the others must stop and remain motionless. Fixed to the very spot from which they called 'freeze', the caller must now throw the ball at one of the 'frozen' others. If the ball touches someone, that someone is given a 'water baby' and must begin the game again from the centre of the circle; if the ball touches no one, the individual who called 'freeze' is given a water baby and must begin the game again from the centre of the circle. Once an individual has received three water babies, they are out of the game. Water babies are also given to an individual who calls the number of someone who is out of the game or who calls their own number.

Water babies can be adapted for an integrated group. Have those who have a visual disability play the game hand in hand with a seeing individual, sharing the ball tossing and catching responsibilities. Those with physical disabilities may require an able-bodied partner – to aid in tossing and catching, as well as moving around the circle. Using eye contact and calling the individuals' names (instead of numbers) may succeed in involving those with developmental and/or learning disabilities. The group dynamic becomes a network of support, with everyone eager to coach any individual through the game, as long as they need help.

The creative work now begins by building performance skills. The following exercises incorporate mask or puppetry dramatically in an improvisational context. The group leader should come prepared with several masks and puppets for use in the workshops. At this stage of the work, it is important to inspire the group with well-made, three-dimensional puppets that are large, colorful and full of character.[6]

Journey through the body[7]

The group begins by lying on their backs on the floor (those who use wheel-chairs need not lie on the floor). With their eyes closed, encourage the group to relax every muscle in the body (guide them though this). As they begin to relax, remind them to pay attention to their breathing rhythms and placement in the body. Then ask each individual to imagine their ideal mode of trans-port. It can be anything from their past, present, future or fantasy life. Allow them to learn everything they can about their chosen vehicle (ask questions pertaining to size, age, color, interior/exterior, speed). At this point, inform them that they are going on a journey through their body, using their vehicle. However, their vehicle will only run on 'breath', so they must stay aware of their breathing to make the journey. Ask the group to put themselves in their vehicles and then either guide them through the journey or leave them to make it in their own time (allow 10–20 minutes for this).

You may need to pair certain individuals with developmental disabilities with a partner for the duration of the exercise. Avoid closing the eyes and lying on the floor. The partner should keep the individual's interest in the exercise stimulated by constant questioning and sharing of information about their vehicles and their journeys through the body. Making drawings or using toy vehicles may prove necessary.

When everyone has completed their journey, ask for volunteers to share their experience with the group. They must do this dramatically, using either a mask or a puppet. This means relating to and through the mask or puppet to engage the group in a storytelling experience. Focus initially on developing the relationship between actor and mask or puppeteer and puppet. Once this has solidified, then gradually encourage interaction between the mask or puppet character and the group. Speech need not be the only form of com-munication here. Other forms such as song, mime or dance may be used effectively in conjunction with mask or puppetry. Remember, in an integrated group there will always be those available to help individuals with a disability to animate a puppet or to share the experience with them before the group if this is necessary. This should be done dramatically, to support the individual and to collaborate creatively in the telling of their story.

Blind drawing[8]

PART 1

Scarves for blindfolds, large newsprint paper, charcoals and 'wet ones' towels will be needed. Begin with the group comfortably seated at a table or on the floor. Ask each individual to tie a scarf around their head, covering their eyes. Do not insist on the blindfold. Those who aren't ready to trust this concept may either close their eyes or focus anywhere but on the paper in front of them. Then, hand each individual a sheet of newsprint paper and a piece of charcoal. Next, give the group a word that will inspire them to draw whatever they associate with that word. Stick to abstract words like love, anger, depth or music, as they tend not to have a single representational picture. Once they 'see' a picture in their mind's eye, they may begin to draw it. No peeking! Once a drawing is complete, remove the blindfolds and share them. Before doing any more drawing, hand out towels to clean the charcoal off hands, fingers, arms, faces, etc.

Those with limited upper body mobility may require a partner to hold the paper for them, support the arm and/or hand as they draw, or even to draw for them. If the last is chosen, have the individual rest their hand on their partner's, moving with them as they draw.

PART 2

For this you will need 6 ft × 4 ft cotton drop(s),[9] high-intensity flashlights, sheets of thin cardboard, markers, Stanley knives, scissors, fishing wire, garden wire, paperclips, rivets and scotch tape.

Divide the group into smaller groups. Have each of these small groups review the drawings and choose one they all agree on. Then give the groups some time to explore moving in a way that the picture suggests to them. Introduce the concept of shadows by giving each individual a chance to move between the cotton drop (held by two individuals) and the flashlight (held by one individual). Taking what they've just learned from using their bodies to make shadows, have each group build a shadow puppet capable of moving in the same way. They will quickly understand what the cardboard, markers and wire are all for and begin tracing and cutting away with great enthusiasm. Allow ample time for this phase, for here the notion of ensemble is put to the test. The groups are thrown into a situation where they must work together, sharing ideas and coming to agreements every step of the way, to produce the final product. They must also learn to integrate by delegating roles and responsibilities based on the individuals' capabilities. Be available to answer questions and offer technical advice, but try to let the groups do any problem-solving themselves. Finally, have each group present their shadow puppet and give a demonstration of what it can do (relating back to the original drawing).

Sock puppets

You will need socks with toes cut horizontally for the mouth; felt-covered cardboard oval shapes for the inside of the mouth; needle and thread or glue gun; assorted odds and ends for facial features; and hair – buttons, felt shapes, yarn, etc.

Sock puppets offer a friendly incentive to communicate and interact with others. They are easy to build and fun to animate. Most sock puppets have mouths used for speaking, but they are also used for grabbing, tugging, lifting, holding, throwing, catching, plucking and digging, among other things. They can rejuvenate a group and bring focus back to the work at hand.

Sock puppets also provide an enjoyable means for developing articulation and rhythm skills.[10] Bring in tapes of popular music that the group can all relate to (the Beatles are always a safe bet). Place a group of puppeteers behind a makeshift storyboard[11] and have the rest observe as audience. Watch how the puppets' lip sync the lyrics and dance to the music. Give everyone a chance to perform and to observe.

Where the puppeteer positions their body in relation to the puppet becomes an important consideration, especially when changing direction. Working behind a storyboard makes everyone sensitive to the spatial relationship between bodies, especially when there are puppeteers who use wheelchairs. Encourage the group to adapt by learning to share space and making room for everyone.

Neutral mask[12]

Essentially, neutral mask technique attempts to wipe the slate clean, so that the actor is left with a neutral base upon which to build a character. Neutral mask is not an end in itself, it is a process. At a glance, the exercises themselves seem fairly straightforward. However, once the expressionless mask covers the face, any extraneous, idiosyncratic movement becomes glaringly apparent. The goal here is not to move like a robot. Rather it is to strip movement down to the bare essentials necessary to complete a given task. This requires that the individual think about each step they make, and its intention. This moment-to-moment concentration on the present toward the future is the actor's thinking process, and must be developed for the sake of ensemble performance.

The workshop leader should come prepared with at least two neutral masks. It is much easier to make them than to buy them (the leather Sartori neutral masks, made in Italy, would cause a pronounced deficit in most budgets). The masks I use are an adaptation of the Sartori masks. I build up a papier mâché form over a three-dimensional styrofoam mould covered with petroleum jelly. I then reinforce the papier mâché foam with plaster of Paris gauze strips and secure an elastic band at both sides (Figure 10.1).

There are several schools of thought surrounding the actual putting on of the mask. Some recommend a period of contemplation, studying the mask for an increased understanding of every layer of its character, before putting it on. Others prefer to work with the mask on right from the start, allowing the character to unfold as the body takes on the rhythm and energy of chosen images. Once the mask is on, some insist on working in front of a mirror, whereas others may rely on the impressions and comments of the instructor

Figure 10.1 A neutral mask.

or director. Either way, it really comes down to a matter of personal preference, based on training, experience and appropriateness for the group in
question.

Once the mask is put on, a visible (to the audience) and tangible (for the
actor) transformation occurs. Those who have worked with mask will often
speak of the 'energy' or 'personality' of the mask, which is no wonder as a lot
of imagination has already gone into the creation of the mask. Perhaps
several actors have already put on the mask, adding to its own personal
history with their creative energies. The mask is a powerful tool for communication and should, therefore, be handled with care and treated with respect.

You will undoubtedly encounter those in the group who either fear the
mask or won't wear it. Never force the issue of the mask. Rather, encourage
those individuals actively to participate by observing others in the exercises
and giving constructive feedback afterwards. Watching others tackle the exercises first may give some the courage they need to try the mask themselves.
Or, you may find it necessary to pair individuals in the exercises. The same
principles of neutral mask would apply. Only now there's the added benefit
of two actors learning to communicate with and be aware of each other in
the work.

There may also be those in the group who haven't full control of their
motor skills and for whom it may appear impossible to exercise any economy
of movement. Neutral mask is a mental and physical challenge for everyone,

regardless of disability. Part of integration involves learning to appreciate an individual's movement as a reflection of who they are. Why deny anyone the right to express themselves or the chance to develop a keener understanding of how their body can serve them creatively?

The first set of exercises allows the individual to discover their neutral base through improvising in a given situation. Feedback on the exercises serves to make the individual aware of what they may be consciously or unconsciously communicating with their body. It may be clear in the mind of the individual what they are doing or feeling, but are they making it clear enough for an audience to understand?

The second set of exercises gives the individual the opportunity to begin building on the neutral base they've achieved in the first exercises. Here, the individual learns to tap into their physical resources by calling upon the body to explore the different rhythms and energies suggested by certain images.

Participation must obviously be limited to the number of masks available. More than four individuals at a time makes it difficult to watch what each one is doing. The defined play area (stage) may only be used by those participating in an exercise. The rest of the group must observe the exercises from the periphery (audience).

First exercises

Ask those participating to assume a comfortable resting position either by lying on the floor or by totally relaxing in their wheelchair, on stage with the masks on. In their own time, they are to do the following:

1   Get up, look at the horizon, then resume resting position.
2   Get up, look at the horizon, see an object (real or imaginary) before you, take it, use the object, place it back where you found it, look at the horizon, resume resting position.
3   Get up, look at the horizon, see your bus before you, move as quickly as you can to try to catch your bus as it is pulling away, watch it drive away, turn and move back to your original position, turn and look at the horizon, resume resting position.

Give everyone in the group a chance to do an exercise before moving on to the next one. Ask those participating to remove the masks once everyone on stage has completed the exercise. At this point, encourage those observing to give constructive comments based on what they saw.

Second exercises

Begin the same way as in the first exercises. Ask those participating to think of an image. It could be anything representational that pops into their mind:

the sun, a cloud, a flower, a raindrop, a brick, a tornado, a camp fire, etc. Once they all have an image, give them time to think about what it might feel like to be the sun or a flower. Whatever feelings come, instruct them to fill the body with those feelings. This provides the impetus for movement. As they begin to explore the movement, they will naturally fall into a set rhythm. Once they have a established a rhythm, ask them to begin moving around the stage. If anyone loses their rhythm, chances are they've lost their concentration and should return to their resting position to rekindle their original impression of the image.

Steer them away from a tendency to fall into clichés. It is not important that they look like a flower; it is far more useful as an actor to understand how it feels to be that flower, and to communicate that fact to an audience. Likewise, discourage them from playing the mask at this point in the work. The neutral mask intentionally takes focus away from the face, forcing the actor to communicate with the body.

The next step involves removing the neutral mask to allow words to come organically from the character emerging from the movement. This step can be made more accessible with the use of animal imagery. Repeat the above exercise, only now ask each individual to think of an animal. Stick to familiar land mammals, birds and reptiles. Fish and water mammals pose a problem because they exist only in water.

Once they begin to move, they immediately take on the nature of their chosen animal, for example, the kitten plays with yarn, the dog lifts his leg, the squirrel collects nuts, the snake slithers through the grass, etc. Being able to relate to the animal's reality makes it easier for most people to begin interacting with the other 'animals' on stage. Encourage them to find a reason to meet. If a particular couple or threesome appears to have tapped a potentially dramatic relationship, coach them from the floor on to their feet. Ask the actors to 'hold' and have several observers go on stage and remove the masks. It is important here for the actor to drop the notion of animals and move on to applying the animal's qualities and energy to the development of a human character.

The actors should continue developing the relationship as they move. The circumstances for the relationship mixed with the animals' energies give the actors the reason to speak. Begin with sound that is released as an extension of the movement, and therefore rooted in the body. Gradually, move to words and watch an improvised scene unfold before your very eyes! Later, commedia dell'-arte masks may be added to objectify and exaggerate the character's qualities.

The process

Now the work becomes more focused. We have been building skills for a purpose: to introduce each individual to the craft of mask and puppetry so that they may now use these skills to explore the art. At the same time, they've learned to adapt those skills to suit the needs of an integrated setting. Further exploration will now unite the group by taking them on a journey that begins with rehearsals, continues through the building of masks, puppets, costumes, sets, etc. and culminates with the actual performance. The process cannot, and should not, be avoided. The process enables the ensemble to grow and mature. The foundation for trust in an integrated group requires a shared commitment covering time and experience. With trust comes confidence in oneself and in others. This must be in place in order for each individual to make the transition from rehearsal to performance.

The decision to rehearse, build and present theatrical performance using mask and puppetry begs one primary consideration. Masks and puppets must begin as an integral part of the concept for the performance. First, masks and puppets are not props. They are the characters of the play, and in some cases even become actors themselves, playing beside their human counterparts. Second, the relationship between mask and actor or puppet and puppeteer must be given the chance to develop. Any inconsistency here would guarantee a superficial performance.[13] This can be prevented if the group becomes comfortable working with masks and puppets (those built for the performance or cardboard mock-ups) from day one. Animation with masks and puppets demands sensitivity and practice. Introducing them as an afterthought would disrupt the harmony of the performance and demonstrates a lack of respect for the art form.

Rehearsals

The following suggestions offer two approaches to building material for a collective performance. I recommend building material over a script for several reasons. In an integrated setting, adhering to a specific text and blocking it (that is setting the actors' stage movements and 'business') might prove too sophisticated a proposition for some groups. The material to be performed must remain flexible enough to accommodate the unpredictable behavior of certain individuals in the group with developmental disabilities. If the words and accompanying movement originate from them, the concept of interacting as characters by allowing words and movement to serve the characters' intention in the action of the performance becomes a less foreign proposition. Also, building material for a performance calls for the active participation of the ensemble at all times. Using a script may persuade some to separate themselves from the ensemble and concentrate only on what they've been given. Therefore, allow the ideas for the performance to stem from group involvement.[14]

Storytelling

Assorted masks and puppets, or cardboard mock-ups will be required. I developed my own approach to storytelling while working with Das

Puppenspiel Puppet Theatre on their adaptation of *Jumping Mouse*. I've since used it for gathering material for collective creations and street theatre performances.

Divide the group into subgroups of three to four individuals. Give each subgroup a structure from which to build their story. This structure is arrived at by plugging in each one of the variables in the box to complete the equation.

Method	*Media*	*Situation*	*Conflict*
Narrator,	Mask	Who, What	
Brechtian,	+ and/or	+ Where and	+ Obstacle
or Realism	Puppets	When	

Under the *Method* heading I've listed three choices. Narrator implies that one character is to tell the story, while the others act it out. The Brechtian method allows for all the characters to switch between narrating and acting out the story. Lastly, Realism simply requires the characters to act out the story with no narration.

An example of this approach was used to create a street theatre perform-ance I directed with an integrated cast. They chose: (Brechtian) + (Mask) + (Mouse, running away from home, to the circus, in the early morning) + (must help his new friend, a Lioness, escape the inhumane conditions and abuse she has suffered at the hands of the ringmaster). From this scenario, the group worked together to flesh out the story, adding other circus characters, improvising sound effects and music and using their bodies as the actual circus tent. The group saw to it that everyone had a part to play, and when they weren't directly involved in the storytelling, individuals would provide the soundscape or become part of the set.

In this particular group, there was an individual with a developmental disability who often grew restless and would wander away from the rehearsal. The group eventually solved this problem by bringing the entire rehearsal to them, thereby refusing to allow the work to be interrupted and reminding the individual of their importance and responsibility to the group. Throughout the rehearsal period, the group used neutral and character mask exercises to harmonize the energy and movement of the animals with the masks.

Theme-based performance

This approach follows a more loosely structured formula. The effect resembles that of a collage: an assemblage of separate scenes that share a common theme. With such compositions, the continuity or throughline becomes the theme itself, and not the chronology of any one story. Theme pieces also lend themselves to an eclectic blend of performing arts, taking full advantage of the spectacle aspect of theatre.

I collaborated on a street theatre performance with an integrated cast, using a carnival theme. The size of the group (over 20 people) permitted us to give each person performance as well as production responsibilities. The following illustrates the breakdown of these responsibilities.

Performance areas

- Punch and Judy scene
- King and Queen of the carnival
- Commedia dell'arte scene
- Clowns
- Sideshow acts
- Maypole dance
- Kazoo marching band

Production areas

- Finding and building

    - masks and puppets
    - sets, props and costumes
    - musical instruments

- Painting

    - scenery
    - masks
    - puppets

- Make-up workshops.

Under such circumstances, I've found that the success of the rehearsal process rests with the ability of the director or instructor 'to provide an atmosphere in which creation can take place'.[15] This can be done in any number of ways, from ensuring a clean and clutter-free rehearsal space to rotating activities to keep the work fresh and interest alive. During this part of the process, every effort must be made to encourage the individual to believe in their ability to contribute in a useful way to the project. The more familiarity breeds a sense of ensemble, the more the individual will feel comfortable with sharing their ideas and cultivating them in a creative way.

Building masks and puppets

There is much to consider before sitting down to build a mask or puppet:

1   How many masks or puppets are needed? Could some characters be

played with a mask instead of a puppet, or vice versa? How many actors and/or puppeteers are required to animate them all? Is it possible for them to play more than one role?

2   Who are the mask or puppet characters? Which of their personality traits should I emphasize? How do I want the audience to feel about each character?

3   How is the mask to be used? Must the actor speak or not? Must the mask change expression or shape?

4   What must the puppet do? Speak? Handle and use objects? Fly or swim? Eat? Come apart? Breathe fire?

5   Where is the performance to be performed? Indoors (with or without lighting) or outdoors? In an intimate setting or a larger venue?

6   What size should the masks or puppets be? Do they fit the scale of the set or storyboard? Do they fit the scale of the venue?

7   What is the required lifespan of the masks or puppets? Will they be used once or twice or over a period of weeks, months or years? Will they be transported from place to place frequently?

8   How much can be spent on materials? Is there a cheaper way to achieve the same desired effect? Can found household objects be cleverly used?

Masks

Suggested materials are: cardboard, markers, Stanley knives, scissors, fabric scraps, trimmings, carpenter's glue, contact cement, 12-inch balloons, pieces of foam core, various styrofoam shapes, cheesecloth, paperbags cut into strips, multicolored construction paper cut into strips, plaster of Paris strips, petroleum jelly, acrylic or tempera paints, small to medium paint brushes, elastic strings and bands.

Masquerade, half-masks

This type of mask was built for the maypole dance sequence in the carnival street theatre performance mentioned earlier. The outline for the mask is drawn with markers on a piece of thin cardboard. Use scissors or a Stanley knife to cut out the face, eye holes and any other details drawn. Poke holes at either end of the mask. Thread the elastic string through holes, knot and staple into place. Apply glue to the front and back of the mask. Stretch fabric over the mask and add trimming.

For a more three-dimensional look, sculpt foam core pieces in the shape of eyebrows, cheeks and noses. Attach the foam pieces to the face of the mask with contact cement. Measure out the elastic band and attach both ends to the back side of the mask with contact cement. Allow to dry before stretching cheesecloth over front and back of the mask. Using a brush, cover the entire mask with a mixture of carpenter's glue and water. Be sure to keep the desired shape of the mask. Allow to dry before painting with acrylic or tempera paints (Figure 10.2).

Character, full masks

Here, I would recommend building the mask on a mould. Ready-made plastic masks make suitable moulds and can be found at the larger theatrical supply or craft stores. You might also check Chinese souvenir shops. A simpler way would be to use an inflated balloon. Blow the balloon up to the approximate size of the individual's head and tie a knot at the end. With a marker, draw on the balloon where the eye, nose and mouth holes will be as well as the perimeter of the mask. Treat the inside of the marked area with petroleum jelly. Dip the paperbag strips in a mixture of carpenter's glue and water and arrange them within the marked area on the balloon. Remember not to cover the eye, nose and mouth holes. Allow to dry before adding the next layer.

Once the second layer has dried, you may want to build up facial features. This can be done by sculpting and arranging pieces of styrofoam on the mask. Set the pieces in place with carpenter's glue and secure them by adding a layer of wet plaster of Paris strips over the entire mask. For a more colorful alternative, cover the mask with several layers of construction paper strips (solid or multicolored) dipped in the same glue and water mixture as before. Once dry, gently lift the mask off the balloon. You may find it easier to pop the balloon. Acrylic or tempera paints can be used on the plaster of Paris

Figure 10.2 Half masks.

masks. Attach an elastic string or band as described above, substituting plaster of Paris strips for the cheesecloth.

You can expedite the process by using the individual's face as a mould. This method takes about an hour, during which the individual must sit or lie still and not move a muscle on their face. Some individuals may not wish to place themselves in what they perceive to be such a vulnerable or terrifying position. However, those who wish to try could donate their masks as moulds for the others to use. Have the individual sit or lie down in a comfortable position. Ask them to tie their hair back from their face and to remove any jewelry. They should either wear an old shirt or wrap an old towel around their neck and shoulders. Spread a thin layer of petroleum jelly over their entire face. Then, apply a single layer of wet plaster of paris strips directly on to their face. Do not cover the eyes, nostrils or mouth. If need be, these areas can be covered with a second layer once the mask is removed from the face. Allow to dry and harden before lifting the mask off the face. I've found this experience most enjoyable and relaxing, particularly if the entire group is involved all at once and there is music playing in the background. You may then choose to add more layers, build up the facial features, add paint or simply leave the mask as is.

Puppets

Suggested materials: *head:* styrofoam balls (4–6 inches in diameter), large cardboard boxes, foam core sheets (1 inch thick), toilet paper and paper towel tubes, various styrofoam shapes, carpenter's glue, straight pins, paperbags and multicolored construction paper cut into strips, cheesecloth, yarn or burlap threads, trimming, acrylic or tempera paints, small, medium and large brushes; *body, arms and legs:* an assortment of colorful and contrasting medium to heavyweight fabrics, cotton muslin, stuffing, wire coat hangers, wood dowelling, pliers.

Hand puppets

This type of puppet was used for the Punch and Judy scene in the carnival street theatre performance mentioned earlier. The head and neck of the puppet consist of a toilet roll tube and a styrofoam ball. Treat one end of the tube with carpenter's glue, then insert it into the styrofoam ball. From here, follow the same basic procedure as with the masks. Sculpt facial features out of the styrofoam shapes and arrange them on the face of the puppet. You may wish to trace the features on to the face first before gluing them on and pinning them in place. Then, use the papier mâché technique described above to add several layers of either the paperbag or construction paper strips to the entire head and neck of the puppet. For such small work, you will need to use smaller pieces of the paper. Allow for drying time between layers. Once dry, the puppet's face, head and neck may be painted. You may wish to attach other trimmings for the eyes, mouth, nose or ears (especially if the hand puppet is an animal). Arrange yarn or burlap threads and glue on to the head for hair.

While one individual or group builds the head, another could build the body of the puppet. Building the body of a hand puppet takes no time at all if you have access to either a sewing machine or a glue gun. A simple smock-like pattern can be traced or cut out and pinned on to double-width fabric (shoulders at the fold). Make sure the length of the smock will cover both the hand that is animating the puppet and most of the forearm. Stitch or glue (right sides together) two side seams, from the underside of the arms down to the base of the smock. Little mitt-like hands can be traced, cut out of cotton muslin, and sewn or glued together in the same manner. Stitch or glue the open wrists of the mitts to the open armholes of the smock (again, right sides together). Now, turn the whole thing right side out. Glue the open neck of the smock to the tube neck of the puppet. Pin, stitch or glue on extra trim for collars, hats, vests, aprons, jewelry, etc.

Rod puppets

Follow the same procedure as used for hand puppets but with a few adjustments. Primarily, this kind of puppet is animated with rods and not with the hand and fingers. Therefore, you will want to make some sort of adjustment to the head and neck area as well as to the body. Try gluing and inserting a piece of coat hanger or thin dowelling into the top or back of the puppet's head. Bend a hook into the coat hanger or add a wooden knob to the dowelling to improve the grip. This kind of adjustment enables the puppeteer to animate the puppet in front of them and on the floor. If you wish to play the puppet overhead, behind a storyboard, use a paper towel tube instead of a toilet paper tube for the puppet's neck. The longer tube now becomes the rod for head animation.

The body of a rod puppet is usually more detailed than that of the hand puppet. So, adapt the smock pattern to include arms, hands, legs and feet. When tracing or cutting the pattern, keep the arms and legs wide and long. Make the body out of cotton muslin. Stitch or glue right sides together, leaving the neck open. Turn right side out and stuff the body with lightweight, synthetic stuffing. I recommend stitching joints for wrists, elbows, shoulders, hips, knees and ankles as you stuff the body. Glue the body to the neck of the puppet. If your puppet has the paper towel tube for a rod, make a slit in the fabric, from lower to middle back, to slip the tube through. Scout the thrift stores, jumble or garage sales for baby and children's clothes to dress your puppet in. Later, you may wish to add two more rods at the wrists or at the elbows, especially if you are animating the puppet overhead.

Larger than life sized rod puppets

These were used for the King and Queen puppets in the carnival street theatre performance mentioned earlier. The heads were cut out of the sides of large cardboard boxes. A layer of thin foam core was glued to the front and back of the cardboard. The foam scraps were sculpted to form facial features. Cheesecloth was then stretched over the head and brushed with the glue and water mixture. Multicolored papier mâché substituted for the actual painting of the faces. Burlap threads served for the hair and beard; Mylar scraps and fancy trim were combined to make the crowns.

The bodies of the King and Queen puppets were basically two crosses, composed of 2 inch × ½ inch slats (shoulders) with a hole drilled through the middle to accommodate long, 1-inch thick dowelling (body). Cardboard tubing had been inserted into the puppets' heads in order to secure them on top of the dowelling. The cotton muslin hands were pinned to two large, heavy pieces of fabric draped over the shoulders as regal robes. Rods were inserted into the hands to aid in animating the arms.

Adapting the process for an integrated setting involves making mask and puppetry accessible to everyone. A strong sense of ensemble, therefore, is necessary to achieve this goal. This support system must ideally meet the needs of every individual in the group. For some, it is a sense of achievement. For others it is knowing that they've helped one another to achieve something. It could be as simple as animating a rod puppet with three puppeteers instead of one, or building a mask and constantly asking for input or suggestions. Time restraints and safety considerations may require that many of the materials be prepared in advance. For some individuals, mixing and matching the finished pieces may prove a more accessible introduction to mask and puppet building.

Performance

Who is the group performing for and why? Again, it comes down to communication. The added element of a private or public audience allows the group to take the process one step further. That is to say, the time has come to share the story with someone new. By focusing on the process and not the product, the group maintains a clear perspective on the work. Process brings us back to ensemble and the notion of working together to produce something. With an integrated cast, ensemble performance becomes a balancing act. It seeks to even out the scales by reducing any disparity in talent or ability.

In the carnival street theatre performance, Judy was played by a puppeteer with a visual disability. Her way of adapting to the experience was to set markers along the inside of the storyboard that she could feel with her left hand, while the right hand animated the puppet. This way, she knew exactly where to make her entrances and exits. The puppeteer who played Punch helped to make puppetry accessible to her by staying in constant physical contact with her and the puppet.

In this regard, it becomes apparent why we bother with mask and puppetry in an integrated setting. Some individuals require the added reinforcement of character that masks and puppets provide.[16] Mask, puppetry and theatre combine to bridge, visually and orally, any communication gap between performer and audience.

The benefits from such a performance reach everyone involved. The experience yields an enormous sense of pride in the performers. It also promotes public awareness. Sharing the work with and for others may eventually succeed in conquering social stigmas surrounding disabilities in general, in favor of a healthier and more productive sense of community.

Notes

1 I use the term integration to describe 'the full, active and equal participation and acceptance of persons with disabilities into the society in which they live. A key to implementing this idea is to provide persons with disabilities the most "normal" environment possible in all areas of social life, which includes, in addition to education, employment, housing and medical care, the ability to participate in social, cultural and leisure activities', quoted in R. Richard, 'A descriptive analysis of two approaches to the use of drama with persons with a disability', unpublished MA thesis, Concordia University, Montreal, 1992.

2 I use the term disability or disabilities to refer to 'a condition which makes the completion of a task or tasks more difficult. This condition may be sensory, intellectual or physical in nature', quoted in B. Warren 'Integration through the theatre arts: responses to theatrical performance integrating persons with a disability', unpublished paper, 1991.

3 I must acknowledge Bil Baird, renowned American puppet master, for this definition.

4 The concepts and exercises presented here stem from my own voice training. I have chosen to adapt and simplify them for the purposes of this chapter. They are discussed in greater detail in K. Linklater, *Freeing the Natural Voice*, New York: Drama Book Publishers, 1978.

5 This game was introduced to me by Dean Gilmour, a Toronto-based theatre artist and clown, to whom I am also indebted for my knowledge of neutral mask, clown and commedia dell'arte. I've adapted his Le Coq-based mask exercises to suit the needs of this chapter.

6 C. Astell-Burt, *Puppetry for Mentally Handicapped People*, London: Souvenir Press, 1981, p. 44.

7 I first did this exercise as a part of my actor voice training with David Smukler at York University. I have since adapted it for my work with mask and puppetry.

8 Enid Kaplan, an artist and a dear friend, shared this exercise with me as a technique for tapping into and trusting one's creative resources. I've chosen to take the exercise one step further, by including the actual building of puppets.

9 I use the term cotton drop (known also in the theatre as a scrim or cyclorama) to refer to any size, white or natural cotton fabric, stretched taut, on to which light and images are projected. In the case of shadow puppetry, the image (puppet) is

animated flush against the stretched cotton drop, with the light source (here, the flashlight) defining the image from approximately 30 to 60 cm away (recommended for a 6 ft × 4 ft drop). The puppeteer(s) should position themselves outside the beam of light; otherwise they will destroy the illusion (with their own shadow) for the audience, viewing the image from the opposite side of the cotton drop.

10 This is actually 'muppeteering' technique, and the exercises were those taught to me by muppeteer Gordon Robertson.

11 A storyboard provides a proscenium style playing area for marionettes, hand and rod puppets. The puppeteers are masked from the audience's view, animating the puppets from behind the storyboard. The puppets play to the audience from inside a picture frame stage (proscenium). In the case of the marionette, the puppeteers animate the puppets from above the stage; with the hand and rod puppets, the puppeteers animate them overhead. The colorfully striped booths used for Punch and Judy shows illustrate a classic example of a storyboard. A makeshift storyboard, therefore, can be any structure used to mask the puppeteers from the audience, to focus attention on the puppet(s). It could be as simple as a table turned on its side, or a cardboard refrigerator box with a picture frame window cut out. The cotton drop described in Note 9 may also serve as a makeshift storyboard.

12 See Note 5.

13 C. Astell-Burt, *Puppetry for Mentally Handicapped People*, London: Souvenir Press, 1981, p. 46.

14 C. Astell-Burt, *Puppetry for Mentally Handicapped People*, London: Souvenir Press, 1981, p. 103.

15 L. Appel, *Mask Characterisation: An Acting Process*, Carbondale and Edwardsville: Southern Illinois University Press, 1982, p. 7.

16 C. Astell-Burt, *Puppetry for Mentally Handicapped People*, London: Souvenir Press, 1981, p. 109.

Chapter 11

Arts for children in hospitals

Helping to put the 'art' back in medicine

Judy Rollins

Hospitalization has long been recognized as a stressful experience for everyone, but research indicates that it is especially difficult for children. With proper support, however, children can survive and even grow from the hospital experience. In recent years we have come to recognize that the arts can play a signifiacnt role in that support[1].

What hospitalization is like for children

A dominating feature of childhood is children's sense of powerlessness and lack of control over what happens to them.[2] Possibly nowhere is this more evident than when children are hospitalized. This sense of powerlessness, added to their illness and limited understanding, increases their vulnerability.[3] Children are not simply smaller versions of adults; they are constantly growing and changing. Thus, not only do they experience illness and hospitalization differently than do adults, but they also experience it differently from one year – or even one day – to the next.[4]

Stressors of hospitalization

Many stressors are inherent in hospitalization. Upon admission, children are required to submit their small bodies to adult control and restriction. They are rarely permitted to refuse or even delay treatments, medications, and procedures. In the passive role of patient, they are poked and prodded, constant recipients of 'things' being done to them, things they may not fully understand, which leaves them feeling powerless and confused. Coupled with limited opportunities to make meaningful choices, emotions often are intense and confusing.[5]

The hospital environment

Hospitals seethe with the unfamiliar. Children hear strange sounds, and also very loud ones, especially in intensive care settings. For the baby in an incubator, even the popping of an envelope when opening rubber gloves can be as loud as a pneumatic drill.[6] High levels of noise can result in disengagement from the environment; extreme noise may further promote a sense of helplessness and powerlessness. However, sounds do not need to be loud to be troublesome. For example, hearing a child crying softly in another room can be frightening for other children. They may wonder why the child is crying, what the child did to cause this to happen, and 'Are they going to do the same thing to me?'

Children are faced with many strange sights when hospitalized. From cords or wires on walls that look like monsters at night, anything can be scary if you do not know what it is. They see many strangers, usually over 50 in their first 24 hours of hospitalization. The observation below describes a common hospital scene:

> The wards are reached through a very long corridor on to which spill visitors, staff, relatives, doctors discussing patients, and patients. There are doors to toilets, more corridors, A&E [Accident and Emergency], wards, shops and operating theatres. Some of the doors have signs which say 'Emergency theatres' and there are people standing around in their theatre greens, very old and ill looking people on trolleys, and people who look like your next door neighbor walking around in their slippers and nightwear. It certainly is a slice of life, some of which will never have been seen before, particularly by young children.[7]

We often underestimate the effects of the sense of smell, which reaches more directly into our memory and emotions than any of the other senses. Medicinal smells can produce anxiety, and unpleasant odors can increase heart rate and respiration. Illness and medication may alter the sense of taste, which is related to smell, so food, if the child is able to eat, may taste bad, or simply be different from that served at home. Further, treatment may require nasty-tasting medicines or preparation mixtures for procedures.

Finally, touch is an important consideration. Although some touches the child receives when hospitalized may be comforting, others may be painful or even confusing, for example, when children are poked in areas they have been told to never let strangers touch.

Dignity

In recent years, discussions about the dignity of the child in the hospital are becoming more common in the healthcare literature. However, a clear definition of dignity is lacking: 'Dignity is a slippery concept, most easily understood when it has been lost.'[8] Although no consensus exists regarding the age at which people believe that dignity becomes an issue with children, research confirms that privacy and dignity are not always respected on children's wards,[9] which, for certain children could be the most difficult stressor of all.

Children's reactions to hospitalization

Although the age of the child is the best predictor, the ways in which children respond to hospitalization also depend on the child's previous experience with illness, separation, and hospitalization; innate or acquired coping skills; seriousness of the diagnosis; and available support systems.[10] Common reactions include separation anxiety, sadness, apathy or withdrawal, fears of the dark or health personnel, hyperactivity, aggression, sleep disturbances, and regression. A typical regression is the potty-trained child having 'accidents'. Children who lose control over a previously mastered skill may feel shame and decreased self-esteem.[11] Behavioral regression frequently continues after hospitalization. Children may not reach their pre-hospital level of development until well after discharge.

Negative outcomes from hospitalization may last as many as ten years or more, especially for young children who undergo multiple, intrusive procedures, experience lengthy hospitalizations, and have parents who are highly anxious or who cope ineffectively with stress. An increasing incidence of post-traumatic stress disorder (PTSD) has been noted in children following life-threatening illnesses or injuries and life-endangering medical procedures.[12]

The arts as tools for coping with hospitalization

Adults who are hospitalized encounter many of the same issues that children face. The difference, however, is that adults typically have the cognitive ability to understand and make sense of their surroundings, and have some skills to cope with their experiences. Children, particularly young ones, usually need some help sorting out the situation. They may feel powerless and yet lack the courage or the words to express their feelings. This is where the arts come in: 'Art can be a way of asking questions, seeking information, provoking thought, communicating, and offering something about the world as perceived by humans.'[13]

Before reviewing some of the ways in which participating in the arts can help children to cope with hospitalization and illness, a distinction must be made between the therapeutic use of the arts and the expressive (e.g. art, music, dance, poetry, drama) therapies:

> In the first instance, artists and other caring adults facilitate children's engagement in expressive activities that may be therapeutic. For example, children may communicate verbally or nonverbally their thoughts, feelings, and concerns through or while engaging in these expressive activities. Expressive therapies, however, are conducted by expressive therapists who receive special training to interpret and prescribe specific expressive activities. A certification or licensing process is involved. Individuals without these credentials can do meaningful work with children,

but they must be aware of their limitations and not cross the boundary into territory for which they are unprepared.[14]

This discussion focuses on the therapeutic use of the arts for children where the artist is facilitator of the arts experience.[15] Participating in the arts with professional artists can help children deal with several realities of hospitalization:

1 *Pain and discomfort*: children can develop new coping strategies and distance and distract themselves.
2 *Limited opportunities to make decisions*: children can make choices and be independent.
3 *Passive roles*: children can be the active ones, the ones in charge.
4 *Emotions*: children can communicate both pleasant and unpleasant feelings, safely let go, and relive and master traumatic experiences.
5 *Physical limitations*: children can draw on their remaining abilities, imagine what they may be unable to do physically, and direct others to achieve their creative decisions.
6 *Unfamiliar environment*: children can do something 'normal' and familiar, share experiences with others, and experience the joy of childhood.
7 *Opportunities for learning and growth*: children can demonstrate understanding of their condition and treatment, experience closure through a completed project, and develop potential for a lifelong interest in the arts and creative expression.[16]

Using the arts therapeutically, artists should avoid initiating conversation about the child's illness, yet be able to listen and to talk about it if the child introduces the topic. This policy provides children with the choice of using the arts to escape their illness and situation for a time. The expressive therapist may have a different goal and thus a different approach.

With the arts, there is no one right way to express something. This reality promotes success and all of the good feelings that go along with it. In the space of a moment or two, the arts can transform a child from victim to victor.

Choices, choices, choices

Perhaps the arts most significant contribution to helping children cope with hospitalization is its intrinsic capacity to provide many opportunities for making choices. The core of the creative process is one of problem solving and decision making. In painting, for example, a child can choose what to paint, what brush or other tool to use, the width and length of lines, colors, etc., and when the painting is finished.

Children unable to physically engage in an activity still may be able to make creative decisions, which the artist can carry out under the child's direction. One rainy afternoon, for example, an eight-year-old boy and I completed a painting together. Only one day post-op, the child had one hand tethered to an IV pole, and generally was very weak. He selected the subject for the painting; the paint colors; the width, length, and other qualities of brush strokes; and decided when the painting was finished. My hands were simply his tools; the piece that emerged was truly 'his' in every important way.

Artists who work in hospitals usually quickly discover that for a number of reasons children may choose *not* to participate in an arts experience. However, by simply offering a creative experience to a child, the artist has given the child an incredible gift: to how many people in the hospital can a child say 'No' and have that 'No' honored? This opportunity may be the first and only one that the child has had that day.

The campfire effect

A child's creative product (e.g. painting, song, dance, story) is often a 'literal' or direct expression of the child's experience. However, at other times the product may serve as a starting point for unrepresented content that the child wants to communicate. This phenomenon – which I like to call the campfire effect – is the result of an activity or experience that provides a focal point shared by the individuals involved that serves to increase conversation in both quantity and intensity.[17] Much like sitting around a campfire with friends, while sitting around the drawing, painting, poem, story, or other creative piece, children will sometimes take this opportunity to share whatever is on their minds – their treatments, medications, worries, hopes, dreams, fears. The transfer of focus from the child to the product seems to relax the child by relieving the pressure of being the object of direct communication.

Research findings

A small but growing body of research supports that physiological processes may take place through contact with the arts. Studies indicate a relationship between arts experiences and the release of endorphins – the body's own pain reliever, relaxant, and mood enhancer.[18] Researchers report significant increases in salivary immunoglobulin A (IgA), an antibody that provides defence against various infections,[19, 20] and oxygen saturation levels, an indicator of respiratory regularity directly affected by the individual's behavioral state and degree of pain.[21]

Technology sometimes makes this visible for the artist. For example, children at our hospital are frequently attached to equipment to monitor oxygen saturation levels. How exciting to step into a room when a musician is strumming the guitar and singing softly, and watch this level slowly rise on the child's monitor. Even when the child is unconscious, the music seems to filter through, and the results are there for all to see just how powerful the arts can be.

Preparing artists to work with children in hospital

Most paediatric program directors agree that although artists may be able to work effectively with adults without preparation, working with children demands more. We use the following formal selection, training, and supervisory process to help to quell the concerns of hospital staff, parents, and even the artist themselves.

Artist selection

Preparation begins with the recruitment and selection of artists. Although each step of the preparation process is important, if appropriate artists have not been selected, no amount of training or supervision can make up the difference. We consider the following qualities essential:

1   Genuine interest in children, a caring attitude, and sensitivity to cultural and ethnic values.
2   Knowledge and experience in a chosen art form.
3   Respect for the child's creative process and products.
4   Appreciation and respect for the power of the arts and an understanding of personal limitations.
5   Flexibility.
6   Sense of humor.
7   Ability to collaborate with others.
8   No health condition that could result in harm to the children or to the artist.[22]

Training

The content and extent of training depend upon the role the artist will assume. Substantive training is needed for artists working as integral members of the healthcare team. Some topics that are frequently included in training are:

- what hospitalization is like for children and their families
- children's psychosocial and developmental needs and ways in which the arts can support them
- communicating with children and families
- relationships with children and families
- safety considerations
- infection control
- confidentiality
- cultural issues
- death and dying

- stimulating creativity
- adapting arts experiences for children who are hospitalized.[23]

Most paediatric hospitals prefer artists who will interact with the children, even one-time performers who primarily see their role as entertainers. Other important considerations regarding entertainment include:

1   Is it appropriate for the developmental age of the children?
2   Could it cause confusion or misconceptions about anything that might happen in the hospital?
3   Might it engender fears or fantasies about being harmed in any way?
4   Does it contain religious themes or content that might trouble some families?
5   Does it avoid any suggestion of violence (including the use of weapons) or death?
6   Does it avoid the use of masks or costumes that might frighten young children?
7   Does it invite children's participation in appropriate and non-competitive ways?[24]

Internship

A clinical internship provides an opportunity for artists to (a) practice their art in the paediatric setting under supervision, and (b) evaluate whether or not this is the kind of work they want to do. We begin the clinical experience by having new artists shadow experienced artists-in-residence for a time or two, and then we schedule three internship sessions for new artists to apply their work in the setting under supervision. The program coordinator role models appropriate interactions and offers the artist interns tips on ways to adapt their art forms to the children's healthcare setting. After conducting the three sessions, we together assess the readiness to end the internship period.

Ongoing education and support

Although artists usually feel fairly confident at the completion of the internship, most tell us that it typically takes about six months to really feel comfortable in the paediatric setting. After the internship period, artists find it helpful to have formal and informal mechanisms in place to provide ongoing opportunities for problem solving, continued learning, mutual support, and growth. We hold regular staff meetings, usually over a potluck dinner, to provide this support and for artists to hear what others are doing, discuss upcoming plans and arrange to work together on certain special events, share information and resources, and to simply enjoy each others company.

Practical activities

Recent research indicates that people who are hospitalized are more likely to engage in arts activities that offer new or interesting experiences.[25] In planning arts activities, it is fun to try something that children would not expect to do in a hospital. For example, one morning I gathered fresh snow in washbasins for children to make snow sculptures, which they then painted. We took photos to capture the memory before the snow melted.

On the other hand, an important concept in helping children cope with hospitalization is 'normalizing' the environment with attention to what is familiar, not unique. This concept drives strategies such as encouraging children to wear their own rather than hospital clothing; to maintain sleep, meal, and other routines as much as possible; to continue schoolwork, etc. Arts activities can follow this approach by focusing on what the child likes to do, incorporating seasonal and holiday themes, 'softening' medical equipment and personalizing the child's room with art, and facilitating a group project to provide a sense of community with other patients, family members, staff, and friends.

Safety is an important practical consideration. Certain art supplies or techniques, for example, can be harmful for children. However, in many cases substitutions can be used to eliminate the risk.[26] Yet, after eliminating obvious hazards for any child, the next consideration must always be 'Is this a safe activity for this particular child?' For example, certain activities, such as printmaking with fruits and vegetables – seemingly quite innocent – can be devastating for a child with a compromised immune system. When in doubt, artists should always ask.

Other factors to consider concerning the child include:

- the child's age
- reason for hospitalization
- anticipated hospital stay
- condition, illness, or injury and level of understanding about it
- physical effects and limitations
- interests
- present mood
- activity restrictions
- recent or upcoming experiences – good or bad
- cognitive disabilities.

A child able to join a group art activity, for example, will likely enjoy the additional element of socialization.

Visual arts

Visual arts activities are popular with children in hospitals. Often only simple materials are required and children can set the pace, working for a time and then putting things aside when tired. On the other hand, materials can be sophisticated. Artists now can bring laptop computers, digital cameras and PhotoShop to incorporate technology into children's art.

See Table 11.1 for a sampling of visual arts activities that are popular with children in hospitals. Many visual arts activities can be extended easily to group projects for establishing a sense of community among children. By helping children symbolically become part of something bigger, such activities help to relieve the isolation they often feel when confined to a hospital room.

Table 11.1 Sampling of visual arts activities

Marbling – floating colours on a liquid, creating designs, and capturing the resultant image in a contact print. Use as background for drawing, greeting cards, covering for boxes, cut into strips and woven, or cut or torn as material for an individual or group collage.

Materials	*Instructions*
• Can of white foamy shaving cream • Liquid watercolour paint • Styrofoam packing trays • Tongue depressors • Paper (with some 'tooth') • Paper towels	1 Squirt shaving cream into the tray. 2 Dribble paint on shaving cream and create design with tongue depressor. 3 Press paper lightly on shaving cream, lift and scrape off excess with tongue depressor. 4 Wipe paper with paper towels and set aside to dry.

Leaf and berry prints* – pounding natural materials to create a design on cloth. Good for children dealing with anger post procedure or on a particularly bad day. For a community project, designate a section of a large cloth for each child and hang as a ward mural or use as a tablecloth for a special celebration.

Materials	*Instructions*
• Cloth, cotton or muslin (old hospital sheets work well) • Freshly picked green leaves • Berries • Waxed paper • A smooth rock that fits into child's hand • Vinegar and water solution (1 tbsp vinegar to 1 cup of water) • Washbasin or other container	1 Have child create a design with berries and leaves (vein side down) on waxed paper. 2 Cover with cloth and have child pound on the cloth with the rock until satisfied with the stains that appear. 3 Dip cloth in vinegar solution to set stains, wring out, and hang to dry. 4 Attach to cardstock and frame, or to a dowel or branch for wall hanging.

Sand candles* – creating candles in a moist sand mold. A recording of the sound of the ocean or some beach music can accompany the activity. An electric skillet on a cart can be taken room to room and plugged in occasionally to keep the wax liquid.

(*Continued overleaf*)

Table 11.1 Continued

Materials	Instructions
• Electric skillet • Empty coffee cans • Candle or canning wax, beeswax rather than petroleum-based because of the fumes • Crayons to add colour • Long-handled spoon • Small white birthday candles • Sand pail or washbasin containing new sand (intended for sandboxes) • Water • Oven mitts • Newspaper	1 Put wax in the coffee cans and the cans in electric skillet that contains a few inches of water, and heat over low to medium heat until the wax is melted. 2 Have child select crayon colour and peel off paper. Add to wax; stir occasionally until melted. 3 Moisten sand with water until it holds a shape, and ask child to make a simple negative shape in the sand. 4 Move mold from child's reach and pour in wax. When wax somewhat solid, insert birthday candle until only wick is showing, at site child selects. 5 When wax completely cool, help child remove candle from sand over newspaper.

Marble painting* – painting with paint-covered marbles. Babies and toddlers love to tilt or shake the container and watch the colours appear. Older children can move the container with more intent.

Materials	Instructions
• Small bowls • Tempera paints • Spoons • Flat container with clear lid • Paper cut to fit the bottom of container • Scissors • Newspaper	1 Pour colours child selects in the bowls and add a marble or two in each to coat with paint. 2 Put paper in the container, scoop a paint-laden marble with spoon, and place marble on the paper. 3 Apply lid and ask child to tilt or shake the container, making trails of paint on the paper. 4 Remove marble and add others until child is satisfied with the results. 5 Place painting on newspaper to dry.

* Adapted from Rollins, J. *Arts Activities for Children at Bedside*, Washington, DC: WVSA Arts Connection, 2004.

Music

Of all the art forms used in hospitals, music seems to have the broadest reach. Music can be used with all ages of individuals under almost any circumstances. Because hearing is still present when an individual is comatose, even the child who is unconscious or dying is believed to benefit from hearing music. Certain music is used to engage children, while other types are intended to help the dying child 'let go' peacefully.

Musicians can offer new and interesting experiences that engage children by bringing in an array of musical instruments from other cultures, demonstrating their use, and helping children play them. Favorites in our program to accompany our guitarist are kalimbas, xylodrums, and shekeres.

Singing requires very little, simply the desire 'to give some small voice to the everyday joy of the soul'.[27] Children and their families may have favorite songs, or the musician can introduce them to new ones. It is also fun to sing certain songs (e.g. 'Are You Sleeping', 'Down by the Station', 'White Coral Bells', 'Three Blind Mice') that, when sung or hummed at the same time, sound beautiful together.[28]

Dance

A dancer trained in the postmodern tradition will best be able to actively engage hospitalized children in dance. Postmodern dance hails the use of everyday movement as valid performance art, and claims that any movement is dance and any person can be a dancer, with or without training. Movement can happen with children standing, sitting, or lying down. Depending on the child's physical condition, dances can be made with movements ranging from eye blinks and nose wiggles to full-bodied jumping and falling, and everything in between. Dancing offers many choices, including the choice of music to accompany the activity.

Children enjoy 'movement conversations'.[29] Face to face with the child, the dancer and the child begin with some body parts touching (fingertips touching, elbows or feet together). The dancer moves for three to five seconds and becomes completely still and frozen, and then the child makes a movement and freezes. Once the basic physical conversation is established, the dancer begins to change the speed and the dynamic of the movement, and perhaps initiate longer movement sentences.

Another favorite is mirroring (see Figure 11.1). This activity allows the dancer to explore a child's range of motion and to support the child's choices physically and verbally. Positioned face to face with the child, the dancer will do what the child does for a while and then the child will do what the dancer does. At times they will work together to make the same motion.

Gathering a group of children together or even drawing in family members or staff at a child's bedside, the dancer can facilitate a group dance. One at a time, each individual makes a movement, which everyone follows. The movement is added to those made before to create a series of movements, a unique and beautiful community dance.

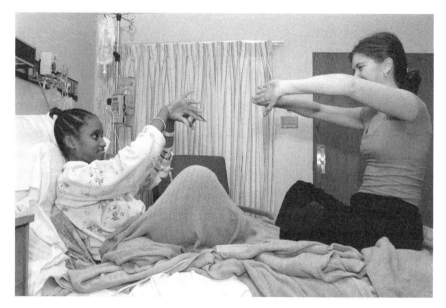

Figure 11.1 Mirroring allows the dancer to support the child's choices physically and verbally.

Storytelling

A well-chosen story allows children to deal indirectly with and discuss if they wish their difficult fears and realities. Some children simply enjoy stories as a fantasy escape. Storytellers frequently dress in costume or use props to further this element of fantasy. Story structure – with a beginning, a middle and an end – can provide a much-needed sense of predictability and closure for children who are ill. Classic stories, such as 'The Three Little Pigs' offer this same predictability. Hearing a familiar story when attempting to cope with an unpredictable illness gives children a sense of comfort and safety.

The storyteller can encourage children's participation by telling stories with chants, songs, rhythm, music, repetitious actions, and vocalizations. Through role play, children become powerful people in control of their destiny. Storytelling gives children 'a chance to play, to create, to imagine, to have sustained human contact, to have choice, to speak, to ask for what they want, to express themselves, to have the time enough to say what is really on their minds, to ask questions, to get the story they really need'.[30] Excellent tips for finding, learning, and telling stories can be found online.[31]

Creative writing

Writing is about discovery and children are often surprised by the insights that emerge as they write. Although paper and pencil are all that is needed, many hospitals now have laptop computers for children's use. In our program we like to give children large hard-cover sketchbooks to use as journals; the absence of lines encourages drawing as well.

Children can write about illness or non-illness related topics, and often need help getting started. Suggested topics could include what they see in their room or from their window, people, animals, something in their room that they don't understand, etc. A 'Top Ten list' – top ten things that make the child laugh, top ten most satisfying experiences, top ten petty annoyances, etc. – also is a popular way to begin.[32]

Many children enjoy poetry because its nature allows them to express themselves in metaphor. Various types of poems – rhyming couplet, quatrain, limerick, chiquan, haiku, shape poems, free form – can be explored. Poets frequently use props to get children started, such as blowing bubbles and asking children what they think of when they see bubbles. Children may enjoy writing music and lyrics as well.

Drama

Children love to dress in costume and be someone else for a time. As a princess, superhero, or other favorite character, a child's experience can be transformative and empowering. Children can act out favorite stories or make up their own, and perform for their families, friends, and staff. A number of children's hospitals now have performing areas for children to act out their roles. Role playing can provide insight for and about a child, and also be an excellent learning tool.

Puppets provide safe, vicarious outlets for impulses, fears, and fantasies, and can be used to educate and to entertain. Children tend to feel unthreatened when speaking for the puppet and assert themselves more than if they were speaking for themselves. Puppets can be made from simple materials, such as socks, paperbags, or even simply a piece of gauze draped over the hand and secured with a rubber band. Colored markers can be used to add features.

Clowns can bring joy and laughter to children, but must be carefully selected and trained. Regarding make-up, most hospital clowns wear little more than red noses to avoid frightening children. As with other artists, hospital clowns focus on engaging the child in the experience (e.g. teaching the child a magic trick), and even have their own code of ethics.[33]

Celebrating children's creativity

A goal of the arts in hospitals is to create good memories to counter the less pleasant ones that children experience. Celebrating their artistic achievements can foster this goal. Consider the following ways to let children know that their achievements are valued:

1 Avoid contests as competition detracts from the spirit of the arts.
2 Frame or mat their paintings or drawings.
3 Create simple anthologies of their poetry or stories.
4 Tape their songs.
5 Take pictures and videos.
6 Display their art throughout the hospital and the community, at places such as libraries, museums, or shopping centres.

The future

Increasing numbers of individuals and organizations around the world (e.g. Society for the Arts in Healthcare in the United States, National Network for the Arts in Health in the United Kingdom) share the vision that some day all hospitals will acknowledge and support the arts as an integral component of healthcare. The arts provide an opportunity for children to achieve tremendous growth while experiencing one of the greatest challenges of their lifetime. Let us hope that this day arrives without delay.

Notes

1 J. Rollins, 'The Arts in Health-Care Settings,' *Meeting Children's Psychosocial Needs Across the Health-Care Continuum*, eds. J. Rollins et al. (Austin, Texas: ProEd, 2005).
2 G. Lansdown, 'Children's Rights,' in B. Mayall (ed.) *Children's Childhoods Observed and Experienced*, London: Falmer Press, 1994.
3 G. Bricher, 'Children in the Hospital: Issues of Power and Vulnerability', *Pediatric Nursing* 26, 2000, 277–282.
4 J. Rollins and C. Mahan, *From Artist to Artist-in-Residence: Preparing Artists to Work in Pediatric Healthcare Settings*, Washington, DC: Rollins and Associates, 1996.
5 J. Rollins and C. Mahan, *From Artist to Artist-in-Residence: Preparing Artists to Work in Pediatric Healthcare Settings*, Washington, DC: Rollins and Associates, 1996, p. 121.
6 G. Grumet, 'Pandemonium in the Modern Hospital', *New England Journal of Medicine* 328, 1993, 433–437.
7 P. Reed *et al.*, 'Promoting the Dignity of the Child in Hospital', *Nursing Ethics* 10, 2003, 62–73.
8 P. Reed *et al.*, 'Promoting the Dignity of the Child in Hospital', *Nursing Ethics* 10, 2003, 62–73, p. 67.
9 G. Rylance, 'Privacy, Dignity and Confidentiality: Interview Study with Structured Questionnaire', *British Medical Journal* 318, 1999, 301.
10 Hockenberry, M. *et al.*, *Wong's Nursing Care of Infants and Children*, Saint Louis, MD: Mosby, 2003.

11 D. Popovich, 'Preserving Dignity in the Young Hospitalized Child', *Nursing Forum* 38, 2003, 12–17.

12 American Psychiatric Association, *Diagnostic and Statistical Manual of Mental Disorders*, Washington, DC: American Psychiatric Association, 1994.

13 S. Baumann, 'Art as a path of inquiry', *Nursing Science Quarterly* 12, 1999, 107.

14 J. Rollins and C. Mahan, *From Artist to Artist-in-Residence: Preparing Artists to Work in Pediatric Healthcare Settings*, Washington, DC, Rollins and Associates, 1996, p. 121.

15 J. Rollins and L. L. Riccio, *ART is the heART: An Arts-in-Healthcare Program for Children and Families in Home and Hospice Care*, Washington, DC, WVSA Arts Connection, p. 48.

16 J. Rollins, 'Art: Helping Children Meet the Challenges of Hospitalisation', *Inter-ACTA* 3, 1995, 36–41.

17 J. Rollins, 'Tell me about it: Drawing as a Communication Tool for Children with Cancer', *Journal of Pediatric Oncology Nursing* 22, 2005, 203–221.

18 A. Goldstein, 'Thrills in response to music and other stimuli', *Physiological Psychology* 8, 1980, 126–129.

19 R. Lambert and N. Lambert, 'The Effects of Humor on Secretory Immuno-globulin A levels in School-Aged Children', *Pediatric Nursing* 21, 1995, 16–19.

20 D. Lane, 'The Effect of a Single Music Therapy Session on Hospitalized Children as Measured by Salivary Immunoglobin A, Speech Pause Time, and a Patient Opinion Likert Scale', Doctoral Dissertation, Case Western Reserve University, 1990.

21 S. Collins and K. Kuck, 'Music Therapy in the Neonatal Intensive Care Unit', *Neonatal Network* 9, 1991, 23–26.

22 J. Rollins and C. Mahan, *From Artist to Artist-in-Residence: Preparing Artists to Work in Pediatric Healthcare Settings*, Washington, DC: Rollins and Associates, 1996, pp. 1–2.

23 J. Rollins and C. Mahan, *From Artist to Artist-in-Residence: Preparing Artists to Work in Pediatric Healthcare Settings*, Washington, DC: Rollins and Associates, 1996, p. 10.

24 Johnson, B., Jeppson, E. and Redburn, L. *Caring for Children and Families: Guide-lines for Hospitals*, Bethesda, MA: Association for the Care of Children's Health, 1992, pp. 245–246.

25 S. Stoner and S. Sahni, 'How do we Know we make a Difference?', presentation, Society for the Arts in Healthcare Annual Conference, Chicago, Illinois, 29 April 2006.

26 M. Rossol, *The Artist's Complete Health and Safety Guide*, New York: Lyons Press, 2001, 366–369.

27 M. Leunig, *The Prayer Tree*, Pymble, HarperCollins, 1991.

28 For an extensive list of songs that go together, see Judy Rollins, *Arts Activities for Children at Bedside*, Washington, DC: WVSA Arts Connection, 2004, p. 69.

29 K. Marty, quoted in J. Rollins, *Arts Activities for Children at Bedside*, Washington, DC: WVSA Arts Connection, 2004, p. 75.

30 S. Gordon, quoted in J. Rollins, *Arts Activities for Children at Bedside*, Washington, DC: WVSA Arts Connection, 2004, p. 57.

31 A. Fraenkel, 'Storytelling tips', *SacredVoices Online* 11 September 2001, 14 May 2006 (http://sacredvoices.com/docs/tips.htm).

32 S. Dion, *Write Now: Maintaining a Creative Spirit While Homebound and Ill*, Teaneck, NJ: Puffin Foundation, 2000.

33 See *British Medical Journal* website (http://bmjjournals.com/cgi/content/full/319/7212/792/a/DC1).

Chapter 12

Friends' Arts in Healthcare Programs at the University of Alberta Hospital

Fostering a healing environment

Susan Pointe and Shirley Serviss

The harpist is in today, I notice as I walk into the hospital main atrium. My feet slow to the melodic notes that float past the patients in wheelchairs waiting to be ushered up to Dialysis. I glance up to admire the many colourful patient window paintings that dot the 55 windows from the first to fifth floor. As I near the Art Gallery, I see a patient looking in the floor to ceiling windows at the art as he adjusts his IV pole. I catch his attention and say, 'Come on in.' In the gallery, a young couple is asking a volunteer about the artists currently exhibiting. Three visitors, outpatients or visiting family members of patients are relaxing, waiting, and lost in their thoughts. A little boy of five and his mom are mining through the art materials seeking a choice project to complete. As I take my seat at my desk, my colleague grins and says, 'We received another letter.' Knowing what she means. I read:

> I would like to express my appreciation to you in relation to your musi-
> cian . . . When I was doing an invasive procedure on a young man with
> Down's syndrome and Al was in the unit playing his guitar and singing,
> I asked Al if he could stay for a few minutes at this patient's bedside to
> serve as a diversion to the patient while I was performing the procedure.
> Al stayed and played for as long as I required him to, and made the
> procedure go extremely smoothly with no requirements for sedating medi-
> cations. This form of therapy is extremely beneficial both for patients and
> families, and staff members alike.
> (Advanced Nurse Practitioner, Cardiac Surgery[1])

At Capital Health's University of Alberta Hospital (UAH) this is business as usual. The arts have become an integral part of hospital life. Unlike any other hospital in Canada today, the UAH hosts a purpose-built art gallery, an art collection of over 1200 artworks, and an Artists On the Wards program where five permanent part-time staff artists work one on one at the bedside with adult acute care patients. This chapter will explore how these services and programs began and how they continue to flourish.

University of Alberta Hospital Art Collection and McMullen Art Gallery

The foundation of the Arts in Healthcare Programs

In 1986, the University of Alberta Hospital finally received its much needed expansion into the newly named Walter C. Mackenzie [WMC] Healthsciences Centre. With over 800 beds, the centre houses the University of Alberta Hospital, the Mazankowski Heart Institute and the Stollery Children's Hospital. It is a national centre of excellence in transplantation, critical care, neuroscience, medicine, renal, emergency and trauma care. The centre has become one of Canada's leading clinical, research and teaching hospital complexes, treating more than 700,000 patients annually from across western and northern Canada.

As the centre was being developed, William McMullen, a University Hospital board member and a group of influential art collectors and artists called for the development of an art collection and a gallery into the hospital plans. The University of Alberta Hospital Board supported the development of a collection under a provincial program encouraging the purchase of artwork with a percentage of provincial capital dollars, and amassed over 750 original artworks to be permanently displayed in the new hospital.

Named for its founder, the 1000 square foot McMullen Art Gallery opened its doors in 1986. Fronted by floor-to-ceiling windows, the gallery is located next to a main hospital entrance, well situated to foster awareness in a large hospital complex.

Friends of University of Alberta Hospitals

This integration of an art collection and gallery into the WMC Centre plans could not have happened without the support of another key player, the Friends of the University Hospitals. In 1986, the hospital looked to the Friends to financially support permanent professional staff to direct the gallery and assist in growing the collection. Being a non-profit organization with a mission to enhance patient comfort, the Friends viewed the gallery and collection as an innovative patient-comfort service fitting well within their mandate.

The Friends responded, by establishing annual operating funds for the gallery and employing a full-time arts professional with experience in public programming and collection management.[2] The Friends also set up a volunteer program, where volunteers (known as gallery guides) would cover weekly three to four hour shifts to provide security for the gallery, and act as educational resources for the visitors.

Under the Friends' direction, the gallery's mandate expanded to serve as more than an art gallery; to serve as a *patient-comfort-zone* that encourages patient well-being by providing an environment that celebrates hope, compassion, beauty, creativity and life. Obtaining patient feedback is very important to the Friends, and therefore we have a visitor comment card that poses the question 'Have we made an impression on you?' Some of our patients wrote:

> Thank you for providing such a healing place in my traumatic time. After being poked and prodded, I come here to calm down before I leave the hospital to face the rest of life . . . I know now, for me, it will be a part of my healing.

> I truly find this one of God's quiet places in the hospital! Thank you so much.

> This is a wonderful healing and nourishing space. It is indeed comforting, health inducing, beautiful, hopeful, and affirming . . . Thank-you.[3]

And other patients' family members wrote:

> It [the gallery] is a place of peace and renewal for me. I first discovered the gallery when my son lay deathly ill upstairs. It was a place of refuge and sanctuary.

> Thank you for a bit of peace for my sick child. He still deserves to see beautiful things even if he can't go outside.

> Coming here with my son has been a reprieve from all the madness and stress from cancer! We relax and enjoy it here! Thank you for having a little piece of heaven here on earth![4]

Under the Friends' direction, the gallery exhibition programming has matured and the art collection has grown. Today, the gallery receives 17,000 patients, family members, staff and public visitors per year.[5] Each year, we select five exhibitions out of approximately 35 submissions. We seek exhibitions that are sensitive in content to the needs of hospital patients and their families – exhibitions that promote emotional, physical, and spiritual well-being, and a diversity of ethnic backgrounds, cultures and heritage. We also endeavor to give a broad range of community groups, curators, artists, heritage and art organizations an opportunity to create exhibitions celebrating diverse aspects of art and culture. In our submissions, we also look for exhibit proposals that outline resources to assist our first-time gallery visitors such as extended labels, artists' statements and visitor feedback opportunities, and provide hands-on or sensory exploration opportunities for visitors. The collection has grown to now hold 1200 pieces of artwork. It is installed in priority in patient and family rooms, waiting areas, public pedways, atriums and staff conference rooms, and offices.

Today, the Friends support two full-time and five part-time staff to manage the collection, operate the gallery, and the Artists On the Wards program. The hiring of the Art Advisor, in 1986, was key in the development of the Artists On the Wards. Unlike most hospitals in Canada, the Friends financed a full-time arts and collection professional for the hospital whose sole mandate was to advise the hospital in gallery management, art collecting and to potentially grow arts programming to meet the needs of patients.

Taking the arts to the bedside

The Friends Artists On the Wards Program

For 12 years the Friends received considerable acclaim for their support and management of the gallery and art collection. However, in 1998, despite strong attendance in the gallery from patients, family members and staff, the Friends acknowledged their dissatisfaction with not being able to reach all acute care patients.

In October 1999, the Friends agreed to fund a pilot project in which three visual artists would be hired to work with patients for a period of four months. The aim was to introduce patients to professional practicing artists, lead patients in talking about art, watching an artist create for them, and creating art themselves. The ultimate goal was that the artist would bring the patient to an interest and comfort level where they would continue to learn about art and ultimately create (draw, paint, sculpt) on their own.

After training on each unit with the nursing supervisors, each artist would work eight hours per week in the pulmonary, cardiology, cardio-thoracic, and the eating disorders units in the University Hospital. The visual artists began by visiting with the patients, and introducing the program. Then, if encouraged by the patient, the artist would guide the patient in painting, drawing or sculpting images or messages of their choice. If patients were physically unable to create, the artist would create for them.

The most popular bedside activities became those where the patient would create a small part of what would become a larger installation in the hospital. Known as the Ceiling Tile Project and the Tile Wall Project, these installations are made up of ceiling tiles and ceramic wall tiles on which patients or family members paint images or messages of their choice. Not only did these projects provide a creative outlet, but they also enriched patient visits. Painting tiles together created a new relationship between a patient and his estranged daughter and enhanced the quality of the visits between an oil-rig worker and his elderly mother as they enjoyed working on a project together. Each tile stands as a powerful testament of the individuals who passed through the hospital. Some tiles act as an important memorial for the family who lost a loved one. The tiles are raw with messages of hope and courage, and have a powerful effect on the viewer.

Within the four-month period we constructed patient feedback and staff evaluation forms which were filled out. Verbal and written feedback from nursing and medical staff was immediate and overwhelmingly positive:

> Patients . . . are under a great deal of stress, very anxious about their lives. The interaction with the artists seems to give them a sense of control, purpose and accomplishment that brings balance back to many of them. Clearly, physical healing is only one aspect of well-being and I think [this] program plays a significant role in the psychological healing associated with disease.
>
> (Dr. Dale Lein[6])

In her nursing evaluation of the program, Carrie Briones also noticed beneficial effects:

> The times that we have observed the artist with the patients, the mood of the patients seems to be brighter . . . The patients have something to do and this may lessen the amount of depression . . . [They] also seem more motivated and determined to get involved in returning to daily activities.[7]

Other nursing staff members wrote:

> The artists have helped patients not only take their mind off their illness but often to express their feelings when they have been unable to do so. It gives a purpose to days and months and a sense of accomplishment to see what they have created. As a staff member I feel it has brought color, and joy to a very serious atmosphere and I enjoy visiting different units to see the works in progress. It has made the UAH a fun place to work. I commend the artists for their work and the Friends of University Hospitals for funding such a worthwhile project. Keep up the good work![8]

> Hospitals/medical personnel concentrate on the body, the medical, the illness. [The artist] provides an opportunity to concentrate on the spiritual, the emotional the holistic. [The artist's] open non-judgmental approach is a real gift. Sometimes they [patients] participate in the artwork and other times just enjoy watching her create. Provides a 'mental break' from other hospital activities . . . Any activity that can improve emotional and/or spiritual well-being can ultimately help to improve physical well-being.[9]

Patient feedback was equally positive:

> Thank-you so much for the art supplies. I spent many hours playing and found that it was great for venting my frustrations. Some of my work

showed a lot of emotion with its vivid colors! This is a great program. Please keep the program going.[10]

I want to express a very heartfelt thank you to Nancy Corrigan. Her timing on stopping into my room to ask if I'd like to contribute to the 'look in your eye' mural could not have been more perfect. I spent a few hours creating in which I forgot where I was. I had a wonderful time.[11]

The Friends were delighted with the success of the pilot, the demand for artists in other units, the annual matching grant support coming from the Alberta Foundation for the Arts and a one-time grant by the Canadian Millennium Partnership Program. The Friends chose to match the incoming grants and committed to ongoing support of five part-time artists. Today we employ three visual artists, one poet/writer and one musician, each working 15 hours per week, servicing 34 nursing units throughout the hospital. These units include the Fire Fighters Burn Centre, the Emergency Ward, Medical Outpatients and Intensive Care as well as Cardiology, Dialysis, Gastroenterology, Hematology, Neurology, Plastics, Psychiatry, Pulmonary, Transplants, Trauma, Urology, and a number of surgical units.[12]

Five part-time artists cannot service 500 adult inpatient beds. However, due to the support of Volunteer Services, we recruit approximately 24 volunteer artists annually who assist our work. They range from art students to professional artists and bring a diversity of personalities, ages, and abilities to the program. The volunteer artists are trained and supervised by the staff artists, and they commit to three to four hours a week for a minimum of six months.

Is this program art therapy?

Art therapy is a psychotherapy specialization formally integrated into a diagnosis and treatment model. Generally, art therapists are clinical practitioners who use art as a tool to diagnose, analyze and interpret a patients' psychological profile. The art therapist uses art to uncover a patient's inner conflict or psychological processes, then assists in addressing the grief, anger, emotional or psychological illness that is present.[13]

The Artists-On-the-Wards program provides patients with the opportunity to work with a practicing artist, journal, write poetry, sing, song write, make art and not be in any kind of therapy. The patients have access to the artists and arts for mere pleasure, and yet the connecting and creating can be, in some cases, powerful in altering the physical, emotional or mental states of the patient. Shirley Serviss, our resident poet, writes:

I started to write poems for patients to reflect back to them the stories they shared with me about their lives and who they really were, not the disease or illness they happened to have. A man, partially paralyzed by a stroke, became once again the commanding officer of a radar unit stationed in the desert in the war as he told me his stories. When the nursing attendant came in to feed him his meal, she could hardly believe the transformation. He was no longer a miserable old man complaining about being uncomfortable; he was smiling.

Another time, I was referred to a patient who had had both his legs amputated and was understandably despondent. I shared some poems with him that spoke to his despair and search for meaning. When the clinical supervisor came in to ask if he was willing to try physiotherapy, he told her: 'I would have said no, but now I'm going to say yes.'[14]

The artists guide the patients to focus on joyful experiences, accomplishments, the future, or simply being well in the moment. From this place, the making of art becomes thoughtful, soothing and almost meditative. Also, these experiences can assist patients in regaining identity and individuality – making their mark in the hospital, broadcasting in the hospital *I exist and I am here*. And what the patients produce often provides them a level of joy if not pride. The realization of one's ability in any form of art is empowering. Therefore the artists also act as teachers or facilitators in bringing patients to a level of comfort in an area where they may continue to learn and create on their own ultimately contributing to their future wellness.

What exactly do they do at the bedside?

Since the program's inception, the artists have spent over 15,000 hours on the wards and have visited over 50,000 patients. They work mostly one on one, seeing between one and three or more patients per hour.[15] It is very important to the Friends that the artists make patient comfort a priority. Therefore, rather than trying to serve a high volume of patients, the artist ensures that each patient receives a quality visit (Figure 12.1).

Music

Our staff musician, Al Brant, plays music for the patients on his guitar. He will sing his own songs for patients, or ones they request. He also composes songs with and for the patients. More and more frequently, Al is requested by family members to play for patients as they are being disconnected from life support.

In support of Al's work, we host volunteer musicians who play a portable keyboard, a harp, the lute, guitar and Native American flutes for patients. Other volunteers simply sing at the bedside in response to patient requests – everything from country and western favorites to operatic pieces in other languages. Al Brant writes:

Music is a wonderful tool for breaking barriers. Whenever I enter a room

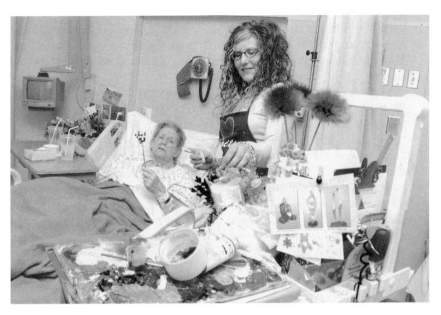

Figure 12.1 For those patients unable to create, the artists will paint to request on windows, sculpt creations to patients' specifications or draw portraits. One of our Visual Artists in Residence, Cornelia Osztovits.

the first thing I do is introduce myself and the program, let them know it is a free service. I usually start by asking what type of music they like; most times they will encourage me to play whatever I want. I usually pick a song that might bring up a good memory of home or just an uplifting song. I find that music can take a person away from their present situation for those few moments; you can see the patients daydream. Often, after the song is done, a conversation will ensue about thoughts that were triggered from the song.

If a patient is willing, I will get into the process of writing a song with them. I usually start this by pulling things out of conversations that occur, for instance if a patient is missing their home I might suggest for them to think about fond memories or funny moments that have happened. I find that most times a song does not get finished but the process is usually a good experience.

A couple of stories:

There was a patient I had played for in Cardiology ICU over a period of several months with no response. Quite often, in this job, you can play for a person one day and the next day they are gone and you usually never know what has happened to them. But one day I was walking past the elevators and this patient looked at me and said, 'I can see clearly now.' I looked at him a little strangely and he said it again. Then he said, 'You played that song for me while I was recovering from a heart transplant.' That song gave him hope. He then said, 'Thank you' and got on the elevator.

There was another patient whom I had been visiting who is a pianist. We would exchange songs, or she would sing a song while I played my guitar, then I would sing while she played guitar. This patient was in for a transplant and while in surgery ended up having a global stoke. The family asked if I would keep visiting her in ICU even though she was non-responsive. This patient did come back and after about three months, when she was out of ICU and in her own room, I would come up with our portable piano and place it in front of her. She started out with single notes and by the time she left for home she was trying to sing again. I recently received an e-mail from this patient; she said her piano playing is 80 per cent, her voice is coming back and she is starting to write songs.[16]

Poetry and writing

Our writer, Shirley Serviss, often begins by reading poetry to patients – her own poetry and that of other poets whose work is uplifting. Many patients have at least one poem from long ago still memorized, and are always delighted to recite – even while sitting in the Emergency.

Many of the poems our writers have written for patients have become treasured keepsakes, and have been read at funerals. Other poems have simply been used for patients and family members to articulate what they want to say to each other. Shirley writes:

At my invitation, a patient waiting for a heart transplant composed a touching poetic tribute to his wife. He went on to write a poem about his hopes for a new heart, and a poem bargaining with God for more time with his family. His daughter expressed her appreciation that her father had been encouraged to write. She had learned things about his thoughts and feelings through his poetry that she hadn't known because they weren't a family who could speak about these things. I encouraged her to write a poem for her father, which she did. Although this patient did not live, his daughter spoke of how poetry became a way for her family to say what was necessary at the time. Today, this family hosts an annual golf tournament in their Father's memory and they donate the monies raised to the Friends Artists On the Wards.

Although engaging patients to write poetry can be challenging, having poetry contests with deadlines has proved to be very inspiring for many patients and staff. The Friends have held four contests to date. To celebrate the winners of the contest, we host a reading in the gallery, where patients, their families and staff attend and read their poems in front of an audience. Whether or not they are winners, the contests encourage patients to put their feelings and experiences into words. Here are two examples:

Bedridden Haiku

All alone in bed
IV line in hand and neck
Uselessness fills me.

Limerick

A young man from the land of the bailer
Ended up with Acute Renal Failure
He'd grow up real fast
Innocence in the past
His new life he would now have to tailor.

In 2001, the Friends published a number of the patients' poems in a collection entitled *Read Two Poems and Call Me in the Morning*, which is still for sale in the gift shop. Since then, contest winners and honorable mentions have been framed and installed along a very busy pedway, known as the Poet's Walk. Woven along the wall, in between each piece, is a poem about writing poetry.

Projects where patients only have to contribute a few words are always successful. In one such project, Shirley outlined a tree on the wall of Medical Outpatients and invited people to write something they wanted to invite into their lives on a cut-out bird and perch it in the tree. They were asked to write something they wanted to release on a leaf and attach it to the wall so it was falling. Many patients confided in Shirley that it was helpful to name their hopes and fears and comforting to see they were shared by others.

Sometimes Shirley involves patients in writing a 'group poem' on a unit whiteboard. After gathering images from the patients in the unit, she composes a poem on the spot to write on the board. The writers also hand out 'Thoughts for the Day' and 'Poetic Medicine' – long, skinny poems rolled up and placed in prescription bottles – to patients, visitors and even doctors when a little poetic inspiration is in order. They give patients blank journals and autobiography duo-tangs containing questions to evoke positive memories with space for the patient to respond.

The writers have also installed a permanent writing desk in the patient library with an open journal where patients, visitors and staff are encouraged to record their experiences. The stories that are written there are very poignant and readers respond to each other with words of encouragement. One woman returned to the library to write in the journal a year after her sister's death in hospital. Another woman wrote:

> I sit here at a desk in the patient library. I'm not a patient but my son is . . . He goes in for heart surgery later today. Small at just over two pounds and almost four months pre-term. I'm scared . . . Even as the car slid off the road, all that was to be thought about was the small makings of the little person in my belly. . . . All that day, through the labor and the tests, I was told over and over again that he might not make it . . . This journal has helped me see that none of you quit and you still have hope.[17]

Visual art

Not surprisingly, the visual artists are the most noticeable on the units. One of our visual artists, Cornelia Osztovits, writes:

> As I wheel my brightly colorful cart on my path to my units, I flash smiles wherever I stroll and inform those I meet of our unique program and free workshops. I ride the freight elevator beside nurses, doctors, maintenance workers and patients with all kinds of medical transport equipment and testing mechanisms. My art cart stimulates curious and creative conversation and eases the silence amongst strangers. Smiles are contagious.[18]

For those patients who are physically unable to create, the artists will paint on windows, sculpt creations of the patients' specifications or draw portraits. One of our visual artists, Nancy Corrigan, writes:

> Once I drew a portrait of a lady who just was in the Burns Isolation area for a long time. Her face was disfigured and she was not in great spirits. I said to her I am going to give you a *makeover*. At first, she was not sure about having her portrait done but a humorous session of giving her pink cheeks, perfect skin and hair in whatever style she so desired, changed her mood and she kept that portrait on the wall until she was discharged.[19]

Nancy has received notes, letters, postcards and verbal feedback about how much the portraits mean to patients and family members. A nursing staff from another city hospital contacted Nancy to tell her that one of our patients had brought her portrait from the University Hospital to the Grey Nuns Hospital and insisted that it be put up in her room. The nurse said, 'You never know Nancy – the things your program can do.'[20] This feedback has taught us never to underestimate the power of creating for patients who cannot create for themselves. After completing a large waiting-room window painting, Nancy writes:

Today was a rare day. For the first time a patient wished to paint on the window. As she painted, a medical intern came over, selected a brush and began painting as well. Behind us gathering was a small crowd to watch us – another intern, nursing staff, other visitors. They were laughing, talking, just being a part of the joy of creating.[21]

The visual artists also involve the patients in drawing, doodling, dream catchers, painting, sculpture, origami, beading, bookmaking, mandalas, mobiles, collage or specific projects such as tile painting, postcards, or gel transfers. The range of projects is limited only by the imaginations of the artists and patients, the cost of materials or their suitability for use in a hospital setting. The artists have found ways to work with patients who are visually impaired or who have limited movement, but must always be sensitive to which materials can be used in particular units. For example, no organic material can be brought into the Hematology unit.

Not surprisingly, the most popular bedside projects are those where the patients create a small piece of a larger project that is permanently installed in the hospital. Nancy has led a simple project where patients and staff trace their hands. Then they imbue these hands with color, images and words. Nancy then proceeds to amass these hands in a large collage for the unit.

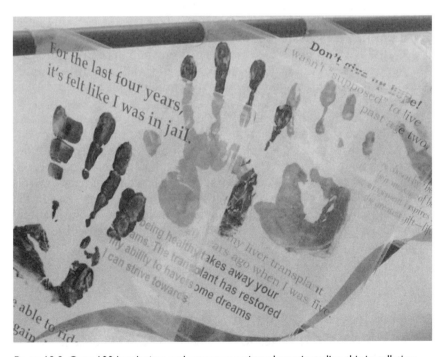

Figure 12.2 Over 100 handprints and messages written by patients line this installation.

Our transplant nursing staff were inspired by the Hands Murals and initiated a wonderful project which they asked the artists to carry out. All recipients of a transplant are invited to make an imprint of their hand on a clear transparency. Beside their handprint they are invited to write whatever message they would like. The handprints and messages are laminated and hang from a permanently installed rod next to one of the nursing stations in the unit. Messages range from expressions of delight over new-found freedom to heartfelt thanks to donor families. One of our kidney recipients wrote: 'Now I can eat watermelon! I'm going to enjoy summer one slice at a time.'[22] Another patient wrote:

> The sacrifice of the donor's family is what I marvel at most – that they would be willing to give of their loved one so that someone else could have a better quality of life. I think of that person and their family often and believe there's going to be a part of that person within me forever.[23]

Hiring artists

Strength comes in facilitation skills, specialty and professionalism

The most difficult challenge in administering this type of program is finding the right fit of artist for the hospital and for the bedside. After seven years' experience, there are four qualities that we feel are strong indicators if an artist is going to be successful in the program. These qualities are superior facilitation skills, demonstrated empathy and sensitivity towards others, formal training or equivalent in an artistic discipline, and a current professional practice.

Excellent facilitation skills are seminal in engaging adult patients. We believe that the superior facilitation skill of our chosen team of artists has been vital in the success of our program. Most often these skills come from artists who have had a variety of teaching and/or coaching experiences. Unfortunately, many Canadians have had a consistent lack of good art education in the school system. As a result some patients are very wary of the arts. Add on to that the fact that adults are much more self-critical and inhibited than children, particularly if previous art experiences were negative. Adult patients often refer to their lack of skill. The artists must be experienced with this initial reaction and able to turn it very quickly into one of comfort, curiosity and confidence. Excellent facilitation skills and years of experience enable artists to handle these situations. Shirley Serviss writes:

> Many people don't feel they are educated enough to understand poetry. An elderly woman I offered to read poetry to expressed discomfort. She thought her daughter would probably get more out of it because she was

a teacher. I chose to read her a poem of mine about women's history being written in rows of washing hung to dry in the sun and canning lined up on cold-room shelves. As I read, she sat up in bed with excitement and stopped me. 'That's my life,' she said. 'You're writing about my life!' Afterwards she told me I'd left out blueberry picking and raking hay. So I wrote her a poem of her own to value her life's experience.[24]

Demonstrated empathy and sensitivity towards others is vital in interacting with patients and families who are dealing with a health emergency, a recent diagnosis, a long-term illness, or an impending death or who simply may not feel up to engaging with the artist that particular day. The artist may be the first contact a patient has after receiving distressing news on a medical condition and must be able to respond appropriately when the patient writes on a piece of paper: 'I will never speak again. I just found out.' Artists must also recognize any situation or set of emotions that should be referred directly to the nursing clinical supervisor. Participation in creative activities by patients and family members can release emotions. Tears from patients are not uncommon while listening to a song or favorite poem or trying to find the words to express what an organ transplant means to them. Our artists have a support system in place beginning with the clinical supervisor on every unit we serve. We also provide the artists with ongoing training by nursing staff and opportunities to debrief at a biweekly 'Artists Rounds'.

Formal training or experience in an artistic discipline is also important to the credibility of our program. If we tell patients and staff they are going to meet an artist, then we are committed to introduce them to a trained professionally practicing artist whose work is of a relatively recognizable caliber. An understandable example is with musicians. Musicians who work at the bedside with a diversity of patients must not only be able play their instrument well, but must also have an extensive repertoire of music. An added bonus for patients is when they encounter a musician who will write a song with or for them.

The same is true for visual artists and writers. Patients and staff recognize lack of skill and they do let us know when they see it. It is through years of training and experience that the visual artists and writers acquire the host of ideas for bedside projects that are mature and engaging enough for adult inpatients. It takes extreme talent to work with such a range of people in often difficult situations and to generate projects that will culminate in a larger installation in the hospital.

Employing artists that are professionally practicing, at least part time, is also critical to the success and credibility of our program. Not only does it ensure that the artists will have a combination of training, experience and talent, but it also means that they are embedded in the arts community. We have found that professionally practicing artists are able to bring a variety of opportunities to the program that others may not. These opportunities include connections with other artists, guilds, arts organizations and associations, and granting agents. These contacts are vitally important when recruiting volunteer artists, initiating new projects, seeking out funding partners and establishing relationships with healthcare professionals within the hospital. For example, when the Friends applied for the first time for an Alberta Foundation for the Arts Grant, we believe that it was the competitive salary and the credentials of the artists in our employ that convinced the grant peer jury members to award us the sum we were seeking. This respect garnered for our program rests on the artists we hire.

The effect we have

Can artists at the bedside assist in reducing patients' pain perception, anxiety, fear or depression? Can artists at the bedside assist reducing the use of pain relief medication and sedatives? After seven years of managing the Friends Artists On the Wards Program at the Walter C. Mackenzie Health Centre, we believe artists at the bedside can reduce the perception of pain and alleviate boredom, loneliness and anxiety, thereby reducing the use of pain medication, sedatives, and antidepressant medication. We believe that artists at the bedside enhance patients' healing, therefore assisting in the reduction of patients' length of stay.

More and more studies are being released in the UK and US supporting the positive physical and emotional effects of creative activities on patients.[25] What we at the University Hospital have are many stories, letters, emails, and comments from staff, patients and family members, and strong encouragement to continue. Today, physicians, nurses, psychiatrists, social workers, chaplains, physiotherapists and occupational therapists stop the artists in the halls to refer patients to the program. While the artists are very careful not to get in the way of treatment and care of patients, they find that their work is also respected. Shirley Serviss writes:

> One day, a doctor came into the room as I was working with a patient. 'I'll be out of your way in just a moment,' I said. 'Stay,' the physician responded. 'I'll just be a moment. What you're doing is important.'

As Bernie Warren has stated, all of these 'stories' are grains of sand. And, in looking at all of the grains of sand we eventually see a beach: a view of something larger that is forming – the realization that invoking creativity responds to individuals' need for self-expression.[26] All of us, who are creative, albeit in carpentry, cooking, sewing, or painting know the profound pleasure, the transcendence, and the power of creating. Creative expression is soothing, meditative, and can reduce the perception of pain, alleviate boredom, loneliness and anxiety. Guided by highly skilled artists in facilitation, the act of making art provides patients opportunities to recapture the joy and respite that comes from losing oneself in an act of creation, watching a piece of visual art emerge, or experiencing live music or words. Through art, poetry and music we witness the will of the spirit to thrive in the direst of circumstances.

Acknowledgements

We would like to thank the Friends Board of Directors for the support, guidance and trust as we grew the arts in healthcare programs; to the Administration Team of the University Hospital, thank you for your encouragement; and to the Shands Arts in Medicine Program for your leadership and inspiration. Particular thanks go to the artists whose journaling made this chapter possible: Al Brant, Nancy Corrigan, Cornelia Osztovits and Shirley Serviss, and to all of the volunteer artists, thank you, your skills are crucial to the success and growth of our programs; and to Michelle Casavant who has worked with us from day one; Diana M. Young who helps us in every way every day; and to Geri Watson who believes in this work.

Notes

1 Kimberly Scherr, letter to Patti Lemieux, Director of Patient Relations, 13 October 2003.
2 Funds to support all of the Friends services and programs are raised through a large and well-designed hospital gift shop which benefits from a highly populated and central location in the University of Alberta campus. In addition, the Friends provide operational funding for the Hospital Volunteer Department (managing over 900 volunteers) in addition to large annual financial gifts to the hospital for patient comfort.
3 Feedback recorded from gallery comment cards collected from 1999–2006.
4 Feedback recorded from gallery comment cards collected from 1999–2006.
5 The Gallery is open from 10 am to 8 pm, Monday to Friday, and 1 pm to 8 pm on Saturdays and Sundays. Admission is free.
6 D. Lein, letter to the Friends, 15 June 2000.
7 C. Brione, staff evaluation, 8 September 2000.
8 J. Tabak, letter to the Chief Operating Officer of University Hospital, 5 March 2001.
9 L. Sanderson, staff evaluation, 11 May 2000.
10 Anonymous, letter to the artist, 10 December 2001.
11 Signed by patient, letter to Nancy Corrigan, undated.
12 Despite the obvious pairing of children and the arts, the Friends consciously chose at this point not to grow the program into the Stollery Children's Hospital for two reasons. One, the positive response from the adult units was overwhelming and the demand from new adult units was increasing. Two, the Children's Hospital had a Child Life Department with eight full- and part-time staff who focused on the leisure and recreation of children which did on occasion include the arts. The adult units had no such programs.
13 M. Samuels *et al. Creative Healing: How to Heal Yourself by Tapping Your Hidden Creativity*, San Francisco: HarperCollins, 1998, p. 13. For more information on art therapy contact the American or Canadian Art Therapy Associations or visit www.arttherapy.org.

14 Shirley Serviss, Artists On the Ward Journal, 2005. Shirley A. Serviss is a published poet, freelance writer, editor and creative writing instructor. Her most recent poetry collection, *Hitchhiking in the Hospital* (Inkling Press, 2005) is based on her experience as an Artist on the Wards for The Friends of the University of Alberta Hospitals.
15 With the exception, two of our artists see psychiatric groups of between three and 15 patients, once per week.
16 Al Brant, Artists On the Ward Journal, 2006.
17 Friends Library Journal, undated.
18 Cornelia Osztovits, Artists on the Ward Journal, 4 April 2006.
19 Nancy Corrigan, Artists on the Ward Journal, 12 April 2006.
20 Susan Scott, personal communication with Nancy Corrigan, May 2005.
21 Nancy Corrigan, Artists on the Ward Journal, 29 September 2004.
22 Anonymous, Hands of Hope, undated.
23 Anonymous, Hands of Hope, undated.
24 Shirley Serviss, 2005.
25 N. Nainis, 'Relieving symptoms in cancer: innovative use of art therapy', *Journal of Pain and Symptom Management*, February 2006, 162–169; R. L. Staricoff, *A Study of the Effects of Visual and Performing Arts in Healthcare*, London: Chelsea Westminster Hospital, 2004, report; S. Walsh, *Art at the Bedside with Family Caregivers of Cancer Patients: A Pilot Study*, Miami: School of Nursing, Barry University, 2003, report; Creative Centre, *Final Report: Satisfaction and Outcomes Assessment, Hospital Artists In Residence Program*, New York: Creative Centre, 2002, report; G. Cohen, *Creativity and Aging Study: The Impact of Professionally Conducted Cultural Programs on Older Adults*, Washington, DC: National Endowment for the Arts, 2004, report. For other studies and research visit the Society for the Arts in Healthcare Website (www.thesah.org).
26 Bernie Warren, personal communication, 2005.

Chapter 13

Healing laughter

The role and benefits of clown-doctors working in hospitals and healthcare[1]

Bernie Warren[2]

Setting the scene

Clowns have worked in hospital settings at least since the time of Hippocrates. Doctors of that era believed that mood influenced healing and Hippocrates' own hospital on the island of Kos supported constant troupes of players and clowns in the quadrangle. In Turkey, several centuries ago, the dervishes who were responsible for the well-being of patients first fed the body and then used their performance skills to feed the soul. At the end of the nineteenth century, The Fratellini Brothers (a famous clown trio) began the current practice of clowns (both amateur and professional) making occasional visits to hospitals, particularly pediatric hospitals.

However, the presence of professional clowns working on hospital wards as part of a healthcare team is a relatively new phenomenon. In 1986, Karen Ridd in Winnipeg and Michael Christensen in New York, separately and unbeknownst to each other, began working with children in large urban pediatric hospitals. Since that time, clown-doctors have fast established a niche for themselves within the healthcare field as this new and exciting artistic practice stirred the imagination and started to take hold in more than a dozen countries around the world.[3] While each program is unique, all value and place a high priority on professionalism, regular training, and maintaining the highest standards possible.

Moreover, the work is not static. While the initial work was focused on children, more recently clowning has moved outside the pediatric unit and beyond the hospital with palpable benefits to patients, families and staff and the community.

In 2001, professional clowns started to work with seniors in hospitals and in that same year Hearts&Minds began their Elderflowers project with dementia patients in nursing homes and seniors' centers in Scotland (Killick 2003). This initiative, and others like it in Europe and Canada, acted as a catalyst for change as clowns started to deliver service to healthcare facilities outside of large urban centers, not only to children but across the lifespan.

More recently Cliniclowns in the Netherlands developed web clowning.

Patients and other interested parties can surf over to the Cliniclowns website (http://www.cliniclowns.nl) and view the clowns in action. In this way, they can help more children than they could ever see personally, particularly as the trend is to keep sick people in the hospitals for shorter and shorter durations.

> Six months after its launch, the fascinating world of clowns is visited by more than 200 children a week. They meet their clown via webcam, chat and e-mail. They also meet with other children. The children are just as enthusiastic as the clowns. The nature of contact is different, certainly, but of the same quality as meeting in the flesh.
>
> (Van Troostwijk)[4]

Before we begin: a few words about clown-doctors

Currently there are several models of practice for clowns who work in hundreds of hospitals and healthcare settings in countries. Professional clowns whose focus is on healthcare *not* just entertainment are called many things (hospital clown, therapeutic clown, clini-clown or simply clown). The focus of this chapter is on the work of Fools for Health's clown-doctors. However, much of what is described may equally be applied to the work of others.

Clown-doctors are specially trained professional artists who work in a hospital. In the same way that ice dancers may be considered a blend of ice skaters and dancers, clown-doctors are a blend of artist and healthcare worker. They work in pairs, wear a red nose, use a minimal amount of make-up, wear a white lab coat and are usually referred to as doctor (e.g. Dr Haven't-A-Clue). Clown-doctors work with patients, their families and the healthcare team to promote wellness and to improve quality of life through the use of music, improvisational play and humor.

Their work requires them to bring together training in music, movement, theatre and other areas (e.g. magic, puppetry) with additional training, orientation and sensitivity to issues related to illness and disease and then, in character, not only improvise but also *interact with their audience*, not on a theatre stage but in a public space where healthcare is delivered.

Clown-doctors are not simply entertainers. Rather, they are accepted as valuable members of the multidisciplinary healthcare team and acknowledged as integral components of the healthcare delivery process.

The development of Fools for Health

Developing clown-doctor programs outside a large city is not without its problems. The experience of developing Fools for Health has something to say to others interested in living in smaller communities or in rural areas who wish to develop similar programs. In April 1999, after 15 years of research on humor in healthcare and an earlier failed attempt to bring clowns to Windsor hospitals,[5] I was invited to present at the First World Symposium on Culture, Health and the Arts held in Manchester, England. While there, I met Caroline Simonds (Dr Giraffe) and learned about the work of the clown-doctors of Le Rire Médecin. For the next two years, as part of research on a book about their work,[6] I made many trips to France to take notes and to shadow clown-doctors in the hospitals. The days of observation were often followed by long discussions on how and what Caroline and Le Rire Médecin do and why they are successful. In May 2000 I had my first conversations about developing a clown-doctor program in Windsor. In November that same year the work on Fools for Health began in earnest.

Windsor is a border town, an urban automotive centre that sits in the shadow of the much larger city of Detroit, which although technically in another country is only about a 15-minute car ride away on a good day. In addition, it has one of the most ethnically and linguistically diverse populations in the country. In many ways it is different to any other city in Canada or anywhere else that I know about.

The Windsor and Essex area health region covers the city of Windsor, in which about 230,000 people live, and Essex County, which is predominantly a rural farming area and home to about another 180,000 people. At the time I was looking to develop our first program, all clown-doctor programs focused on children. Most often these services were delivered in large specialized pediatric units or hospitals. However, in 2000–1 while Windsor did have a 60-bed pediatric facility,[7] the provincial government was knee deep in healthcare reorganization.[8] As a result, I was told that a pediatric program was unviable at the time. Looking back, I see this as one of those 'think of the solution, not the problem'[9] moments, one of many in the six years since Fools for Health began. In many ways, Fools epitomizes the notion that 'necessity is the mother of invention'. To remain viable and provide stimulating employment, Fools for Health has had to look at developing new frontiers.

From the start, Fools for Health was unusual. Besides being the first Canadian clown-doctor initiative, its first program, launched in July 2001, was delivered on the adult inpatient rehabilitation unit at the Western Campus of Windsor Regional Hospital. Since then, clown-doctors have worked regular shifts in various local hospitals on oncology, palliative care, complex continuing care, intensive care unit, medical, surgical and pediatric units. They have also worked occasional shifts in emergency, outpatient clinics and even operating rooms.

In 2002, Fools for Health started to offer programs in nursing homes. In 2003, the first familial clown program was launched and in 2004 clown-doctor and familial clown programs started to be delivered in smaller, more rural settings throughout Windsor and Essex County. One result was the development of a model for service that targets the whole hospital rather than a single ward or unit. Currently, Fools for Health delivers clown-doctor programs at five hospitals and familial clown programs at five local area nursing homes/long-term care facilities not only in Windsor and Essex but also Chatham-Kent Health regions.

Personnel and training

Developing a clown-doctor program in this area is a much different proposition to developing one in a large urban centre such as Paris (Le Rire Médecin) or New York (Big Apple Circus Clown-Care unit), or Sydney (The Humour Foundation). While we have a university with excellent performing arts programs[10] and a thriving arts community, we do not have the resources or job opportunities for graduates available in larger centers. Few professional performers choose to move to Windsor to seek a career and upon graduation most local graduates usually move to Toronto, Los Angeles or New York to seek fame and fortune. To keep someone in a smaller centre like Windsor, a program needs to provide stimulating satisfying full-time employment.

Fools for Health was one of the first clown-doctor companies to work across the lifespan, and even today works with adults and seniors as much as if not more than with children. This variety certainly provides more work opportunities and a variety of experiences. However, while each population has its own joys and challenges, this work necessitates that the clown-doctors be enthusiastic, empathetic, good with all ages, non-judgmental, and multi-talented as a performer. It is difficult enough to learn to work with one population, but the Windsor clowns have the harder task of learning to work with all the populations, and to be able to switch from one population to another, sometimes on the same day.

The work in Windsor requires a great deal of training. In the first four years, I trained 30 different clowns to work in hospitals using several different models of training. In part this was because of the factors cited above and in part due to lack of adequate funding. In the last couple of years things have stabilized. Funding has been more secure and I have worked with the University of Windsor to develop the first English language university-based training for students wishing to work as clowns in a healthcare setting. The training to work with Fools has several phases:

- First, there is an audition and interview to assess the individual's level of performance skills, their physical and mental health and their aptitude/ potential for the work.
- Once selected there is extensive training in clown, improvisation, character development, musical repertoire and an orientation to work in healthcare that covers medical and psychosocial factors and the culture of healthcare facilities.
- Each clown-doctor develops their own character through a series of training games and exercises that enable them to come up with a characteristic

voice, walk and personal traits and then create a costume and name to complement these characteristics.

- Before ever working in the hospitals, clown-doctors get a taste of the intensity of the work through observation and shadowing senior clowns. This observation and shadowing is at first done out of character, then later in clown.
- Regular round-table meetings and in-service training sessions are conducted with the clowns to improve and maintain their skills. The meetings allow other clowns to find out what is happening on the floor, share stories about what has been happening with the patients, and air concerns.
- The in-service training is run by both the company and guest speakers/workshop leaders and covers performance skills (clown, song, music) and medical/psychosocial aspects of the work such as dealing with death, or working with those with dementia.

A typical day

Each day the team follows the same pattern. After arriving and signing in they go, out of clown, to get the daily census and to receive notes from and ask relevant questions of the healthcare contact for the unit, usually an experienced nurse, charge nurse, or in Leamington a chaplain who initially trained as a nurse.

The pair proceed to the 'clown office' to change into their clown-doctor characters. The process takes about 30–45 minutes. During the process of transformation the partners talk a little about the mood of the ward, the types of problems present that day and possible strategies for working with each patient. Then they warm-up vocally and physically and finally get into character and leave the room.

Once in character they will spend from two to six hours as a clown-doctor at the hospital. At the end of the day the partners change back into street clothes and make detailed notes about the day's work. They then spend time debriefing with their healthcare contact about the events of the shift sharing any especially important events and observations.

Working across the lifespan

From the start, Fools for Health was unique. They began their work with a two-month pilot project at an inpatient rehab ward rather than the well-established route of clowning on a pediatric ward. Since then, the wide variety of settings that they have worked in means that they have interacted with patients ranging in age from newborns to centenarians.

The development of recent work in small rural hospitals has often involved the clown-doctors having to clown to all age ranges within a single day. Each population has its own joys and challenges. Thus, the clown-doctors have to be multitalented. It is challenging enough to learn to work with one population, but Fools for Health clown-doctors have the harder task of learning to work with all populations, and being able to switch from one population to another.

When working with children, the main concern is finding time to visit every child on the ward, while still providing extra attention to those who need it most. Although this is difficult, when they succeed, they are incredibly beneficial not only for the patients but also for the staff. A pediatric oncology nurse shared the following anecdote:

> We have one Oncology little girl who gets her chemo every week, and she's got a port . . . I was having a lot of problems with her, I wanted her to lay down, and she wanted to be sitting up . . . I couldn't feel the port effectively, I needed her to lay down so that I could push down on it, and she just was not going to do it, she was just being really cantankerous . . . the clown-doctors came, and within about two minutes, she was laying down and I accessed her port. And, then, we had appointments with them – they would come back . . . on Wednesdays – that's her day to come for chemo, so . . . make a point of [them] coming down to be with her.

When working with adults, one of the biggest challenges for the clown-doctors is to overcome the 'clowns are for kids' mindset. Many adults believe that clowns have nothing to offer adults, as they are meant to entertain children only. The clown-doctors have to show the adults that clowns are for everyone. The benefits when the adults realize this are wonderful, as reported by one clown-doctor: 'The husband of the woman on Oncology told us that last time we were in, his wife was complaining about pain but after we left, the pain was gone.'

Research

Overview

Fools for Health is unique in other ways. The organization began as a collaboration between Windsor Regional Hospital and the University of Windsor. From the beginning, Fools for Health kept records of its work in order to track its successes as well as determining areas of possible improvement. It remains committed to systematic, rigorous and continuous research[11] on factors that influence the efficacy of, and limits to, the role and benefits of clowns working in the healthcare system and effects of the work on the clown-doctors and familial clowns themselves.[12] In general the research we have conducted over the last several years suggests the following:

- Smiles and laughter have the capability to cross all barriers (age, gender, language, illness, pain).
- No two patients/residents, healthcare team members or units are the same.
- Patients/residents, nurses and doctors are part of the community in which they live, and they're all interconnected. Moreover, each hospital is a focal point of the community, especially in a small rural community.
- Clown-doctors, like 'mail carriers' in a small village, interact with all members of the 'village', spreading smiles and creating community in each room, ward and throughout the hospital.
- Each facility (hospital, nursing home) should be considered a unique 'living organism' and each clown-doctor program needs to be designed to try to meet the unique properties of that facility.

More specifically our research has already shown that clown-doctors help to:

- 'reset the clock' (i.e. reframe perceptions of time) for patients and staff – especially valuable in emergency waiting rooms and for patients waiting for surgery
- take the minds of patients and families off illness
- brighten the mood of nurses, doctors and other healthcare staff
- reduce anxiety in young children awaiting surgery
- act as a distraction during minor bedside procedures (e.g. inserting an intravenous drip, or a Ventolin treatment)
- extend the range of motion for stroke and aphasia patients
- encourage patients with a tracheotomy or aphasia to speak
- reduce the use of pain and antidepressant medication
- reduce the overall length of stay in the hospital
- increase staff morale
- reduce staff absenteeism
- increase satisfaction with rehabilitation programs.

In reflecting upon the work in the hospitals, the clown-doctors came to understand that beyond the individual benefits they brought to the people they saw, their work helped to improve the overall environment of the hospital in a number of ways. Talks with healthcare staff working at these locations further substantiated these beliefs (Figure 13.1).

Clown-doctors help to humanize the healthcare experience

Clown-doctors often work hand in hand with pastoral care, helping to humanize hospitals stays. As one hospital chaplain observed, 'Clown-doctors provide moments of respite from pain, depression and boredom.' They do not forget a patient's illness but always try to focus on those parts of the

Figure 13.1 'You'll never know, really know what your visits have meant to me . . . I will never forget when you came to visit me as I was going for my surgery and how you said that OR meant Over the Rainbow. It helped me a lot and I even think I was saying that in recovery after . . . am I over the rainbow!'

individual that are healthy. They help remind family members and the healthcare team that a patient is not simply their illness. They spread smiles and laughter wherever they go and make being in a hospital or nursing home a more pleasant experience for everyone. As one hospital CEO once put it: 'I don't need statistics to see the good you do in this hospital. Everywhere you go, you bring sunshine, not just to the pediatric unit but to the hospital as a whole.'

Clown-doctors help to improve healthcare delivery

Patients and visitors are often more relaxed and comfortable with the clown-doctors than other staff and open up to them more. The clown-doctors record what they observe and what is told to them, and report this valuable information to the healthcare team. This information is used to improve a patient's treatment.

Our research has noted the problems that the staff and clown-doctors have in communicating with patients from other cultures so we developed training workshops on how to reach out to patients from other cultures. These involve learning songs and phrases in the main languages used in each healthcare facility that help the clowns communicate with patients in the patient's own language.

Clown-doctors work with physiotherapists, occupational therapists and speech therapists to help with a patient's rehabilitation. As the manager of a rehabilitation unit notes:

> Patients have commented that the clown-doctors made them work harder in therapy . . . and also that they allow them to have a bit of normalcy to their lives, for a few moments. When clown-doctors are near, smiles are everywhere. There is an infusion of endorphins into the air. Staff sing with them, react with them and if needed are quiet with them.

Clown-doctors make hospitals more accessible and user friendly

They create a sense of community in a room, a ward and throughout the hospital (Figure 13.2). There is a ripple effect to the work of the clown-doctors. As one patient put it, 'They bring sunshine and laughter. They put a smile on your face and it lasts the rest of the day and when you think of them {the clowns} it {the smile} comes back. They leave good feelings behind.'

Those who come into contact with the clown-doctors experience an uplifting of their mood which may then carry over to others they meet during their day. When patients or family leave the hospital this sense of community

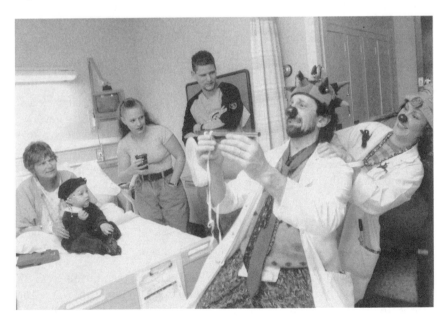

Figure 13.2 Oncology: 'Boy, you've got to carry that weight!'

continues on with them into the community at large. Student nurses, who train in many facilities throughout our region, often comment about seeing clown-doctors in other facilities and how much the patients, families, and staff look forward to their visits.

Clown-doctors benefit the hospital as an institution and community partner

Over the past few years clown-doctors have on several occasions been involved in the process of hospital accreditations. Accreditors have cited the clown-doctors as:

- one of the major reasons a rehabilitation program was given an 'excellent' rating
- an example of 'best practice' recommending other 'hospitals provide this service for their adult patients as well as pediatrics'.

Moreover, the physician recruiter for the Windsor/Essex community, a much under-serviced area, reports that the presence of clown-doctors in local area hospitals has helped in the process of physician recruitment.

In a little over five years, clown-doctors have become accepted as valuable members of the multidisciplinary healthcare team and are acknowledged as integral components of the healthcare delivery process. In this short time clown-doctor programs have helped to reduce healthcare costs through decreased use of medications, shorter hospital stays for patients and less stress on and fewer sick days taken by hospital staff. As one hospitalist put it, 'The presence of clown-doctors improves the attitudes of the staff both to the patients and to each other and inspires confidence in hospitals and in the patient's healthcare.'

Chatham-Kent Health Alliance's Annual Report 2005–06 states that clown-doctors 'reduce stress and anxiety and improve clinical outcomes'. They have helped to improve the quality of life for countless patients, residents, visitors and staff. Healthcare workers, families, patients, and even members of the community who have never seen clown-doctors and familial-clowns at work, have come to see the value of humor in healthcare.

Other developments

Familial clowns

The familial clown program was begun in 2003. During the previous year we had worked extensively with seniors on a complex continuing care ward. The clowns found that their interactions were positive, from the point of view of both the patients and the clowns. The decision was made to pursue more opportunities to work with seniors, particularly with dementia patients. Fools for Health expanded their work to local seniors' homes. There they found that the persona of a doctor had to be discarded. Unlike in the hospitals, in this environment doctors are not a typical fixture, and their presence was alarming rather than expected. Familial clowns are like clown-doctors except that they:

- do not wear white coats or carry stethoscopes
- use relatively little 'medical shticks'
- 'age' their characters
- are *not* called Dr, rather they are called by a single name, e.g. 'Buddy' or 'Sweetie'.

These changes were inspired in part by the Hearts&Minds' Elderflowers program.

As many nursing home and long-term care facility residents experience cognitive difficulties (such as dementia, Alzheimer's disease), familial clowns employ laughter, music, storytelling and 'reminiscence' techniques to stimulate memory and improve cognitive functioning. Familial clowns aim to increase the quality of life for seniors by engaging them in activities that help rejuvenate creative, expressive and communication skills and that help residents connect the past to the present and be present in the here and now. They ask stimulating questions, motivating the resident to engage in a conversation. They encourage the resident to take the lead in the interaction, telling the clowns what to do or sing; returning the power to people who have very little control over their lives. This engagement is especially important for residents who do not receive many visitors.

Since the beginning of the program, Fools for Health has put familial clowns in six different assisted living homes across the Essex County region. Within these six settings, the familial clowns have interacted with seniors, as well as their visitors and the staff. Familial clowns' work has shown that they help seniors to:

- connect to their immediate surroundings
- recognize family members
- remember the past
- improve cognitive functioning and communication skills.

In addition, they help to increase the quality of life for seniors, their families, and the healthcare staff who work with them.

Junior clown-doctor program

In addition to its impact on healthcare facilities, Fools for Health's work extends into the community. In 2004 we created, in partnership with the

Hospice of Windsor and Essex County, a 'junior clown-doctor' program designed to alleviate emotional stress for the siblings and children of cancer patients.

The premise behind the junior clown-doctor program is to provide children whose relatives are battling with life-threatening illnesses with the skills and self-esteem to become clowns in their own right. They are taught the benefits of using humor in the face of serious illness, and how to incorporate that humor into their daily life. The initiative:

- helps to build self-esteem in the children
- gives the junior clown-doctors a 'tool' (humor) to deal with their own feelings of stress and depression
- allows them to feel like they are doing something for their ill relative
- helps to expose and hopefully foster a love of the arts in the child.

Modified versions of the training used with professional clown-doctors are adapted for work with younger participants. They are shown how to find a voice, find a costume, find a walk and a name, and taught how to work in pairs. They are given pointers on developing a clown character. Once the training is complete, their families are invited in for a special performance. The newly minted junior clown-doctors give an improvisational performance in pairs.

Clown-doctor clinics

Often the most salient way of explaining our work is to have people experience it for themselves. In 2003, in part as a result of a collaboration with Dr Christine Thrasher on a health promotion she organized for the Faculty of Nursing,[13] Fools for Health began developing health promotion programs that deliver 'clown-doctor clinics' at local elementary schools, health fairs and other community events. Clown-doctors are sent to these various events around the region where they:

- perform more, and in a 'larger' style, than they would at the bedside
- choose an audience member or two to be their 'patients'
- perform some of the more popular medical shtick with the 'patient'
- describe (or have another staffer describe) the work of the clown-doctors.

All those who attend these events can see for themselves how the clown-doctors can help to make them feel happier and bring joy. As another way of spreading the word about the work of the clown-doctors and the benefits of humor in healthcare, this initiative is concerned with health promotion.

Developing and delivering clown programs in hospitals and healthcare

The success of Fools for Health has shown that even in smaller, less arts-oriented centers clown-doctors can survive and flourish. Organizations simply have to be creative and 'think outside the box'. Those who are contemplating the development of such a program in their own locations would do well to consider the following advice:

1 Learn from others' successes and mistakes.

- Do your homework, read any relevant journals/articles, visit the websites of the numerous clown-doctor companies around the world, and if possible, talk to them.

2 Choosing a site can be tricky and may take a lot more time than you anticipate.

- You may have to meet with several people and make many 'pitches' of your idea before you connect with the right contact who can open doors for you.
- Prior to delivery of the program, make sure to meet with senior management.

3 Give a general presentation on the value of the work, backed up with any research data or anecdotes from other reliable sources.

- Do not make extravagant claims you won't be able to back up later.

4 Design a program that you feel meets the needs of the hospital culture and the unit on which you work which you can deliver.

5 Remember that no two situations are the same.

- Each hospital, ward/unit and healthcare team has its own unique challenges and ways of doing things.
- Each patient, visitor, doctor and nurse is unique and may respond differently to the clown-doctor's interactions.
- Each clown-doctor is unique, with his or her own strengths and weaknesses.

6 Ensure that you can adequately fund each project.

- Ideally secure at least partial funding from the host site as this financial commitment usually transmits to support for the program, especially during the often bumpy initial phase of the program delivery.

7 It is often a tall order to find just the right person, but choosing the right people is crucial to the success of the work.

- If you live in a large city with a thriving performing arts community, there are many ways to find and interview potential clown-doctors. In smaller communities you may have to be creative.
- Placing interview/audition notices with job banks, local theatre groups, universities, colleges, and even high schools with performing arts programs or social services organizations may produce just the person you are looking for.

8 As a word of caution, do not be blinded by technical skill; simply being a good singer or accomplished stage actor does not necessarily make the person a good clown-doctor.

- Look for qualities in a person that make them a good person first and a good clown-doctor second. When it comes to clowning in healthcare facilities, maturity and life experience often outweigh talent.
- Look for someone who is a 'good enough' performer, but one who is positive, empathetic, good with people, a good listener, a giving improviser, willing to learn new songs, approaches and ideas, and is generous to others.

9 Having chosen the right people, make sure you provide appropriate preliminary and in-service training.

- Enlist the services of your site contact to provide the appropriate orientation to new facilities and local healthcare professionals (doctors, nurse practitioners, nurse clinical educators, hospital chaplains) to provide guidance and training on particular healthcare problems.

10 Visit the facility at least a week before the first day of program delivery.

- Spend time walking around the facility.
- Talk to and get to know any and all staff who will be involved with your program. If possible, meet again with senior management and the hospital board.
- Insinuate yourself and the clown-doctors into the healthcare team as much as possible; arrange to attend rounds and interdisciplinary team meetings and have lunch in the staff lunch room.
- Determine who would be your best contact and secure them as your 'point person'. Formalize a 'check in/check out' time.

11 During program delivery, be sure to listen with 'all antennas up': that is pay attention to sights, sounds and general 'energy' of each moment.

- Working as a pair really helps. What one partner misses the other usually picks up which helps to avoid most major problems.

12 Share information with the healthcare staff as you may be in a position

to notice important information about the patient that the staff didn't see.

13 Most importantly, keep good notes and try to learn from your mistakes.

Conclusion

In order to thrive, clown-doctor companies need to be flexible and creative. Thankfully, this is part of a clown-doctors' nature. In this chapter, I have outlined how Fools for Health have expanded their work beyond the pediatric ward, where most hospital clowns are found, and beyond the typical notion of clown-doctors to include familial clowns and junior clown-doctor trainers. In the next two chapters Magdalena Shamberger and Peter Spitzer present how they have expanded upon their traditional clown-doctor work.

Notes

1 This chapter is based in part on research conducted as part of an SSHRCC grant 'What is the Value of a Smile'. The grant is jointly held by Dr Warren and Dr Peter Twohig of St. Mary's University, Halifax.

2 I wish to thank my research associate, Nicole Gervais, who wrote sections of the original drafts of this text and without whom this piece would not have been finished and my research assistant, Candace Hind, who helped by reading the final draft and making many useful suggestions about its improvement.

3 There are many hospital clowning programs around the world and some of these are Theodora Foundation (Europe, South Africa, Hong Kong and Belorussia), Le Rire Médecin (France), Die Clown Doktoren (Germany), Payasospital (Spain), Soccorso Clown (Italy), CliniClowns (Europe), Doctors of Joy (Brazil), Fools for Health (Canada), Zdravotni Klaun (Czech Republic) and Humour Foundation (Australia).

4 T.D. von Troostwijk, 'The hospital clown: a cross-boundary character', in B. Warren (ed.) *Suffering the Slings and Arrows of Outrageous Fortune: International Perspectives on Stress, Laughter and Depression*, Amsterdam, New York: Rodopi, 2006.

5 In 1992 I wrote several grants for 'Prospero's Fools' (an Integrative Theatre company) to develop a pilot clowns in hospitals program. Unfortunately adequate funding was not available and the idea was shelved.

6 *Le Rire Médecin* published by Albin Michel in 2001 and later in English as *The Clown Doctor Chronicles* by Rodopi in 2004.

7 The unit provided first line medical and surgical care not only for all the usual suspects of childhood (i.e. upper respiratory and gastrointestinal illnesses, accidental injuries, diabetes, etc.), but also for more problematic conditions (e.g. childhood cancers, cystic fibrosis, rare 'syndromes'/diseases). If after an initial diagnosis children needed more specialized care, they were stabilized and then moved to larger centers in London and Toronto and occasionally Detroit.

8 At the time there was one hospital in Leamington and four hospitals in Windsor. The Windsor hospitals were reorganized into two hospital corporations, each with two sites. Duplication of services was phased out as were emergency departments at two hospital sites. Pediatrics was assigned to move from one hospital corporation to another, although this move eventually took five years.

 9 Zedd, in T. Goodkind, *Wizard's First Rule*, London: Gollancz, 1995.
10 My day job is as a Professor in The School of Dramatic Art.
11 Currently two research projects are under way, 'What is the Value of a Smile? An Investigation of the Impact of Clown-doctors on the Lives of Patients, their Families and the Healthcare Team in Windsor Hospitals', funded by SSHRC, and 'Down Memory Lane: Work with Seniors', on the work of familial clowns, funded by Ontario Trillium Foundation.
12 N. Gervais, B. Warren and P. Twohig (2006) ' "Nothing seems funny anymore": studying burnout in clown-doctors', in B. Warren (ed.) *Suffering the Slings and Arrows of Outrageous Fortune: International Perspectives on Stress, Laughter and Depression*', Amsterdam, New York: Rodopi, 2006.
13 Currently Nursing Professor Christine Thrasher and I are developing a course to train 'standardized patients' for clinical programs in nursing and medicine.

Chapter 14

Songlines

Developing innovative arts programmes for use with children who are visually impaired or brain injured

Magdalena Schamberger

Background

Hearts&Minds is an arts-in-health organisation based in Edinburgh, Scotland. The aim of the organisation is to promote the quality of life for people in hospital and hospice care using clowning and the performing arts. Hearts&Minds currently runs two programmes: the Clowndoctors programme for children in hospital and hospice care (launched in 1999); the Elderflowers programme for elderly people with dementia (launched in 2001). Both aim to contribute to the physical, mental and emotional well-being of participants and use clowning and the performing arts (including music, puppetry, dancing, etc.) as a starting point for communication with the participants and as an outlet for their creativity.

The artistic style of Hearts&Minds' work has its roots in the European theatre clowning of Jaques Lecoq, Philippe Gaulier and Pierre Byland. We use the red nose, 'the smallest mask' in the world, to aid the performer to connect to his or her own curiosity, playfulness, openness and naïveté. This can enable the creation of profound linkages with the participants beyond the spoken word.

The context of our work initially was highly visual and often non-verbal. From the outset this proved to be a particular strength and led to a further development of the Clowndoctors programme, called the 'Special Branch'. The Clowndoctors 'Special Branch' was developed specifically for children with multiple special needs, fully dependent children and children with terminal illnesses in residential care. With contributions from physiotherapists as well as speech and language therapists, this development created a new set of tools elaborating on existing successful Clowndoctor interactions. It also highlighted a different set of challenges when working with children who were partially sighted, blind or had acquired brain injuries – who, due to physical restrictions, could not fully appreciate these activities.

The beginning of Songlines

The idea was born to create a new project which would be tailored for such children and benefit those who could not participate in visual stimulation or for whom this stimulation could be overpowering and/or even painful. Within this new development the idea was still to follow the basic principles of the Hearts&Minds Clowndoctors programme, which are:

1   *Using a person-centred approach.*
2   *Using clowning and the performing arts as a starting point.*
3   *Delivering activities in Clowndoctors character* (with a red nose, no make-up and a yellow doctors coat), and as a duo. Two Clowndoctors interact with individual children with the aim being to facilitate the child's responses.
4   *Providing individual visits:* rather than providing ward or group entertainment – individual children are referred to the Clowndoctors by healthcare staff for a specific reason.
5   *Using a referral system:* in advance of their visits, Clowndoctors receive basic information on the children (name, age, illness, special needs, communication needs, special interests) and when appropriate more detailed information on their emotional state and family situation, etc. The Clowndoctors are therefore able to make an informed decision on a planned approach. A written record is then produced which contains both the plans for each individual session at the beginning of the day as well as the outcome of each interaction at the end of the day.
6   *Gathering feedback:* feedback from healthcare staff and Clowndoctors practitioners is gathered through a strategic programme review process twice a year, while feedback from participants is gathered on a more informal basis.
7   *Undertaking evaluation and monitoring:* end-of-day summary sheets with relevant non-confidential information are forwarded to the Hearts-&Minds offices after each Clowndoctors visit. This information is used to provide statistical information and provides a mechanism for quality control. The Artistic Director makes onsite supervision visits at each of the units at least twice a year.

From the idea to the project proposal

When forming the idea it was essential to clarify the exact context for the Songlines project and to set the following parameters:

*   deciding who exactly the project should benefit
*   identifying the challenges of working with this particular client group
*   describing the expected benefits

- potential challenges within the interactions and areas of need for our Clowndoctors (e.g. information, training, assessment tools)
- potential content of research phase and development
- considering timing of research, development and training
- considering potential training contributors, potential training content and expected outcomes.

Decisions on context and content were made after discussion with our team of existing Clowndoctors practitioners as well as healthcare staff. This was followed up by onsite artistic observations of regular Clowndoctors visits with the potential target client group and conversations with organisations such as Sense Scotland and the Child Brain Injury Trust (CBIT).

From the non-verbal to the non-visual

We embarked on this exploration from the highly visual and non-verbal to the non-visual. The plan was to develop and deliver interactive music, sound and storytelling activities for children who are visually impaired or brain injured. I decided to give the project the name of Songlines and the choice of title seemed to inspire the content of activities.

The Songlines project takes its inspiration from Aboriginal tradition, which describes songlines (or Yiri in the Walpiri language) as tracks across the landscape created by mythical Aboriginal ancestors when they rose out of the dark Earth and travelled, creating mountains, valleys, waterholes – all the physical features of the land. As the ancestors underwent various adventures, the laws for living, and hunting skills were established. Ceremonial songs, which pass on these stories, are described as 'songlines'.

From its inception Songlines aimed to create music, sound and individual story maps for, and with, each participating child – a 'map' representing paths or landmarks of each child's physical, creative and emotional environment. Hearts&Minds aimed to promote these musical and vocal 'areas of success' for participating children, opening up channels of non-verbal creative expression and humour through sounds, voice, rhythm, fragments of words and letters rather than elaborate speech.

Project: timing, research and development

We started our research in August 2003 with financial support from the Scottish Arts Council (SAC). This was followed by a period of development (September to mid-November 2003), and then training (mid-November to January 2004) culminating in the delivery of the activities from February 2004 onwards.

I started by gathering useful information from relevant organisations such as Sense Scotland, the Child Brain Injury Trust (CBIT) and Royal National

Institute for the Blind (RNIB) and participated in a conference organised by Sense that was inspirational and gave a valuable insight into the world of potential participants.

I made onsite visits in several of our regular hospitals and residential houses for children with multiple special needs and watched Clowndoctors interactions with children who could potentially benefit from our Songlines project. I observed and noted details of those activities that worked, as well as the shortcomings and challenges of some of the interactions. Furthermore, I attended a day at the Royal Blind School as I was interested in seeing and hearing a participant's sound world outside their regular Clowndoctors visit and away from their residential setting.

Trainers and training contributions

Very early on it was clear to me that as well as creating brand new approaches, techniques and routines, we would be able to build on existing routines and materials. Three trainers were chosen to contribute to the Songlines project. I met with each of them, clarifying the aims and objectives of the project as well as outlining their training briefs.

Drawing on the expertise and practical experiences of the Hearts&Minds Clowndoctors programme and focusing on some time-tested Clowndoctors principles, the three trainers helped us 'translate' our highly visual activities into a non-visual context. They were James Robertson, a music therapist, Naheed Cruickshank, a professional musician and music educationalist, and Pete Vilk, a professional musician and Clowndoctors practitioner at the time. All three trainers were asked to contribute to the creation of a training programme for Clowndoctors Songlines and were provided with the following training briefs.

James Robertson

- Provide an insight into the basics of Nordoff-Robbins Music Therapy[1] – theory, strategies, approaches, instruments, teaching material, training plan.
- Share experiences from a music therapy setting: playful approaches and strategies.
- Help contextualise music therapy approach for the Clowndoctors work.
- Explore the use of musical instruments and voice: improve Clowndoctors' confidence to improvise (individual, group and duo).

Naheed Cruickshank

- Explore the use of voice: training, repertoire, confidence to improvise.
- Create a bank of Songlines repertoire (music and rhymes).

- Explore the use of graphic notation, including basics of Kodály system.[2]
- Share experiences from educational settings: (as above) playful approaches and strategies.

Pete Vilk

- Explore the use of voice and musical instruments (practitioner's own, new instruments and self built instruments).
- Help adapt the existing Clowndoctor's artistic themes/repertoire and find new strategies/musical approaches.
- Research the needs of target groups.
- Assist in the creation of sound scenarios and events.
- Explore the use of sound signifiers and sound symbols.
- Assist in the purchase of instruments and their use. These instruments would later make up the content of the Songlines case.
- Explore storytelling using musical instruments and sounds.
- Contextualise graphic notation, scoring and recording.
- Help contextualise all material created in sessions with other trainers.

In addition, Pete and James were asked to help evaluate the project.

Training content and training sessions with Hearts&Minds practitioners

The aims of the training sessions for the practitioners were as follows:

- To prepare the ground for the Clowndoctors for this additional focus on music and voice and to establish a basic musical vocabulary.
- To discuss the use of potential instruments (bought and made).
- To discuss and plan the actual making of instruments.
- To explore musically different themes and stories.
- To design multisensory Clowndoctors coats to be worn as part of the costume and explore the use of suitable multisensory props. This included the idea of creating wristbands for the practitioners bearing their Clowndoctors names in Braille.
- To research the existing 'sound world' of participating children and to discover starting points in regards to music and sound in order to develop sound scenarios as well as sound conflicts.
- To explore the possibility of sound recording of the interaction and to make an attempt to create a notation of creative symbols to provide written/drawn record of the interactions between the Clowndoctors and the child.

In the practical training, James led the exploratory sessions. He focused on improvisation – and on simplicity, space and selflessness. Naheed's work helped build the Clowndoctors' confidence in using music and voice and on creating a bank of Songlines songs and rhymes. Pete, due to his experience working as a Clowndoctor, was a practical collaborator who helped translate the activities into concepts that his fellow Clowndoctors could understand and use. The other Clowndoctors also contributed their practical experience of working with the target children in a residential setting.

Philosophy and approach

The Hearts&Minds practitioners' approach to the Songlines interactions are informed by the Clowndoctors' approach to visiting children in general and are as follows:

- *Using different rhythms for each Clowndoctor* (steps, sounds and movement) to make it easy to distinguish between individual characters and to make them easily recognisable, even if a child is unable to see. This enables games such as siding with one or the other Clowndoctor, losing and looking for a Clowndoctor, etc.
- *Using clear and strong rhythms within their musical approaches* to provide simple and clear suggestions for starting points and games. Establishing rules enables the freedom of playful interaction.
- *Being aware of the importance of a strong/confident entrance.* The Clowndoctors often play music when approaching from afar to announce their arrival in the hallway and create anticipation for their visit. However, once they enter a child's room/space they use a strong clear entrance – so the child knows it is their turn. This also helps to distinguish chosen sounds from other background noise such as televisions, music players, etc. and provides a clear starting point for the interactions/play.
- *Taking a moment of silence to tune in with the child* at any particular time at a given location. This includes reading their needs and exploring their likes/dislikes, etc. – rather than just filling the air with 'busy' sounds.
- *Using the child as a starting point to create Songlines.* The sounds and/or rhythm of movement/voice of a child, even a fully dependent one, who is unable to verbally communicate, can create a starting point for a musical exploration of their world. The surrounding environment can influence the sound scenario – using the sound of drawers, water taps, light switches, etc.
- *Allowing silences throughout the visit.* Silence is an essential marker before changing any activity. In theatrical clowning, silence allows for the arrival of 'the flop' – the moment of failure when nothing happens and the clown shows his or her humanity through their failure – and has the generosity to share this failure with the audience. This gives the audience, even an audience of one, time to observe, understand

and react to the failure (often through laughter). The same applies here.

- *Playing with distances and spaces to change the perceived environment.*
- *Remembering the importance of simplicity, space and selflessness.* In clowning, the simplest suggestions (simple – as in not complicated) are the strongest and best. They are the easiest to pick up and develop.
- *Allowing for physical and musical space gives the participants time to join in and respond.* The interactions are about facilitating the individual child's needs rather than for the Clowndoctors to show off their skills (e.g. playing the flute):

> Dr Superdoc and Dr Pavlova were visiting a child who suffers from mild seizure activity. From previous visits the Clowndoctors knew that the child loved physical and oral slapstick, such as falling over or making the sound of falling.
>
> The child was genuinely enjoying his visit, laughing during the visit in between the mild seizures (lasting no more than 30 seconds). Every time a seizure arrived the Clowndoctors would stop and wait until it had passed and then continued with their visit.

- *Using simple language.* Both verbal and musical vocabulary should be simple allowing for it to be repeated and developed at a later stage or further session. Comic timing and play are generally created by setting up an expectation (i.e. a rhythm) and later 'destroying' it by changing it. These 'ruptures' often cause laughter (Figure 14.1).
- *Taking risks.* Dr Superdoc and one of his colleagues were visiting an eight-year-old boy Adam[3] at a children's hospice. Adam has multiple special needs and can't see very well. He is generally very passive. Initially the Clowndoctors were very careful, initiating interaction by playing gentle music during a series of visits. As there appeared to be no great response they took the risk of a very different avenue. They started a visit by stamping their feet loudly accompanied by the use of a kazoo. In this way they discovered that the child seems to love loud rhythmic music and responds very well to this. Another approach would be to start gently and increase the volume. The boy is now starting to physically move along with the music, he smiles and his eyes light up.
- *Linking different visits with sounds.* When there is more than one participant in the same room, the Clowndoctors often link these visits with particular sounds/instruments. Rather than stopping and starting they use these sounds to 'balance'/connect the group while giving individual attention.
- *Leaving with sounds after ending the visit.* Just as it is beneficial to approach a child playing music to announce yourself, we realised that children seem to find it soothing if the departure is also still accompanied with sounds/music.

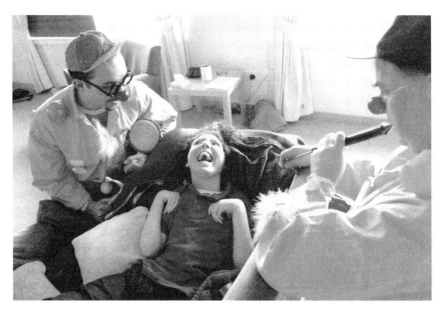

Figure 14.1 A musical rupture.

- *When in doubt, listen.* When the plans you have made don't work, then stop, wait and listen. Rather than overpowering a room or an entire visit with sounds and ideas, start with the child from 'nothing' and let a new idea arrive.
- *2:1 sessions vs. group sessions.* In general most of our Clowndoctors and Songlines sessions are 2:1 (two Clowndoctors will visit one referred child). However, sometimes children and young people can find the amount of attention disconcerting. They find it easier to participate when the focus is not directly on them. With children that have multiple special needs and/or are fully dependent, these preferences might be harder to read:

> Dr Molotoff and Dr Pavlova found it hard to achieve any reaction from Susan, a 16-year-old fully dependent girl in one of the residential units we visit. The only means of communication for her is eye movement during very close up eye contact.
>
> During one of their Clowndoctors visits they came across Susan in the living room with another couple of residents. Being unsure how to develop activities with the teenager, the two Clowndoctors decided to treat the visit as a group session. They started creating a sound world for another child, when Susan, to their great surprise, joined in by vocalising along with the sounds and becoming part of the sound world being created. The Clowndoctors incorporated her contribution and also managed to link it to a third resident child.

During a further visit the Clowndoctors wanted to give Susan individual attention but had to realise that she prefers participating as part of a group.

Songlines referrals

The stages and techniques used by the Clowndoctors in working with an individual child include:

1 *Create a Songlines record card* for each participant with the help of healthcare staff. This becomes the children's 'passport' to their Songlines journeys.

2 *Receive Songlines referral* with updated information from staff.

- *The Songlines referral card* (which we adapted from the Clown-doctors referral system and which was also influenced by patients' cards which the healthcare units already used) and referral sheet (end-of-day summary) provided the basis and a record of all activities we provide.
- It contains basic information such as name, age, ability level, likes and dislikes and communication needs.
- In addition we use photographs of the children and add additional information such as effect of medication, abilities, disabilities, range of vision, range of hearing, range of physicality, preferred physical position, signs for approval, signs for disapproval, signs of relaxation, signs of discomfort.
- Following several visits with an individual child we would then create and record a *Songlines sound control*: preferred musical instruments and style; signs for yes, no, stop, go, again, more, less, louder, quieter, faster, slower.

3 *Prepare and plan* Songlines activities.

Dr McFlea and Dr Molotoff were going to see Jason, a boy with multiple special needs and very limited vision. Jason spends most of his time in a wheelchair in his room or the living room. The Clown-doctors made a plan to take him on a journey through the corridors of the residential home using sounds.

4 *Initiate interaction with child, with the help of musical triggers.* They initiated contact and suggested the idea of a journey by using a tri-tone whistle as the starting point to a train adventure.

5 *Listen and translate* – enabling participation and facilitating exchange, enabling a creative and emotional outlet for participant: the Clown-doctors played with distances. They responded to and explored sounds Jason was vocalising himself.

6   *Share own musical experiences with the child*: in addition to the journey sounds and Jason's vocalising, Dr McFlea and Dr Molotoff also used their musical abilities to increase the musicality of the 'adventure'. In this case, they added some jazz elements to the tri-tone whistle and incorporated instruments (tambourine and harmonica) into the story.

7   *Reflect and report* – working to build a long-term relationship with the child, enabling success for participants. At the end of the day the Clowndoctor practitioners produce a written record on the activity and outcome of the session:

> Songlines storyline (a 'train journey'); activities and games (leading and following; playing tag, hide and seek with sounds).
>
> Positive response (Jason was alert and vocalised). Negative response (Jason started shaking his head when the train journey took him into the bathroom).
>
> Significant developments (Jason made direct eye contact for the first time during a visit – when anticipating train sound; he held eye contact for several seconds).
>
> Successful sounds and instruments (Jason responded particularly well to the tri-tone whistle in combination with the harmonica).

8   *Creating a written Songline for each individual child* as a part of the referral system to create an artistic and playful 'world' for the child. At the end of the day, in addition to the written record, the Clowndoctors would attempt to create a drawing of a musical/sound score/storyboard of the journey – so it could be re-created and built on at a later stage. This proved to be the most difficult part of our explorations and mostly we had to rely on written description instead.

Songlines' artistic repertoire

Exercises and improvisations

In training, we identified various aspects of the patient's sound world that the Clowndoctors could work with to enhance their sensory experience. As most of our Clowndoctors are not trained musicians, we were trying to explore the use of creative notation to find a way of creating a record or visual score of what was going on musically during the Songlines session. We wanted to be able to pass on the information, repeat it or build on it during future visits (most of the children we see in Songlines are visited over a period of several years on a weekly basis).

We only succeeded to a small degree as the creativity of the process left too much room for individual interpretation. This made it hard to create universal rules. However, I would recommend attempting the exercises as they were a lot of fun and of great help in developing a musical relationship within the partnerships.

Connotations of various musical instruments

Very early on, we embarked on an exploration of different instruments, noting connotations and possibilities of sounds. These possibilities are outlined in the chart found in the Appendix to this chapter.

Sound signifiers

Personal musical signatures were created for all Clowndoctors and/or children using a particular musical instrument to distinguish between the different Clowndoctors. We created simple and clear phrases for: yes/no; confusion; hello/goodbye for each of the Clowndoctors with their sound signifiers. These would always be used in the same way. It is not important what the actual sound is, only that it is consistent, clear and can be repeated.

Dr McFlea used her tambourine and would use the following musical vocabulary:

- to indicate a *yes*, she would slap on the tambourine once
- to indicate a *no* she would scrape the skin of the drum
- when confused, Dr McFlea would hesitate (long pause) before scratching the drum skin
- to say hello she would shake the tambourine as it rises and flick the skin with two fingers at top
- to say goodbye she would reverse the above downwards and also reverse the order.

Dr Superdoc always used his song whistle in the following ways:

- to indicate a *yes* he would use the stick for a quick curl up
- to indicate a *no* he would mouth the word 'uh-uh' (no)
- when confused, Dr Superdoc would use several quick phrases on his song whistle
- to say hello he would use the whistle going from high to low
- to say goodbye he would reverse from low to high.

Ceremonial songs

By using the preferences of individual participants, such as favourite words, the child's name or the name of a pet or special interests, etc. and combining them with the child's favourite musical style, the Clowndoctors would create a 'ceremonial' song for each individual child, which could be recorded and repeated. This could become their 'special song' and a starting point to each visit. One girl insisted that every Clowndoctors visit would start with her name being sung in an operatic style of music also incorporating the names of all other people present in her room. This would give her the security of knowing exactly who was around and she could relax and join in with other activities.

Sound symbols

The Clowndoctors use sound symbols as rituals signifying the beginning and end of each of the sessions. This can be as simple as:

*   using the same musical instrument such as a gong or cymbals for each of the children
*   using the child's preferred instrument to provide a 'frame' for the visit
*   using the Clowndoctors sound signifiers
*   using a hello and goodbye song
*   using a ceremonial song
*   using a special rhythm of knocking at the door.

Sound events

Created by other 'users' of the same or adjoining space – the Clowndoctors would react and respond to the sounds of the actual physical environment of the room or the building: water; gargling water; monitors; doors; keys; windows opening/closing; cleaning windows; curtains being drawn; doorbells; ringtones; phone conversations; footsteps; chairs; radio players; bed wheels; intercom; washing machines; etc.

Everyday sounds

Mapping the room

Use is made of the actual sound environment by creating a sound map of the individual rooms of participants and their contents, for example: washing basin; bin; stereo; television; cupboards with drawers; cupboards with sliding doors; beds; windows; soap dispenser; door opening and closing; clocks; crisp packets; sounds on shoes; tapshoes; squeaky shoes, etc.

Sound-making qualities

Some of these sound discoveries were planned, some incidental. During one visit Dr Spritely took several instruments out of the Songlines case, some of which were protected with bubble wrap. While unpacking the instruments, one boy responded particularly strongly to the sound of the bubble wrap.

Therefore Dr Spritely explored using the sound of the plastic and also misused it by playing the bubble wrap as if it was cymbals – which led to additional slapstick.

Soundscapes

The Clowndoctors would often embark on musical journeys using the sounds of the child's actual environment. They would create sound maps of these musical 'landmarks' in the child's environment. In addition, they would use these sounds to create different moods and atmospheres, therefore changing the actual environment: for example, letting the source and choice of sounds turn the child's room into a kitchen, a playground, or a storm:

> Dr Molotoff and Dr Sprout would create an age-appropriate soundscape with Mary (16) using the sounds of objects in the room (such as CD player, glasses, water, window), including the acoustics of the adjoining bathroom (echo, steps).
>
> One theme, 'A Night on the Town', was an attempt to take the girl out of the hospital environment. It included: meeting with some girlfriends; walking to a club and standing in line to get in; inside a club (music, conversations, too loud, etc.); going back out for a breath of fresh air; returning inside; walking back home and returning to her room.

Sound scenarios

Using musical instruments and voices, the Clowndoctors would take the children on imaginary journeys such as to the bottom of the sea, the circus, to the moon, on top of a mountain, to the farm:

> Dr Spritely and Dr McFlea visited Sarah (7), a fully dependent girl at Rachel House. Sarah is blind, but her hearing is unimpaired. The Clowndoctors decided to create the sound scenario of a farmyard and farm animals using a variety of instruments and voices.
>
> The animals were introduced by their different sounds and moved around the room. They were also told off by the Clowndoctors for eating the plants. Different materials were used to let Sarah touch the animals. She loved the cow in particular, which kept knocking into her chair. Her mother and carer were present and soon became involved in the play. Sarah's mother was laughing and playing along as various animals too.
>
> The visit concluded with a variation on the song 'Old McDonald' using the girl's name. Finally, the animals were put on a bus and sent back to the farm for their dinner.

Both soundscapes and sound scenarios offer opportunities to accompany, mirror, or contrast the movements, sounds and rhythms of the child. This allows the practitioners to support, lead or follow the suggestions of the participant.

Sound slapstick

Sound slapstick includes: musical accidents; counterpoints; contrasting rhythms and ruptures – setting up a rhythm/pattern/song and then breaking/interrupting/changing it; starting a song together slapstick – too early, too late, too fast, too slow, etc.

In comic timing a very simple exercise is to set up a movement a couple of times and then make a mistake the third time. The same applies to musical clowning. Set up a musical pattern, play it correctly twice and then make a mistake the third time. Play a melody well and then make a mistake. Make a mistake thrice and then play the melody well, making a new mistake at a different time than expected. Experiment with using strange/surprising sounds that arrive spontaneously.

> Dr Superdoc had regular visits with Holly, a fully dependent eight-year-old girl. Holly responded particularly well to odd sounds – which she found very funny. Dr Superdoc would play a beautiful tune on his song whistle. One of his colleagues would interrupt the song with a vibra slap. This rupture would make Holly laugh every time. At times the anticipation of the rupture would be enough.

In our experience, sound slapstick (as well as visual slapstick) works particularly well with fully dependent children, those with multiple special needs and those who are generally very ill (such as children on oncology or neurology wards). These children, because of the nature of their illness, often spend a lot of their time in isolation cubicles and the silence and 'carefulness' of these environments tend to remain with them. The children seem to particularly enjoy when this silence is broken (Figure 14.2).

Sound narratives

These are stories and conversations between musical instruments and/or singing voices of distinctly different sound qualities such as:

- replacing verbal communication: i.e. using a harmonica and a drum instead of words to converse, to lose and find each other, have an argument, resolve it with a happy harmonious ending
- playing the child's body parts (different body parts touched make different sounds, accompanied by second Clowndoctor)
- playing the child's environment (scratching of chair, tent, etc.)

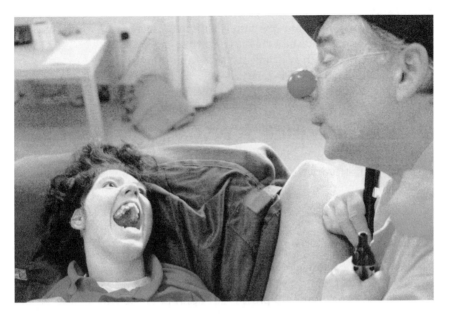

Figure 14.2 A non-verbal conversation.

- interpreting movement of child with sound
- telling an existing story with musical accompaniment.

Sound dynamics

Explore different sound dynamics and their connotations, for example: pop, stop, clutter, silence, surprise, rhythm, discord, harmony; create communication tools such as yes/no, stop/go, louder/softer, slower/faster, for each child.

Body sounds

These sounds may be: yawning, coughing, sneezing, breathing, smacking lips, eating, drinking, gargling, kissing, smelling, body percussion.

Musical instruments

As a starting point I would generally recommend the use of acoustical rhythm instruments combined with a range of whistles, mouth organs, vibra slap, and might use them as follows:

- to play a song
- to tell a story
- as accompaniment within a story being told

- for songs and instrumental pieces
- making rhythmical improvisations with instruments and voice using the rhythms and sounds of a child as a starting point
- Hide and Seek with Instruments: hide from sounds
- follow the sound: look for the other Clowndoctor or Clowndoctor sound
- instruments – qualities of sounds, preferences and aversions.

Home-made instruments

Suggestions for home-made instruments might include: water bottles; sound of water going from one vessel to the next; ping pong balls; kitchen instruments; salad spinners; thimbles; graters; thunder sheets; tray of sand; balls (graduation – different tones); elastic bands; sound tubes, etc.

Different styles of music

There is an endless range of music styles to choose from: opera; reggae; jazz; swing; rap; barber shop; crooning; etc. Different musical styles and parodies may be used. For example, to provide age-appropriate activities for teenagers we would explore rapping their names, interests, etc.

Voice

Use of the voice might involve:

- storytelling
- foreign languages; accents; laughing; talking; describing; using animal noises; words:

> Two Clowndoctors were working with Brian, a young boy with complex special needs, in respite care. Brian was quite unresponsive. The Clowndoctors experimented with a range of different things, none of which was successful. They persisted and by chance Dr Superdoc started using the word 'Ouch'. Brian responded very strongly in a positive way. He appeared to like the sound quality. Dr Spritely joined into an improvisation of 'pain sounds', which turned into a pain song and a very successful visit.

- silences – silence speaks loudly too.

Singing

Singing might involve:

- operatic singing, rapping, film theme songs (e.g. *Blues Brothers, Mission Impossible, James Bond*)
- misusing songs (i.e. insert different lyrics to well-known songs, getting lyrics wrong)
- lullabies
- using song repertoire – 'Moses supposes' change Moses to child's name
- sing child's name in different styles
- can't stop singing – keep holding notes for too long.

Bank of ideas for storytelling and soundscape visits

Touch and sound

For their work with Songlines, the Clowndoctors use multisensory coats. These are standard yellow Clowndoctors coats covered with Velcro patches to which can be attached a selection of tactile objects (e.g. carpet patches, shells, sponge) and fabric that can create a tent between two Clowndoctors and a child. In addition, each Clowndoctor will have Braille name bracelets. Other materials and props, such as tubes filled with a selection of different grains (e.g. rice, couscous, lentils, peas, etc.), coloured card, foil, crepe paper, acetate, card, ribbon, mini-fan, smelly bubbles, sticky balls, magic wands, will help to make the visit multisensory and to link touch with sound. Use of the tactile objects might involve:

- feeling materials such as stone, velvet, vinyl, suede, shells, leaves, bubble wrap, fluffy material, sandpaper
- feel these, which one feels like the sound
- place them in hand of child or use in tactile play (e.g. stone and Tibetan bowl)
- play the sound of an instrument (e.g. child 'creates/conducts' music by having different materials in tactile play).

Very small babies who are fully dependent and children with acquired brain injuries seem to enjoy gentle and beautiful music and singing. These gentle sounds can be combined with touch in the rhythm of the music: for example, touch their hand/arm with an object such as a soft toy, so they can feel the rhythm of the music in addition to hearing it. These objects can become little beings/small animals dancing on their hands and arms.

Words

In our experience using naïve verbal narrative ('Wow!' 'Oh!' 'Good!' 'Yes!') works better than description as the children get plenty of descriptive narrative from other sources. Obviously the Clowndoctors will be the best judge of this in each individual case.

Stories and journeys

The quality of a sound can give a visual feel and/or describe a motion. It can also indicate whether objects and/or people are stationary or moving as well as the quality of movement (quick, slow, ponderous, flowing, etc.). Words and stories/journeys can be woven together, but also allow room for silence.

Patients controlling Clowndoctors with sound

• Magic wand as sound control by child.

> Dr Foot-Twanger and Dr Soundsgood were visiting 12-year-old Martin on a Neurology ward in a participating paediatric hospital. At the time, due to an acquired brain injury, Martin had no speech and no movement aside from being able to wiggle one of his thumbs.
>
> The Clowndoctors decided to take the entire Songlines instrument case into the boy's cubicle. Martin's thumb became his 'magic wand' with which he was able to conduct the Big Band consisting of Dr Foot-Twanger, Dr Soundsgood, parents, grandparents, visiting friends, staff members, etc.
>
> Martin thoroughly enjoyed the control given to him and became very animated during and after these repeated visits.

• 'Sleepdoctors' with musical instruments: a control game where one of the Clowndoctors would not be able to stop himself or herself from falling asleep and whereby a child with limited movement could use an instrument to wake him or her up.
• Child directing Clowndoctors with sounds; movements, etc. – natural movements become musical instruments.

Play each other's movements

The set-up for this exercise is as follows. Two Clowndoctors work together at a time and all other practitioners keep their eyes shut to listen to the music/ sounds created. One at a time, the pair musically accompany each other's movement:

• Play the movement/dance of the other Clowndoctor: sound – silence – reaction – silence; the physical movement/gesture creates the sound.
• Play the movement of the child in hospital: the Clowndoctors play the movement of eyes, hands, feet and other parts of body.

- Place a wand in the child's hand and move it for them/with them so the child can conduct the second Clowndoctor playing.

Assessment games

- Identify which part of the child's body *and* what degree of their movement they are using to consciously control the clown's sounds.
- Eye movement: even though a child may be blind or partially sighted, tracking is still common when alert and engaged in a visit.
- In the case of involuntary seizures, we can still treat these as signals and give them some significance. Giving control to something that is essentially out of their control can be empowering in some cases.
- Clowndoctor changes the dynamic variable as a rupture (e.g. child may only have one signal, *stop/go*, so change it to *loud/quiet*).

Conclusion

I believe that some of the successes of the Songlines project are as follows:

- Our practitioners have found additional ways of communication with participants through the use of music and sound.
- We have gained experience in the use of a range of musical instruments (contained in the Songlines instrument case).
- We have created a repertoire of songs and rhymes to be used.
- We have created a common musical vocabulary to be used in our Clowndoctors partnerships.
- We have found means of clowning and expressing humour through the use of music and sounds.
- We have explored multisensory coats and Braille name bands as part of our interactions (the portable tent proved highly impractical).
- We explored creative notation, which is the only point that did not find its way into the delivery of the programme.
- We have successfully translated existing visual Clowndoctors activities such as physical/visual slapstick (e.g. falling off chairs) into sound slapstick.

Although the Songlines project has had a limited lifespan and was officially concluded in 2005, the experiences and explorations we made have had lasting impact in the ongoing delivery of our Clowndoctors and Elderflowers programmes. It has not only given us further tools to communicate with children who are visually impaired, blind or have acquired brain injuries, but has also taught us to have the patience to wait even longer for responses. It taught us never to expect any responses at all and nevertheless continue exploring, trying and listening. It has taught us to keep taking risks. If responses do happen we have learned to notice what triggered them so we can use this in future. Most importantly, beyond any disability is always the ability and whatever it may look like the child is in there.

Acknowledgements

A special thanks to Ian Cameron (Dr Superdoc), Fiona Colliss (Dr Spritely), Clark Crystal (Dr Foot-Twanger), Zoë Darbyshire (Dr McFlea), Virginia Gillard (Dr Pavlova), Maria Oller (Dr Molotoff), Pete Vilk (Dr Soundsgood) and Elizabeth van Zwet (Dr Sprout). These Clowndoctors contributed to the development of the Songlines project and continue to deliver Songlines activities within the Hearts&Minds Clowndoctors programme.

Appendix

Vibra slap	Fun accident; earthquakes; rattlesnakes; woodpecker; a marker; wake up (when played side on creates a muted earthy sound).
Elephant bells	Create little melodies; solitude; serene, gentle vibration.
Swirl xylophone	Wheels; wagon; motion; time passing; sand in hourglass; rain; dripping; underwater; little people, walking; arriving; good alongside storytelling.
Hand chimes	Strong/deep physical resonance in vibrations; establishing a sound world; warm, cuddly, comforting; bells; markers for storytelling; conversation one to one (third person drops in as a comic rupture or to expand harmony).
Vibratone	Outer space; question mark; submarine; valleys; echoes; distance; chasing the quirky sound.
Sound tubes	Wind; mountain top; ghostly; play like a didgeridoo; talk through them.
Frog drum	Ship creaks; alien; doors opening; small curious creature; insects; frog conversations between the two; too intense close up.
Nightingale whistle	Birds of the Amazon; cover hole for bubbles sound; cover hole and gently release whilst sucking in air creates subtle sound.
Goongroos	Tied to ankles for entrances; Rudolph/Christmas; huskies in the snow; circus; soothing close up.
Ocean drum	Sea; water; waves; holiday at the beach; big dynamic range; raindrops increasing to a storm; little drummer boy.
Tibetan bowls	Falling asleep; arrival of a character; dreaming; calm; serene; strong/deep physical vibration in the space; healing; intense warm sound close up; call for lunch; slapstick 'it's beautiful here' then rupture with a silly sound.
Hand fan	Flight of the bumble bee; fly; mosquito; landing; the wind (watch out for hair!).
Tri-tone whistle	Train; steam engine; boat; departure or arrival in story; singing/blowing jazzy phrases through it; clip the sound to make it vocal.

Electronic keyboard	Happy birthday; nursery rhymes, ruptures well with the electronic laughter bag.
Anticipation and using silence	Create anticipation with lovely melody, then break it. Countdown, then forget or play unexpected sound.

Notes

1 Nordoff-Robbins Music Therapy evolved from the pioneering use of music as therapy developed by the late composer Dr Paul Nordoff and special educator Dr Clive Robbins. Robbins says: 'Music is the most basic way to reach handicapped children. It is the one thing that transcends all human emotion and feeling. Though there is so much these children can't do, what we want to know is what they *can* do.'

2 Zoltán Kodály (1882–1967) was a music educationalist, born in Hungary. Kodály's approach to music education is based on teaching, learning and understanding music through the experience of singing, giving direct access to the world of music without the technical problems involved with the use of an instrument. The Kodály approach to music education is child centred and taught in a logical, sequential manner. There is no 'method' – more a series of guidelines. Tools used according to Kodály guidelines are relative solfa, rhythm names and handsigns.

3 All names of participating children were changed.

Websites

www.britishkodalyacademy.org
www.clowndoctors.org.uk
www.heartsminds.org.uk
www.nordoffrobbins.org

Chapter 15

LaughterBoss

Introducing a new position in aged care

Peter Spitzer

It is the job of the LaughterBoss, via open-heart surgery, to touch the soul and give it room to smile and laugh.

Introduction

LaughterBoss originates from the philosophy that laughter is the best medicine. The positive power of humor is well known and bringing humor and laughter into aged care assists staff to more creatively meet quality of life and psychosocial care issues of residents. The LaughterBoss is also well placed to help reduce staff stress and improve staff morale.

The LaughterBoss is the modern-day equivalent of the court jester. They bring together the art and the medicine. Ideal candidates for training are staff members who have intimate knowledge of residents, families and staff as well as a thorough understanding of the environment and culture of the facility. Training to become a LaughterBoss does not make the applicant a professional performer. They remain a healthcare professional who has developed creative skills in introducing humor and laughter into their facility. This chapter explores how to train and introduce a LaughterBoss into aged care.

Clowning and evidence-based medicine

Gelotology is the study of humor and its effect on the human body.[1,2,3,4,5] The Association for Applied and Therapeutic Humor (AATH), founded in 1988, defines therapeutic humor as 'any intervention that promotes health and wellness by stimulating a playful discovery, expression, or appreciation of the absurdity or incongruity of life's situations'.[6]

Clowning has a long history of being an art form that invites play, interaction and, above all, laughter. Many studies on the effect and benefit of humor and laughter have been published.

Laughter affects the mind and the body. There are many reasons why laughter makes us feel good and a recent study has found that humor and laughter triggered the brain's reward centres.[7] Other studies show respiratory and cardiovascular effects. Laughter stimulates respiration, relaxes arteries and improves blood flow as well as oxygen saturation of peripheral blood. After a transient rise there is a drop in blood pressure. Positive effects on hypertension and diabetes have been noted. A relaxation response is experienced after laughter. Laughter has been researched in the field of psycho-neuroimmunology and studies have shown a drop in serum (cortisol) stress hormone and enhancement of immune system functioning. Laughter reduces pain. Laughter is also studied in the field of positive psychology and positive effects on performance, mood, optimism, anxiety and depression have been observed. Laughter enhances communication and is positively associated with emotional stability.

There are many published studies on the impact and place of humor and laughter in aged care and a small number is referenced here.[8, 9, 10, 11, 12, 13, 14, 15, 16, 17]

Aged care issues and depression

Not that long ago, life expectancy was in the 40 to 50 range. Now, it is common to be caring for people who are in their eighties and nineties. This group suffers from a multitude of losses such as loss of physical and mental ability, loss of power, loss of friends, loss of control in their lives and loss of independence.

Depression is common at this late stage of life and brings with it significant morbidity, which when left untreated is associated with higher health service utilisation.[18] Depression is a major public health problem. It is common for depressed older adults in residential care not to receive optimal help as depression is often under-recognised by health professionals and other carers.

A crucial issue in health promotion intervention is to increase participation in both mental and physical activity. Common health education messages include: depression is not an inevitable part of ageing; depression is not a spiritual or personal weakness and non-pharmacological treatments can be effective when used alone.[19] Multifaceted interventions have been recommended due to complexity of depression in residential care as well as the potential for synergy between different elements of possible interventions.[20] However, cost of funding is a common factor in introducing intervention programs.

With an increase in the aging population, the aged care health sector is under growing pressure. Staff stress, lowered morale, burn-out, staff turnover and absenteeism are recurring problems. In summary, implementing effective depression interventions can positively affect quality of life and reduce physical and psychological morbidity and consequent patient transfers to higher levels of supportive care.[21]

Background to the LaughterBoss concept

In Australia, the Humour Foundation charity is the only national organization delivering hospital clowning to children and adults through its Clown Doctor program.[22, 23] This includes episodic visits to aged care facilities.

Whilst we see and feel the impact of Clown Doctor visits, we are not able to make regular visits, which limits the impact and connection with everyone in the facility. The commonest complaint is 'Why don't you come more often?' This signals an inadequately met need. With the inability to meet increasing demand for Clown Doctors to visit aged care facilities, the author developed the LaughterBoss concept under the LaughterWorks arm of the Humour Foundation. LaughterWorks provides education and runs seminars for healthcare providers in using humor in patient/carer relationships. In this initiative, we would teach a staff member humor intervention skills to deliver, on a regular and opportunistic basis, the positive power of humor and laughter.

The LaughterBoss model was presented at the First National Conference on Depression in Aged Care: 'Challenging Depression In Aged Care' at the University of New South Wales, Sydney, Australia in June 2003.[24]

Who and what is the LaughterBoss?

The court jester (or fool) was a particular type of clown associated with the Middle Ages. In those days they were thought of as special cases that God had touched with a childlike madness. They wore bright, motley-patterned costumes and floppy cloth hats with three points, each having a jingle bell at the end. They also carried a mock sceptre. Medieval medicine considered health to be largely governed by four humors (sanguine, melancholia, choleric and phlegmatic). Imbalance of the humors produced distinctive emotional states and the court jester was specifically employed by the court to help rebalance the humors. For example, the court jester would be summoned to lift the monarch out of an angry or melancholic mood:

> Above all he used humor, whether in the form of wit, puns, riddles, doggerel verse, songs, capering antics or nonsensical babble, and jesters were usually also musical or poetic or acrobatic, and sometimes all three.[25]

The tradition of court jesters lasted about 400 years and they worked in the royal courts of Europe, the Middle East and Asia.

The LaughterBoss is a modern-day equivalent of the court jester. The main role of the LaughterBoss is to bring play, humor and laughter into the facility. This role originates from the philosophy that laughter is the best medicine. The healing power of humor is well documented.[26, 27, 28] Sharing a smile and a laugh reduces anxiety, positively impacts on the immune system, improves circulation, modulates the mesolimbic reward centre,[29] reduces depression and creates an atmosphere of positivity and warmth.

While the main focus of the LaughterBoss is on the residents, a positive impact on staff, visitors and general community has been reported. The LaughterBoss can reduce staff stress and improve morale as well as assist staff to better meet quality of life and psychosocial needs of residents. This is done through assisting communication, increased support, giving residents cognitive control, providing positive diversion and generally increasing the 'smileage' factor.

Ideal candidates for LaughterBoss training are facility staff members who have an intimate knowledge of the people (residents, staff and families) and a thorough understanding of the environment and culture of the facility. The LaughterBoss position is added on to the 'day job' of the staff member. This not only reduces costs but also addresses and enhances recommended multifaceted interventions.

After training, the LaughterBoss is a new identity in the facility. They should be easily recognisable and available to do their work at a moment's notice as the need arises. They also lead the way in introducing themes, special days and events. Training does not make the applicant a professional performer. They remain a healthcare professional who has developed creative skills in introducing humor and laughter into their facility.

Given that training involves play, improvisation, engagement, humor and laughter, the ideal trainer would have performance background with teaching experience including the ability to deliver scientific data. Performers who also do hospital clowning have the benefit of working in the healthcare system as well as having the backing of their organization. This adds to depth of experience as well as professional credibility. Trainers do not have to be medical practitioners in order to deliver LaughterBoss training.

Feedback about quality and appropriateness of training given by our performers who are also hospital clowns has been enthusiastic and very positive.

LaughterBoss training

The initial training is a full-day experiential program.

Selection

Applicants usually self-select and are motivated to attend training. They must have the acknowledgement and support of senior staff and management. Applicants have included CEOs, directors of nursing, nursing staff, diversional therapists, occupational therapists, recreational therapists and the clergy. Often, training grants cover the cost of training.

Group size is limited to 20–30 people and training is held on a weekday, typically from 8:30 am to 4:30 pm. Commonly, one person takes on the role of liaison and administration assistant and this person also arranges refreshments as well as audiovisual needs.

Advertising is usually via in-house, local newsletters, aged care journals, within the allied health specialty groups and word of mouth.

Location

The space must be large enough to seat 30 people comfortably. Chairs are often positioned in a semi-circle at the periphery. There must be space to hold exercises. Lightweight chairs are used as some exercises are performed seated in groups of two and three. Natural light and fresh air are preferred. Noise and laughter levels can rise and this is factored in. Loose and comfortable clothing is recommended.

Course materials and teaching aids

Each trainee receives a resource pack. It contains information on the Humour Foundation Clown Doctor program which opens discussion on introducing new models into the healthcare setting. There is a paper on the LaughterBoss written by the author. There is a summary of the therapeutic effects of laughter; review of laughing at vs. laughing with someone; humor resources; a list of creative ideas; taking steps towards an optimistic state of mind and a paper on the health benefits of optimism; a nursing journal paper on the 'Use of Humour in Patient Care'; a paper on 'The Therapeutic Power of Humor' and an academic and therapeutic reference list on humor and gerontology.

Humor resources and creative ideas give busy healthcare professionals a practical summary of what material is available, how it can be used as an intervention and where it can be sourced. This includes reading materials and (local) internet access.

The scientific material and video clips are delivered using PowerPoint/laptop computer/data projector. Usually a whiteboard is available. One or two tables are used to hold reference books and materials as well as a variety of props. One source for scientific material as evidence is our own site, (www.humourfoundation.com.au: select Resources then Humor References followed by Therapeutic Humor and Physiological response). See also Notes at the end of this chapter for further references.

Providing a summary that includes both the psychological and physical benefits of laughter helps to support with scientific evidence and to under-pin the validity of LaughterBoss. The author typically presents information on psychoneuroimmunology, stress hormone reduction, immune system benefits, circulation benefits, and information on reduced depression, positive cardiovascular benefits and the effects on the mesolimbic reward centres.

Questionnaires

Three questionnaires are used. These are valuable in assessing the program and can form stepping stones to future research. The first questionnaire is filled prior to training. The second questionnaire is filled in at the end of the training day. The third questionnaire is filled in at the half-day follow-up workshops which are held every few months.

Training content

Training brings a number of elements together by:

- introducing the science behind the 'laughter is the best medicine' quote
- exploring the 'art of medicine' and how to introduce humor and play
- stimulating creativity and developing new skills
- networking between like-minded healthcare professionals.

Training is delivered over four sessions in the day. *Session 1* includes: pre-training questionnaire; introduction to the LaughterBoss concept and introduction to each participant; group activities to have some fun and play with each other; introduction to the Humour Foundation Clown Doctor program; the science and psychoneuroimmunology underpinning laughter and humor; video clips and stories from the coalface.

Video clips, when available, give visual cues to laughter/play interactions. Photos are also used and give similar cues. Both open the door to delivering stories from the coalface. Stories are a very important way of translating the theoretical to the transformational reality.

Session 2 includes: group play; developing a new view of the aged care space; introduction to the play basket, the humor noticeboard and resource material; brainstorming in groups of three on creative ways to humor oneself, residents and staff.

Group play includes a number of exercises that stimulate play. This is valuable experientially to balance the intellectual activities. Group plays show the value of brief interventions and are a good way of linking the participants. Group plays are introduced in all the sessions. There are many appropriate group plays available. A good resource is *Playfair* by Matt Weinstein and Joel Goodman.

The play basket is in itself a play resource. A strategically placed basket can have a variety of colorful props such as scarves, wigs, hats, lightweight balls, etc., ready to be used at a moment's notice. Local businesses and community groups can connect with the facility by donating equipment.

The humor noticeboard is also strategically placed. It invites humor. Residents, families and staff can add jokes/humor articles/photos. The LaughterBoss maintains and supervises this space.

Resource material can be donated or made by the local community. This includes materials for the play basket as well as items such as puppets, balloons, etc.

The brainstorming exercise is a way of including others in creative thought and expression. This is a safe and non-judgemental exercise in lateral thinking.

A selection of books on humor is on display throughout the day.

Session 3 includes: more group play; using props as communication tools; using polaroid and photography; examples of brief humor interventions; humor during entry and exit; introducing love heart tennis as an example of fun play that can incorporate residents, staff and family. In this play six people (or more) participate. Equipment needed is chairs, one red heart balloon (the ball), four soft fly swatters (the rackets) and a roll of toilet paper (the net). Two people sit facing each other holding the rolled out toilet paper. Two players sit side by side on each side of the net facing the players on the other side. The aim is to get the love heart balloon over the net to the other side. Scoring is strictly ad hoc. This play is quickly set up and very rapidly changes the mood of the environment (see Figure 15.1).

A variety of props can be used to induce play, laughter and enhanced communication. These are on display and the 'schtick' is shown. Colourful, close-up magic or puppets often work well. Participants can experiment and play with the props during breaks in the training. Polaroids/photography add a dimension to play and leave a positive visual reminder of the activity/play.

Given the busyness of the day, brief improvisations/interventions make a

Figure 15.1 Love heart tennis – score: love all

difference, make sense and are achievable during a busy shift. These are shown and discussed. For instance, it may be possible for the resident to team up with the LaughterBoss to play a 'trick' on the family.

Entry and exit to the facility, the staff room, the dining room and the resident's living space are areas where the LaughterBoss can trip over themselves literally – a way of acknowledging human frailty even in the staff. This is theatre 'on the go'; this is brief intervention; this invites reaction and comment; this is play.

Session 4 includes: group play; planning and introducing themes; exploring fun musical opportunities; aligning play to the resident's history; exploring the possibilities of the humor/play cart and the potential to connect with the broader community; different ways of being funny on excursions; dealing with dementia; question and answer segment and post-training questionnaire.

Themes for the day, the week, the month and a variety of special occasions are explored. For instance, how does the LaughterBoss make Funny Fridays happen? Ways of engaging residents, their families and staff are discussed. One facility put together a 'Funny Day Out' where residents had the opportunity to dress funny on a bus outing. This was also great for photo opportunity. Photo opportunities can easily find their way to the residential or local newspaper. The message is that residential facilities are a part of the community.

A variety of musical/fun opportunities is explored. There is a variety of ways of forming an 'instant band'.

Taking the time to listen to the resident's history gives the opportunity to introduce appropriate play. The resident will give the cues.

Like the humor basket and the humor noticeboard, the humor cart is another opportunity of introducing play. The medication trolley brings medicine. The humor trolley brings play. This can have props as in the humor basket as well as things like polaroids, puppets, magic, balloons, etc. These can be sourced from the local community, schools and businesses – again linking the facility with the broader community.

Throughout the four sessions participants experience the Massage Train. This massage activity connects the group in a quick, enjoyable and light-hearted way. In essence, the group forms a close circle facing the centre. Everyone turns to the left and massages the upper back of the person in front. After a couple of moments everyone turns in the opposite direction and again massages the upper back of the person in front. This activity can include residents and may be used during staff handover/shift change (see Figure 15.2).

Each participant receives a colourful completion of training, the Laughter-Boss certificate. Often a graduation photograph is taken.

Figure 15.2 Rub my back and I rub your back

Follow-up workshops

These workshops are recommended every three to six months. Senior Clown Doctors experienced in teaching lead them. They introduce their artistic professionalism in taking the LaughterBoss role forward. The workshops last half a day and include fun play, introducing new performance elements and review and feedback of LaughterBoss activity. They finish off with the questionnaire.

The training day and follow-up workshops also give an opportunity to meet healthcare professionals from other facilities and to establish LaughterBoss networks.

Evaluating the LaughterBoss training

Broadly based evaluation using a series of questionnaires takes place during initial training and at the follow-up workshops. A fairly typical training is reviewed here. Twenty-six people took part in this initial training. They came from 14 different organizations that included government community health services, nursing homes, hospitals, carers and artist-in-community. Participants held 15 different positions. The majority were registered nurses. Activities officers, nursing aides, a social worker, speech pathologist, physiotherapist, artist, diversional therapist, an adult day care manager and a nursing unit manager also attended.

Reasons for attending included: to improve the atmosphere at work; to introduce humor to reduce work stress; curiosity; to expand knowledge and skills; to develop one's own humor skills; to increase skills working with dementia and have more fun and laughs with residents. Fifteen out of the 26 participants had no prior performance training.

Some thoughts on what the LaughterBoss could bring to the workplace included: improved patient care; a more enjoyable workplace; reduced staff stress; improved communication; permission to encourage laughter; certification and validation of this new position; improved staff morale and team building. Eighty per cent had the support of their organization to attend training, while 8 per cent were organization independent.

One hundred per cent agreed that training met expectations: 96 per cent felt training gave sufficient skills to begin LaughterBoss work; 88 per cent felt training gave enough confidence to begin LaughterBoss work; 100 per cent had fun.

Thirteen (50 per cent) attended the follow-up workshop three months later. Management had totally accepted LaughterBoss in 70 per cent of cases and partially accepted in 30 per cent. Thirty-one per cent of other staff totally accepted LaughterBoss with 69 per cent giving partial acceptance. Some felt it was too time consuming and interfered with normal routine.

Of residents 54 per cent totally accepted LaughterBoss, with 46 per cent giving partial acceptance. Comments included: always have to gauge whom you can use it on; have to choose the right time; humor creates an instant bond when meeting someone with dementia. Of families/carers 85 per cent partially or totally accepted the LaughterBoss role. Comments included: families need explanation on the role of the LaughterBoss; good feedback from volunteers; it is now okay to laugh in here.

Comments on the wish list to maintain creativity and develop skills included: have regular LaughterBoss meetings; LaughterBoss position for a month – shared amongst all staff; time to fit creativity into a very lousy job; attending magic and juggling courses.

Engaging residents with dementia in humorous interactions varied with the level of dementia. Those with mild dementia engaged 69 per cent often/most of the time. This was at 31 per cent for moderate dementia and 23 per cent for advanced dementia. Of those working with people with dementia 46 per cent felt improved level of confidence since introduction of the LaughterBoss.

Finally, some general comments included: love watching the pleasure on their faces, even those not directly involved; I'm committed to getting a laugh every day; proves that humor can be a positive therapy for people with dementia.

Conclusion

The creative challenge is in becoming comfortable with and learning to appropriately shift between health professional and LaughterBoss role. The positive benefits of humor and laughter in the aged care setting have been acknowledged. The 'art of medicine' as practiced by the LaughterBoss in the new millennium is alive, well and needed in the aged care sector. Laughter-Boss training is a step on the way to allowing the court jester to emerge.

Notes

1 L. S. Berk, S.A. Tan, W.F. Fry, B.J. Napier, J.W. Lee, R.W. Hubbard, J.E. Lewis and W.C. Eby, 'Neuroendocrine and stress hormone changes during mirthful laughter', *American Journal of the Medical Sciences* 298(6), 1989, 390–396.

2 K.M. Dillon, B. Minchoff and K.H. Baker, 'Positive emotional states and enhancement of the immune system', *International Journal of Psychiatry* 15(1), 1985–6, 13–18.

3 W.F. Fry, 'The biology of humor', *HUMOR: International Journal of Humor Research* 7(2), 1994, 111–126.

4 W.F. Fry and W.A. Salameh, *Handbook of Humor and Psychotherapy: Advances in the Clinical Use of Humor*, Sarasota, FL: Professional Resource Exchange, 1987.

5 M. Gelkopf and S. Kreitler, 'Is humor only fun, an alternative cure or magic? The cognitive therapeutic potential of humor', *Journal of Cognitive Psychotherapy: An International Quarterly* 10(4), 1996, 235–254.

6 The Association for Applied and Therapeutic Humor (www.aath.org).

7 D. Mobbs, M.D. Greicius, E. Abdel-Azim, V. Menon and A. Reiss, 'Humor modulates the mesolimbic reward centers', *Neuron* 40, 2003, 1041–1048.

8 A.L. Barrick, R.L. Hutchinson and L.H. Deckers, 'Humor, aggression and aging', *Gerontologist* 30(5), 1990, 675–678.

9 R.A. Dean, 'Humor and laughter in palliative care', *Journal of Palliative Care* 13(1), 1997, 34–39.

10 K. Fox, 'Laugh it off: the effect of humor on the well-being of the older adult', *Journal of Gerontological Nursing* 16(12), 1990, 11–16.

11 W.F. Fry, 'Humor, physiology and the ageing process', in L. Nahemow and K. A. McClusky-Fawcett (eds) *Humor and Ageing*, Orlando, FL: Academic Press, 1986, pp. 81–98.

12 J.R. Hulse, 'Humor: a nursing intervention for the elderly', *Geriatric Nursing* 15(2), 1994, 88–90.

13 F.A. McGuire and R.K. Boyd, 'The role of humor in enhancing the quality of later life', in J. R. Kelly (ed.) *Activity and Aging: Staying Involved in Later Life*, Newbury Park, CA, Sage: 1993, pp. 164–173.

14 F.A. McGuire, R.K. Boyd and A. James, 'Therapeutic humor with the elderly', *Activities, Adaptations and Aging* 17(1), 1992, 1–96.

15 J. Richmond, 'The lifesaving function of humor with the depressed and suicidal elderly', *The Gerontologist* 35(2), 1995, 271–273.

16 J.J. Simon, 'Humor and the older adult: implications for nursing', *Journal of Advanced Nursing Practice* 13, 1988, 441–446.

17 H. Williams, 'Humor and healing: therapeutic effects in geriatrics', *Gerontion* 1(3), 1986, 14–17.

18 R. Llewellyn-Jones, 'New approaches for late life depression in aged care', *Challenging Depression in Aged Care Conference*, Sydney, Australia, 2003.

19 I. Hickie, 'Depression in older persons: challenging community attitudes and providing appropriate treatments', *Challenging Depression in Aged Care Conference*, Sydney, Australia, 2003.

20 R. Llewellyn-Jones, 'New approaches for late life depression in aged care', *Challenging Depression in Aged Care Conference*, Sydney, Australia, 2003.

21 R. Llewellyn-Jones, 'New approaches for late life depression in aged care', *Challenging Depression in Aged Care Conference*, Sydney, Australia, 2003.

22 The Humour Foundation (www.humourfoundation.com.au).

23 P. Spitzer, 'The clown doctors', *Australian Family Physician* 30(1), 2001, 12–16.

24 Hammond Care Group (www.hammond.com.au/dsdc/conferences.php?conference=2003).

25 B.K. Otto, *Fools Are Everywhere. The Court Jester Around The World*, Chicago: University of Chicago Press, 2001.

26 W.F. Fry, 'The biology of humor', *HUMOR: International Journal of Humor Research* 7(2), 1994, 111–126.

27 H. Williams, 'Humor and healing: therapeutic effects in geriatrics', *Gerontion* 1(3), 1986, 14–17.

28 Hammond Care Group (www.hammond.com.au/dsdc/conferences. php? conference=2003).

29 D. Mobbs, M.D. Greicius, E. Abdel-Azim, V. Menon and A. Reiss, 'Humor modulates the mesolimbic reward centers', *Neuron* 40, 2003, 1041–1048.

Resources

Training

At this time of writing there is an abundance of formalized programs available for people who wish to train to be a professional 'art(s) therapist'. While programs that prepare artists to work in hospitals and healthcare settings do exist, these tend to be less formalized than those that train art(s) therapists. As training requirements are different in every country and because programs tend to spring up and/or close regularly I have resisted making a list of every university and college that currently offers a training program. Rather what follows is a partial list of contacts for English-language based organisations committed to *Using the Creative Arts in Therapy and Healthcare*. Many are national organizations that oversee training and/or regulate professional accreditation in that country. Also most of these sites have links to others.

Artists in hospitals/healthcare

Arts for Health
http://www.mmu.ac.uk/artsforhealth/

Australian Network for Arts + Health
www.anah.org.au

National Network for the Arts in Health
http://www.nnah.co.uk/index.html

Society for the Arts in Healthcare
http://thesah.org

Creative/expressive arts therapies

International Expressive Arts Therapy Association (IEATA)
www.ieata.org

Irish Association of Creative Arts Therapies
http://www.iacat.ie

National Coalition of Creative Arts Therapies Associations (USA)
http://www.ncata.com/

Art therapy

American Art Therapy Association
http://www.arttherapy.org

Australian and New Zealand Art Therapy Association
http://www.anzata.org/mambo/

British Association of Art Therapists
http://www.baat.org/

Canadian Art Therapy Association
http://www.catainfo.ca/

Dance therapy

American Dance Therapy Association
www.adta.org

Association for Dance Movement Therapy (UK)
www.admt.org.uk

Dance-Movement Therapy Association of Australia (DTAA)
www.dtaa.org

Drama therapy

British Association for Dramatherapists (BADTh)
www.badth.org.uk

National Association for Drama Therapy
www.nadt.org

Sesame Institute for Drama and Movement Therapy
www.sesame-institute.org/

Music therapy

American Music Therapy Association
www.musictherapy.org

British Society for Music Therapy
www.bsmt.org

Canadian Association for Music Therapy
www.musictherapy.ca

Play therapy

British Association of Play Therapists
www.bapt.uk.com

Canadian Association for Child and Play Therapy
www.cacpt.com

United Kingdom Society for Play and Creative Art Therapy
www.playtherapy.org

Poetry therapy

National Federation for Biblio/Poetry Therapy
www.nfbpt.com

Name index

Subject index